MONUMENTAL INSCRIPTIONS

in the

BURIAL GROUND

of the

JEWISH SYNAGOGUE

at

BRIDGETOWN,

BARBADOS.

TRANSCRIBED WITH AN INTRODUCTION

BY

E. M. SHILSTONE

THE JEWISH HISTORICAL SOCIETY OF ENGLAND
UNIVERSITY COLLEGE
LONDON
W.C.1

LIST OF CONTENTS

ILLUSTRATIONS

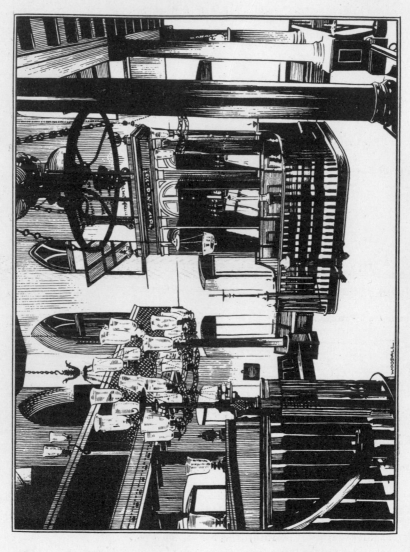

View of Interior of Synagogue, Bridgetown, looking towards the Ark of the Law. (1927)

FOREWORD

to the

AMERICAN EDITION

Tombstone inscriptions have long been a major source of Jewish history. While the data supplied by such epigraphic evidence are largely limited to names and dates, they have the great advantage of contemporaneity and authenticity. For this reason not only students of ancient epigraphy, but many other scholars interested in tracing the early history of Jewish communities have diligently gathered whatever material of this type has survived the ravages of time.

Jews of the Western Hemisphere, however, even if living in large and affluent communities, have thus far paid little attention to these important sources. Owing to their lack of interest, they have allowed many old monuments to sink into permanent oblivion. In fact, it is but a few years ago that, in his *Portraits Etched in Stone,* Dr. David de Sola Pool was able to present a first comprehensive study of an old American Jewish cemetery and its contribution to the knowledge not only of the persons buried there, but also of the entire community in which they lived.

Jewish cemeteries situated in less favoured communities have suffered from even greater neglect. Jewish scholarship is deeply indebted, therefore, to Mr. Eustace M. Shilstone for his untiring and devoted endeavours carried on for many years faithfully to transcribe and elucidate all the extant inscriptions on the island of Barbados. The history of the Jewish community of that island goes back to the same chain of events which led to the establishment of the first organized Jewish community on the North American continent in 1654. Fortunately its future, which looked quite dismal a quarter century ago, now seems assured by the rise of a new, active congregation, and one may look forward to its further contributions to American Jewish life. But beyond the confines of Barbados the story of its beginnings, as it unfolds here from these inscriptions, as well as from the work done on them by Messrs. Shilstone, Richard D. Barnett, and Wilfred S. Samuel, will shed much new light on the early stages of Jewish communal evolution throughout the Western Hemisphere.

Salo W. Baron.

New York,
March 15, 1956.

PREFACE

In a 1934 lecture, published in 1936, "A Review of the Jewish Colonists in Barbados in the year 1680", I appealed for other historical workers to make further contributions to the history of British West Indian Jewry.

Fulfilment has come, and it is with unbounded satisfaction that I indite this foreword to Mr. E. M. Shilstone's "monumental" work - the most recent of these contributions.

I have been in friendly correspondence with Mr. Eustace M. Shilstone ever since 1936, when I learned with amazement and admiration that this busy Barbados lawyer, at that time I believe also Deputy Clerk to the Legislative Assembly, was accomplishing the arduous task of copying all the Jewish epitaphs - ranging over the centuries - in our ancient grave-yard in Synagogue Lane, Bridgetown. He had no Jewish interests or connections, but as one of the founders of the Barbados Museum and Historical Society, he had decided that on an Island where frequent hurricanes destroy historic buildings the flat monuments of the Jews were well worth preserving. He seems to have been alone in realising that in the horizontal tombstones of its Jews' Cemetery Barbados possessed three centuries of history, and he stout-heartedly proceeded to record it. The tangible relics of the departed Sephardim of Barbados have encountered many vicissitudes during the past twenty years, in all of which Mr. Shilstone has battled for their preservation, often with a success to which this volume bears witness, and especially in its author's introduction.

In 1936 the Spanish and Portuguese Jews' congregation on Barbados was dying out after having been on the point of expiring for close on a hundred years. But about twenty years ago as a result of Nazi persecution in Europe a trickle of Jews reached Barbados and after

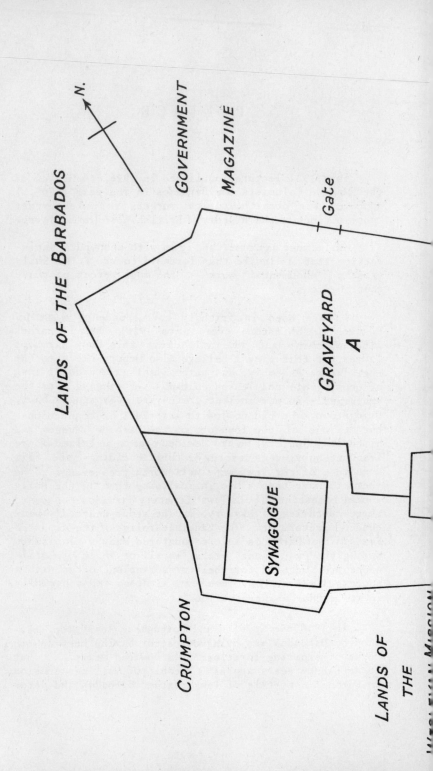

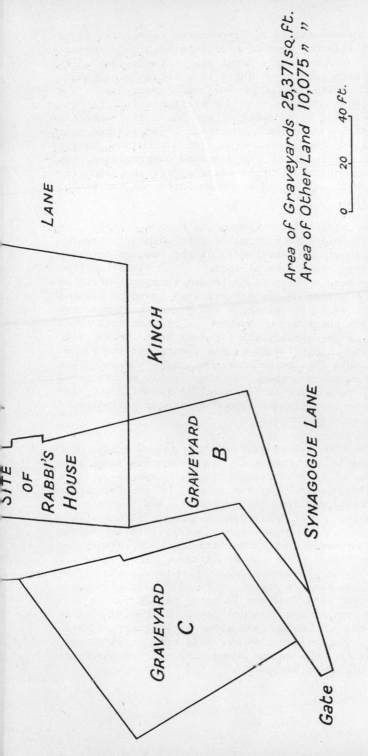

PLAN OF THE JEWISH CEMETERY, BARBADOS.

LANE

KINCH

SITE
OF
RABBI'S
HOUSE

GRAVEYARD
B

GRAVEYARD

SYNAGOGUE LANE

GRAVEYARD
C

Gate

Area of Graveyards 25,371 sq. ft.
Area of Other Land 10,075 " "

0   20   40 ft.

a struggle contrived to secure a modest commercial footing on the Island. None of them were Spanish or Portuguese or for that matter English. To-day Barbadian Jewry has been reborn. There is a sizeable congregation which meets regularly for public worship. The ancient Jewish burial ground is available for its use, and Mr. Shilstone is a member of its Board of Trustees - as representing the Barbados Historical Society; so that "Bevis Marks", the parent synagogue in London, having inherited the funds of the deceased congregation, has been able to repay them to the new congregation, who will be using the Burial Ground which Mr. Shilstone has tended so lovingly.

A few additions and comments may be permitted on some of Mr. Shilstone's valuable conclusions. New information about the settlement of the Jews on Barbados has been very recently published.[1] A historian from Curaçao has been working on Amsterdam synagogal archives for nearly a year - in pre-war days leave to examine these was invariably refused - and we now know that two Scrolls with their appurtenances, a reading desk cover and curtains (presumably for the Ark) were handed over at Amsterdam in April 1657 to the agents for the Barbados Jews (Abr. Chillon and Abr. Messias), who undertook to obtain payment for them. Another Scroll was supplied to a different agent in September 1657, which suggests that perhaps the Island's second synagogue at Speightstown had indented for it.

Another recent writer[2] who has gained access also to the Amsterdam Synagogue's muniments has shewn that the founder of the Bridgetown Synagogue, Joseph Jessurun Mendes, alias Lewis Dias, was active in the Pernambuco (Recife) Synagogue from 1649 to 1652. The historian of Curaçao shews him at Amsterdam - with his father - as a recently joined synagogue member in August 1654. Allowing that Cromwell had authorised another refugee Jew from Dutch Brazil, "Abraham de Mercado, M.D. Hebrew ... to exercise his profession ..... (in) ..... the Barbadoes" - the pass is dated April 1655[3] - it is not impossible that this foreword is being penned in the Tercentenary Year of the Barbados Jews. Public worship for the Jews of London came about in February or March 1657, but in his introduction Mr. Shilstone shews grounds for selecting 1654 as the commencing year of the practice of Judaism on Barbados.

Right up to Queen Victoria's accession it was held in certain English legal circles that a Jew could not hold land. It is interesting to note that the Jews of Barbados were already in the 17th century freeholders on a fairly extensive scale. One can instance the brothers de Caceres in 1653, and David Namias and David de Acosta, plantation owners by 1680. In that year the Barbados congregation with its synagogues at Bridgetown and Speightstown could not have been greatly inferior in numbers to London's synagogue in Creechurch Lane - the precursor of Bevis Marks Synagogue, not opened until 1701. With regard to Mr. Shilstone's estimate that at the close of the 17th century about 250 Jews were living on Barbados, by 1710 a certain T. Walduck, writing from Bridgetown to London[4], records a far larger number. He held that there were 150 Jewish families in Bridgetown and a further 20 families at Speightstown to its north. Reckoning only 4 Jews to one family, that would give a total of 680 Jews, or 8% of the total white population on the island. In 1684 a Dutch visitor to London listed all the members of the Creechurch Lane Synagogue. Children included, they numbered 414[5].

In the "House of Life"[6] (a pious euphemism) of the London congregation was a small burial plot usually near the Keeper's house and designated "behind the boards". There were interred those Sephardi Jews deemed by their co-religionists to have lived or died or been born ignobly. Communal tradition has it that actors, bastards, felons, prostitutes, pugilists and suicides were interred "behind the boards", no entries being made in the burial registers so that no positive information on this gruesome subject has survived. It may well be that the small graveyard mentioned in Mr. Shilstone's introduction ("enclosed by the buildings fronting on Swan Street, White's Alley and James's Street") is of this category, although one would scarcely expect such graves to be marked with tombstones. As against this, Mr. Shilstone wrote in a recent letter:- "It was a common practice for owners of plantations to be buried in their estates and not in churchyards. Many tombstones can still be found in sugar-cane fields in plantations." A cognate incident is revealed by a somewhat grim entry in the Bridgetown Minute Book :-

"Friday, 15 Ab. 5552, 3rd August 1792 ---- agreed "that no Person or Persons that stands on the list

"as a Pensioner should be concerned in aiding or
"assisting in digging her (Lunah Arrobus') grave
"or washing her, and should any one of such persons
"attempt in aiding or assisting they shall be
"immediately taken off the list of Pensioners ....
"it was also further agreed that upon application
"to the Parnaz [7] to know where she is to be buried,
"that he shall go and show the place in the Nook
"and if they will bring negroes to dig her grave
"they are at liberty to do so, at the same time
"it was directed that a way should be built to
"divide the Nook from the Bet Haim [6] and a door to be
"put at the end in front of the street so that that
"part shall have not communication with the other."

Notwithstanding that Lunah Arrobus had been conver-
ted to Christianity, the Jews had apparently been ordered to give her burial. The costly manoeuvre described
in the Minute had the effect of creating a separate, if
tiny, non-Jewish cemetery, and "to divide the Nook from
the House of Life [7]" was to be effected by making a special path and perhaps also by boarding-off the Nook.

Persistent attempts to convert the Jews on Barbados to the Friends' form of Christianity were made by
the Quakers, who were at one time numerous on the Island.
As far back as 1686 George Fox, the Quaker leader
(1624 - 1691), had sent out a printed letter in somewhat
curious Hebrew for circulation among the Jews. It was
in connection with this that the following report was
sent to London from the Island :-

"Inform dear G.F. that I copied over divers of
"his Hebrew papers which were writt to the Jews;
"And by reason many of them did Not understand
"Hebrew; them I writt Spannish copies. The
"2 Hebrew printed papers were delivered to the
"Jews at their 2 synagogues; at the one they
"were indifferent moderate to Friends; but at
"the other they were Not. Some denied the
"Truth of the Papers as to Substance, and also
"said that it was Not rightly printed; but as to
"that they were but some Litteral mistakes; and
"as for the Substance I have undertaken the proof
"of it by Scripture. And some of the Jews did
"grievously Raile at, and abuse G.F. "

A further extract from this report which is dated

27th December 1685/6 is worth quoting for the unexpected picture it gives of the humbler sort of Bridgetown Jews:-

> "I had at, and before the time of the delivery of
> "those papers, a Jew for my Usher; who used to
> "hear my Schollars read the New Testament, and to
> "hear the Children read, and say by heart the
> "Child's Lesson and Cathechism in G.F.'s Primer;
> "But after the delivery of G.F.'s Papers to the
> "Jews did much Vex and Perplex him; and particu-
> "larly his Father told him (as he himself told me)
> "that if he could Not get his Liveing unless he
> "lived with a Christian then he should Not live in
> "this Island; by reason of which he was very urgent
> "with me to acquit him of my Service (for he had
> "covenanted with me for about 6 months) and after
> "many entreaties I granted his request; but first
> "got him to write one of G.F.'s Hebrew papers,
> "divers Testimonies relating to the Messiah, etc."
> "I have at times had severall Jews, both Men and
> "Children, which I have taught in G.F.'s Primer,
> "etc.   One of which being a notable lively boy,
> "had learnt part of the Child's Lesson by heart
> "(chiefly, I believe, by hearing the other Child-
> "ren say it) and would say it at home to the
> "People of the house and his parents.   I goeing
> "one day to the Jew's house his Father called
> "his Child, and bid him say it: And he began
> "very prettily and boldly to say, Christ is the
> "Truth; and so went on till his Mother began to be
> "very angry and called him Dog, and bid him hold
> "his tongue.[8]"

The trading activities in the late 17th century of one section of the Barbadian Jewish community have received some light from the hostile writings of Samuel Hayne, an English Customs' official under Charles II and James II. In a rare pamphlet[9] he reports that in 1680 the Jews were "removing the staple of Commerce from England to Holland, most of their cargoes for the planta- tions being made up of the growth, product and manufact- ure of those parts, and none of English", i.e. instead of paying dues in accordance with the Navigation Act on Dutch wares imported to and re-exported from England, the Jews were avoiding payment and underselling their com- petitors. He further instances the ship *Experiment* of London "bound from the Island of Barbadoes" which docked in October 1680 at Falmouth en route for Amsterdam with much Sugar, 3 hogsheads of tobacco and three great Brass or Copper guns "which were taken abroad the said ship at Barbadoes; the sugar and merchandise do really belong to Jews and particularly to Aaron Barscoe, Abraham Barrase, one Rodrigo and Lewes Deus and some other Jews whose names are unknown to the Deponents[10]." These goods ostensibly the property of a Falmouth merchant were reloaded at Falmouth for Amsterdam without paying duty. Hayne having arrested the ship, he found that he had writs taken out against him by the gentile owners as well as by 'Gomasera & Losado'.

The history of the Barbados Jewish Community during the 18th and 19th centuries has not yet been written. In a rare book by Mr. E. S. Daniels[11], who was the main pillar of the Congregation in Victorian times, were sketched the progressive steps whereby full emancipation was reached in the island, and it is to these steps that Mr. Shilstone in his admirable introduction has alluded.

The present series of epitaphs should facilitate the task of future students of Barbadian history. It does not tell the whole tale, which is one not only of immigration but emigration too. To take an example: In the second half of the 17th century Rowland Gideon was resident in Barbados coming from St. Kitts. He settled in London ca. 1690. He is remembered in Anglo-Jewish history as the first Jew to become a freeman of a City Company. He became the father of Sampson Gideon (1699 - 1762), the financial magnate, who for years was Sir Robert Walpole's adviser in money matters.

These epitaphs, however will enable the historian to trace many families which had and preserved extensive connections with London (the Lindos, Barrow-Lousadas, and others) and with New York (Valverde, Messias, Peixotto).

For 1777 one notes the Burial Register entry "Haham Raphael Haim Isaac Carigal 48 years". This Rabbi of Bridgetown had been born in Palestine and had taught in the Bevis Marks *Medrash* for two and a half years (from 1768). Before visiting the American Plantations and the West Indies he had wandered through Persia, the Ottoman lands, Germany, Italy and France. He bequeathed his Barbados library and oriental wardrobe to his wife and son at Hebron, and one wonders whether the London executor - Abraham Levy Ximenes - ever contrived to have them delivered.

Other picturesque Jewish figures flitted across the scene at different times in the history of Barbados Jewry without settling on the Island or leaving any permanent trace of their passage. There was, for instance, Benjamin Franks, who had in 1697 deposed in New York that he was a West Indies trader who had lived in Barbados. In the previous year he had been a passenger in the galley "Adventure", as he designed to settle in India as a trader in jewels. The master of this ship, the notorious Captain Kidd, turned pirate on a considerable scale and was hanged, largely on the evidence of Benjamin Franks, who had taken no part in his piracies[12].

* * * * *

In sponsoring this publication the Records Committee of the Spanish & Portuguese Jews' Congregation in London (Chairman, Dr. Lionel D. Barnett, C.B., M.A., F.B.A.) has had the generous help of the Jewish Historical Society of England as well as of confrères in the United States, viz., The American Jewish Historical Society of New York, the American Jewish Archives of Cincinnati and the Spanish & Portuguese Jews' Congregation (Shearith Israel) of New York. Private individuals in Brazil and Curaçao have also supported the Publication Fund. It is due to the initiative of a recently deceased member of the Records Committee, the much regretted Albert M. Hyamson, O.B.E., F.R.Hist.S, that this invaluable assistance was procured.

The illustrations have been drawn in London by Mr. Douglas Woodall from photographic snapshots furnished by Mr. Shilstone.

It would have been more appropriate had Mr. Shilstone's "monumental work" been introduced by Mr. Richard D. Barnett, M.A., F.S.A. the Honorary Archivist of the Spanish & Portuguese Jews' Congregation, London. For it is he who has borne the arduous work of editing it and seeing to the indispensable indexing. He has also unearthed the register of Jewish burials on Barbados, which contains some 800 names, and has checked this London material - which came from Barbados - with the Shilstone material. This register in London seems to have been compiled about 1750 from the tombstones and thereafter kept up to date. All who use this work will have good

cause to be grateful to Mr. Barnett as well as to Mr.
Shilstone for their unselfish labours. A word of
thanks is also due to Mr. Cyril Moss, of the British
Museum, for checking the texts of the Hebrew epitaphs.

Wilfred S. Samuel.

London.
1st August, 1955.

FOOTNOTES

(TO PREFACE)

1. By Dr. I. S. Emmanuel of Curaçao in *American Jewish Archives*, (Cincinnati, Jan. 1955).
2. Dr. Arnold Wiznitzer: *"The Records of the Earliest Jewish
   Community in the New World"*. (New York 1954 – Am. Jew. Hist.
   Soc.)
3. Calendar of State Papers (Domestic) 1655, xi. 583.
4. Brit. Mus., Sloane MSS. 2302
5. L. D. Barnett, *Bevis Marks Records*, Part I, p. 20.
6. i. e. graveyard, in Hebrew *Bet Haim* as in line 12 page viii.
7. Parnas = Warden.
8. Professor Henry J. Cadbury in *Bulletin of Friends' Historical Association*, (Swarthmore, Pa., 1940).
9.   AN
                       ABSTRACT
                      of all the
                       STATUTES
                    Made Concerning
                    ALIENS TRADING
                          IN
                       ENGLAND
                        ALSO

9. *(Cont'd)*

Of all the Laws made for Securing
our Plantation Trade to our Selves

With Observations thereon, proving that the Jews
(in their practical way of Trade at this time)
Break them all, to the great Damage of the King
in His Customs, the Merchants in their Trade,
the whole Kingdom, and His Majesties Plantations in America. . . . .
. . . .
. . . .

By Samuel Hayne, sometime Ryding-Surveyor for His Majes
ties Customs and Surveyor for the Act of Navigation in
the Countries of Devon and Cornwal.

Printed 1685.

10. For Barscoe understand Pacheco, for Barrasse – Barrassa or
De Barrios, for Deus – Lewis Dias; Rodrigo was probably
Anthony Rodriguez (the alias of Aaron Levi Rezio).   The
London agents were doubtless a Gomez-Serra and a Lousada.

11. *Extracts from various records regarding the settlement of
the Jews in the Island of Barbadoes* (privately printed,
Bridgetown 1899).

12. Publ. No. 31, Am. Jew. Hist. Soc. (N.Y.1928).

INTRODUCTION

I

About three of the clock on a bright and sunny afternoon in the month of March, 1833,[1] the people of the Hebrew Nation in Bridgetown, Barbados, commenced to assemble in the courts and avenues of their Synagogue, and in the course of an hour, they were joined by a number of the most respectable inhabitants, and ladies of grace, fashion and beauty (admitted to the galleries) to witness the interesting and impressive ceremony before them. "It was a day that would ever stand eminently distinguished in the annals of the Hebrew community of the town", prophesied the editor of the *Barbados Globe*.[2]

The occasion was the consecration of the new Synagogue, built to replace a former building on the same site within whose hallowed walls, for possibly two centuries "they had long been accustomed to assemble and chaunt a solemn worship in an ancient tongue, with ceremonials and religious observances that constantly re-animated their high enthusiasm into holy joy". The former synagogue, like so many of the churches of the island, had been so shattered by the calamitous hurricane of 1831, that it was found necessary to raze it altogether to its very foundations. Through the liberality of their community, the indefatigable exertion of the leading members, and the unwearied zeal of a select committee of their body, this remnant of the ancient congregation, *Nidhe Israel* - "the dispersed of Israel", had provided a new structure of exquisite taste and chaste design, for the exercise of their faith and worship.

The building occupied an area of two thousand square feet, being fifty feet long and forty feet wide. It was thirty-seven feet high and received considerable strength

View of the interior of the Synagogue, looking towards the Reader's Desk. (1927).

from the rounding of the angles of the walls which were capped with large antique censers, uniting a balustraded parapet all around, the roof being hardly visible.

The windows were lancet shaped, and tastefully harmonised with the proportions of the building: a double flight of stone steps on the north side covered with a gothic hood led to the gallery within: the whole exterior was lightly tinged of stone colour and scored out in blocks, and the appearance altogether was classical and chaste. The high enclosure walls which had hitherto rendered the passage to the old synagogue so dull and sombre had been recently lowered, so as to afford a general view of the whole at the entrance of the avenue.

The court-yard around the building was well drained and neatly paved with imported squares of English manufacture: and a handsome marble fountain[3] occupied a niche within the inner court, railed off with an iron trellis.

On entering the building, one beheld on his right the Ark[4] (or sacred depositary of the Pentateuch) on which was inscribed in Hebrew characters, *'Know in whose presence thou standest'*, having the tables of the Law, surmounted with the regal crown, placed on its top; a splendid star, in glowing transparent colours of stained glass, being directly over the whole. On the left stood an imposing Reader's desk,[5] sufficiently elevated to give a conspicuous view of the persons officiating; and immediately in front the warden's stall, of highly polished mahogany, presented itself. On three sides of the interior ran a gallery of light construction[6], supported by doric columns suitably decorated. From the ceiling was suspended at each corner in front of the gallery, a fine brass chandelier, of eight lights each, and in the centre one of a similar nature containing twenty-four[7]. There were numerous Sheffield plated sconces ranging round the walls, and to the splendour of the consequent illumination was added the light from the massive candlesticks and wax candles on the railing of the reader's desk and enclosure of the Ark.

The building was paved in alternate squares of black and white marble, and the ceiling painted in relief. It was designed to hold three hundred persons.

The cost of the new structure was £4000 in Island currency.

I I

In a solemn and impressive ceremony, the new synagogue was dedicated - *HOLY TO THE LORD* - by the reader , the warden, and other officers of the congregation. The door of the synagogue was thrown open on the pronouncing of the words - *Open to me the gates of righteousness* during the singing of Psalm cxviii by the reader and choristers.

Then followed the prayer - *Blessed art Thou, O Lord! our God! King of the Universe! who hath preserved us alive, sustained us, and brought us to enjoy this day!* The congregation then entered the building and the ceremony proceeded. The assembled Jews were about ninety-three in number; and many people of distinction in the life of the island joined them in witnessing the joyful but dignified ritual of consecrating their new place of worship. Among persons of note, there were present the Speaker and several other members of the House of Assembly, the Attorney General, the Solicitor General, the Judge Advocate, the Chief Baron of the Exchequer, the Treasurer, the Secretary of the Island, the Collector and the Comptroller of Customs, Colonel Sir F. Smith, commanding Royal Engineers, and many other military gentlemen, and a goodly number of the principal merchants of Bridgetown.

I I I

There is no exact record of the earliest existence of a synagogue in Barbados. In a deed of conveyance of land adjoining the Jewish property, dated 1 September 1664, one of the boundaries mentioned is "the Jewes Synagogue". And as one of the muniments of title to the same land there is preserved a plan, dated 4 July 1664, made by Andrew Norwood, surveyor, with a sketch of the synagogue building shown as a boundary.[8] It is interesting to note that the synagogue there shown occupies the exact position of the present edifice.

Facts concerning the acquisition by the Jews of the site of the synagogue and the lands of the burial grounds attached are buried in obscurity. No such records exist; and, until the year 1869, there is no evidence to disclose in whom the property was vested.

The presence of Jews in Barbados soon after the English settlement of the Island in 1627 has been alleged by more than one commentator. Schomburgk, the author of the *History of Barbados,* published in 1848,[9] states that according to the best information obtainable, the settlement of the Jews there dates from 1628. Doubtless this statement was based upon a letter, dated 22 September 1628, preserved among Colonial State Papers[10] from Abraham Jacob, writing from London, to the Earl of Carlisle, Lord Proprietor of Barbados, wherein he complains of the island business as having been exceedingly unprofitable. The letter discloses no evidence in support of the inference that the trade was with Jews.

Definite evidence of their existence is found in the Minutes of Council of Barbados[11] for November, 8, 1654, when it was "Ordered that the consideration of the jews and foreigners brought from Brazele to the Island be presented at the next sitting of the Governor and Assembly". Evidently, before that time, Jews and foreigners seem not to have been present in sufficient numbers to attract attention. At a subsequent meeting of the Council, in January 1655, the matter came up for consideration, and the following Order is taken from the Minutes - "Upon the Petition of several Jews and Hebrews, inhabiting in and about this Island, it is Ordered, that the Petitioners behaving themselves civily and comformably to the Government of this Island, and being nothing tending to the disturbance of the Peace and quiet thereof, during their stay, shall enjoy the privileges of Laws and Statutes of the Commonwealth of England and of this Island, relating to foreigners and strangers".

The Jews were the subject of a "presentment" by the Grand Jury of Barbados in 1656;[12] and on notice thereof being taken by the Council, it was decided that "the particulars relating to the Jews presented by the Grand Jury at the last General Session held for this island, (the Governor and Council) will take the same into further consideration at the next sitting".

Early mention of the presence of a Jew in Barbados is made by Richard Ligon in "*A true and exact history of*

Barbados", published in London in 1657, second edition, 1673. Ligon sojourned in Barbados between the years 1647 and 1650. Referring to the failure of the trials by the inhabitants in making bricks, the author says: "there was an ingenious Jew upon the Island whose name was Solomon, that undertook to teach the making of it, yet for all that when it came to the touch his wisdom failed and we were deceived in our expectations".[13]

There is documentary evidence that previous to the year 1655 Jews had emigrated from England to Barbados. The document is a Petition of the Jewish Nation in America to the Dutch West India Company, dated January 1655.[14] And in April of the same year, a pass was issued by Cromwell to Dr. Abraham de Mercado, and David Raphael de Mercado, his son, to go to Barbados to exercise his profession.[15]

The Barbados congregation, "the scattered of Israel", although mainly Portuguese, were gathered from all parts of the world. They increased in numbers as years rolled on, and towards the end of the seventeenth century there were about 250 Jews living in the island. Thus a considerable community existed, eventually to join their forbears and fellows in *Beth Haim*, the House of Life, as more than one testator referred to his last resting place in the instructions for burial contained in his will.

The removal of all civil and political disabilities at the commencement of the nineteenth century finally increased the tide of prosperity which they had enjoyed for the past fifty years. On the other hand, their extensive loss of property in the great hurricane of 1831, followed by the emancipation of slaves in 1834, very definitely contributed to the closure of the period of their affluence. Moreover, about that time, many prominent Jewish families went to settle in England, whence they tried to maintain a trade and correspondence with the island. These trade relations gradually waned under increasingly active competition from local interests until they reached a vanishing point. Also, many families migrated to the United States, and more or less lost touch with the Barbados assembly.

The final decline of the community seems to have been marked by the rebuilding of the synagogue in Bridgetown: or was it only coincidental ?

In 1848, there were but 71 Jews in the Island, 38 of whom belonged to the congregation;[18] and by the opening of the present century there were less than twenty people all told who claimed or acknowledged the Jewish faith.

As will be noted later on, there came a time when it was declared that only one Jew then remained, and it was not many years after that he was gathered to his fathers.

IV

The transcripts submitted for publication, are of the inscriptions on the tombstones in the burial-ground attached to the Jewish synagogue in Synagogue Lane and Magazine Lane, in Bridgetown.   The grave-yard lies in the heart of the town, and in close proximity to the business section, where the Jews lived and had their shops.   Swan Street, a block away, was formerly called "Jew Street", because the Jews gradually acquired nearly all the houses there and absorbed that entire business section.   It is quite natural that the Jews should have chosen to live near the synagogue, but the fact that there was a grave-yard attached to their place of worship and in view of the surrounding houses calls for comment, since it is alleged that this circumstance is altogether unusual in a Jewish community.[17]

There was another small burial-ground enclosed by the buildings fronting on Swan Street, White's Alley, and James Street respectively.   Practically all the backyards in that section opened upon the little plot of land.[18]   It is mentioned as a boundary in conveyances of Swan Street buildings and land about the early nineteenth century.   There were many tombstones still visible in this small burial-ground when in the year 1928 officials of the Jewish congregation in London sold the buildings in James Street which had belonged to the Barbados congregation.   These buildings and all the land (including the small graveyard) are now in private ownership.   As for the tombs in this burial-ground, it is understood that all have been laid level and covered with

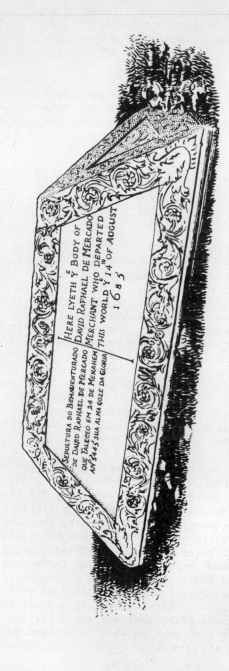

Here lyeth ỹ Body of
David Raphael de Mercado
Merchant who departed
this world ỹ 14ᵗʰ of August
1685

Sepultura do Benaventurado
de David Raphael de Mercado
que Faleceo em 24 de Menahem
Anᵒ 5445 sua alma goze da Gloria

Tombstone of David de Marcado, 1685. (No. 178, page 81.)

earth to remove all traces of them.   Visitors are now denied access to the area.

Burials in the small graveyard are said to have been contemporary with those in the large burial-ground attached to the synagogue.   In accounting for the ex- istence of this small exclusive graveyard, the reason is given that a Jew buried therein had either died by his own hand or that he was not of the Portuguese and Spanish congregation.   These are points which require elucidation by those competent to discuss them.

Schomburgk states that there were five burial-grounds of the Jews, three of which were completely filled at the time of writing his *History*, although he makes no attempt to identify them.   Most certainly, he would or could have seen the graveyard in the synagogue grounds, and perhaps the smaller one in White's Alley, and poss- ibly the burial-ground which received the bodies of the Speightstown congregation in the Parish of St. Peter, more that twelve miles away.   Where were the other two ? One may hazard the guess that the historian was misled into assuming that the two Quaker burial grounds, one in St. Michael and the other in St. Philip, both by that time in disuse, were indeed Jewish graveyards, filled and abandoned.   Schomburgk mentions the Quaker congre- gation which had formerly existed in Barbados, but he makes no reference to their burial grounds.

A careful survey of the Synagogue graveyard revealed that the oldest tombstone (No. 230) records the burial in 1660 (9 Adar 5420) of Aaron de Mercado. Mr. Wilfred Samuel, in his excellent and scholarly treatise on the Jews in Barbados, notes this as the first Jewish burial. In this assertion he is supported by the Record of the Burials of the Jews deposited in the Registration Office at Bridgetown.   The record is supposed to be a copy of the Jewish records preserved in the synagogue at Bridge- town, although there is no official statement to that effect, nor is the compilation certified in any way by the person in whose custody the original records were kept, or indeed by anyone else.

The compilation forms part of the records of sectar- ian bodies, records of the military stationed in the Garri- son, and Jewish records, bound together in two volumes and classified as baptisms, marriages, and burials.   It is believed that these records were deposited during the eighties or nineties of the last century, purporting to be copies made from originals in the custody of the church or synagogue.

As regards these burial records of the Jews, after careful inspection and deliberation, one arrives at the conclusion that the copy so deposited was not transcribed from original entries in a register made at the time of each event, but was specially compiled for deposit with the central authorities from the then visible tombstones. Errors in dates, names, descriptions of the deceased (e.g. "wife" for widow, and *vice versa*) are of frequent occurrence, and fully support that view. Moreover, during the one or other of my tours over the grounds, by the removal of a considerable amount of earth, memorials in the graveyard were exposed which must have lain buried for two centuries. In every such instance, comparison with the entries in the volume showed that there was no corresponding record.

V

To revert to the relation of the preservation of title to the synagogue, and its graveyard, and the subsequent loss of authority over them by the Jews. About the middle of the last century, the Barbados community seem to have been aware of the necessity for some active steps to be taken to preserve their legal interests. Realising the decay in their numbers, and the importance of making provision for the future protection of the synagogue and burial-grounds besides the other freehold properties in James Street belonging to the congregation, some of the most prominent members took steps to set the matter at rest, with the intention that so long as there was a professing Jew in Barbados a place of worship and also of burial among the people of his faith would be assured.

Consequently, on May 6, 1869, a deed of settlement was made and executed by Michael Baber Isaacs, Joshua Levi, Benjamin Cohen d'Azevedo, Solomon Baber Isaacs,

Jacob Lindo, Edward Daniels, Benjamin Lobo and Daniel
Lobo (all Barbados Jews) of the one part, and Isaac
Benjamin Elkin, Nathaneel Lindo, Samuel Taylor, Charles
Thomas Cottle, the said Edward Daniels and Michael Baber
Isaacs, of the other part. [19] By that document the synagogue and graveyard in Synagogue Lane, Bridgetown, were
conveyed upon trust for the use of the Hebrew community
in the island of Barbados until there should be no person of the community residing in the said island; when
it was to be conveyed to the warden and other officers
of the Spanish and Portuguese Hebrew Community and Congregation of Bevis Marks, London. In 1905 the trustees
of the said settlement being all dead, the whole property
was conveyed by John William Lackland Craig and others
(executors of the Will of Edward Daniels the last surviving trustee) to Joshua Baeza and Edmund Isaac Baeza (two
Jews, brothers, prominent merchants in Bridgetown) by deed[20]
upon trust for the use of the persons mentioned in the
indenture of 1869.

Joshua Baeza died, and Edmund Baeza, claiming to be
the sole male member of the Hebrew faith in Barbados,
suggested the time had arrived for winding up the trust and
disposing of the Jewish property in Barbados. Seeming-
ly, the London authorities approved of his suggestion,
and he received a power of attorney[21] from the wardens
and treasurer of Bevis Marks community empowering him to
represent the London trustees in negotiating and com-
pleting sales of the Jewish properties.

It is suggested that the extent of the powers granted
was most unusual in the case of trustees, and definitely
not in accordance with the legal maxim - *delegatus est
non potest delegare.*

V I

Then on April 27, 1928, Edmund Isaac Baeza made a
sale of the property by private treaty with Henry Graham
Yearwood, a Bridgetown solicitor. The deed, dated April
27, 1928,[22] was made between the said Baeza, surviving
trustee, of the first part, Edward Lumbrozo Mocatta,
Ellis Saleh Manasseh, Jonathan Pinto, Frank Isaac Afriat
and Leon Benham Castello, the wardens and officers of

the Spanish and Portuguese Hebrew Community or congregation of Bevis Marks acting therein by the said Baeza, their attorney, of the second part, and Henry Graham Yearwood of the third part.   The price of the entire property was stated to be £600; and the document contained a grant by way of assurance of the. fee simple of the synagogue and a dwelling-house (the ruins of the rabbi's house) *and also the graveyard* containing 25,247 square feet of land, according to a plan thereof annexed to the deed.   The purchaser covenanted for himself and the successive owners for the time being of the property, with the vendors, to keep the wall enclosure around the burial ground in repair and from time to time to replace the same; and also to keep in proper order and condition the burial-grounds, and not to use or permit the same to be used for any purpose whatsoever, with the right of the vendors or their agents to inspect the property from time to time to see that the covenant is being performed.

Mr. H. G. Yearwood purchased the synagogue intending to present it to the Barbados Government for use as a library for the members of the legal profession, the proposal being to transfer the law books from the Carnegie Library to the synagogue building.   Apparently the thought of legal practitioners being obliged to look upon a collection of ancient tombstones while pursuing their researches in the law was disturbing, and a suggestion was made and communicated[23] to the Bevis Marks officials that the graveyard would be improved by levelling the graves and removing the broken tombstones.   This suggestion, far from finding favour with the London Mahamad, provoked an expression of their refusal[24] to sell at the price of £600, or indeed at any price on the terms offered and the declaration "that the Mahamad cannot on religious and sentimental grounds be party to the destruction of existing memorials", and Baeza was asked to "find means of disposing of the property on conditions which do not affect the burial-ground in the manner suggested".[25]

About that time, the writer offered to purchase the synagogue for preservation as a national memorial to the Jews of Barbados, and because of its historical and antiquarian connections, but the proposal was rejected by Mr. Baeza on the ground that the price offered was less than the offer in hand, the amount of the first offer, however, not being divulged.

Being favoured with the right of perusal of copies of the lengthy correspondence which passed between the Mahamad and Mr. E. I. Baeza I am left in considerable doubt as to the final intentions of the parties in the light of subsequent developments. Early in 1928, Mr. Baeza reported to the Mahamad that he had agreed to sell the building and the land on which it stood, but not the graveyard, for the sum of £600. "The graveyards are excluded from sale and remain in possession of the Bevis Marks Congregation".[26] Apparently, the proposed transaction on those or similar lines had the approval of the Mahamad, and it must be assumed that the graveyards were to be excluded from a sale, for simultaneously the Mahamad authorised the expenditure by Mr. Baeza of £30 in repairs to vaults and in putting the ground in presentable condition.[27] The clearing of the ground and the general improvement in its appearance was supervised by the late Miss Margaret Packer, M.B.E., an indefatigable worker in the cause of civic improvement, to whom I remain indebted for securing for me the favour of being allowed to copy the inscriptions on my first tour of the grounds. Through her unfailing co-operation and direction of the removal of the tangled vines, shrubs and undergrowth (and above all, through her success in removing the spirit of opposition to the task I had undertaken) my work was considerably lightened. Moreover, it was made more interesting by her magnetic personality and sympathetic interest and influence during its early stages, and indeed, until her lamentable demise.

As has been stated, the declared intentions of the parties to the sale negotiations do not seem to coincide with subsequent developments. Following the sequence of events, it seems that in February 1929 an inquiry from the Mahamad concerning the upkeep of the burial ground[28] brought the reply from Mr. Baeza[29] that the graves had all been levelled to one height and only a general cleaning up was necessary. In view of the purchaser's covenant in the conveyance, Mr. Baeza thought any further expense unnecessary as the cost of repairs to the enclosure walls and upkeep of the burial grounds was thrown on the purchaser.[30] It is difficult to reconcile these circumstances with the Mahamad's former views.

The Government refused Mr. Yearwood's offer to present them with the building for a law library; and in

Marble fountain for washing the hands,
at the entrance to the cemetery.

reporting the circumstances to Mr. Baeza, Mr. Yearwood wrote[31] - "I will ask Miss Packer, who is in charge of the Military Cemetery, if she will undertake to look after the Jewish Cemetery for the Mahamad". One can only conclude that although he was the owner of the graveyard, Mr. Yearwood considered the responsibility of its maintenance still rested with the London trustees.

The synagogue building was sold with all its furniture and fittings used in synagogue worship. The purchaser afterwards made a sale of the chandeliers and wall sconces for export to the United States. In May 1934 Mr. Yearwood died after a short illness, and on the 4th of June following Mr. Baeza died.

Subsequently, a public sale was held of the furniture and fittings then remaining in the synagogue, and not long afterwards the entire property changed hands again. It was acquired by Mr. W. St. C. Hutchinson, a Barbados solicitor, who made some alterations to the main building and let it in offices.[32] The old and magnificent timber trees were felled, and garages erected in certain portions of the grounds. The old approaches from the street were closed and new ones made of more convenient widths for motor traffic.

The subsequent owner of the property repudiated the burden of the covenant to keep the burial ground in proper order and repair, etc. resulting in unhappy differences which have only recently been settled. Meantime, Mr. Hutchinson also died.

With the lapse of time, a considerable community of Jews has been again established in Barbados, who sought the right of burial in the graveyard. They were willing to assume control of the ground and to take all lawful measures for vesting it in trustees so that it might never again fall into secular use. After protracted negotiations over a period of years the graveyard has been brought under control of trustees drawn from the local Jewish congregation and also a representative of the Barbados Museum and Historical Society by virtue of a Statute passed by the island legislature on the petition of the Bevis Marks authorities and others. A sum of money in hand from the sale of the property was delivered over to the trustees the income whereof is devoted (along with contributions from the congregation) to the preservation and upkeep of the graveyard.

VII

The synagogue and graveyard had ever been a place of wonder and mystery to me. I remember as a child of about eight years of age being taken by one of the daughters of the late Mr. E. S. Daniels (the last reader of the synagogue) to see the building, and having the meaning of its various appointments explained to me. Subsequently, for eight years I had offices in a building in James Street exactly opposite the entrance gate of the synagogue, which was regularly opened every Saturday morning by an old woman who lived in the shabby ruins of the rabbi's house within the confines of the yard. Frequently, I dropped in to enjoy the peaceful scene and to read in a casual way one or two of the inscriptions on the tombstones bordering upon the flagged pathway leading to the edifice. It was always a source of pleasure to conduct a visitor over the synagogue and grounds who had a taste for the antiquities and had been unaware of the existence of the synagogue and its treasures.

My decision to decipher the inscriptions on the tombstones and to copy them was originally taken for their antiquarian interest and not with any idea of publishing the results. In the midst of a busy life, the time that one could devote to it was at first indeed inconsiderable, but later on as the work progressed I became so engrossed in the effort that I decided to enlist the help of a friend, Miss Eileen Leacock, who, as I cleaned and deciphered the inscriptions, English, Portuguese and Spanish, very kindly wrote at my dictation and afterwards typed them neatly for revision. I knew not a single Hebrew character and made no attempt to copy inscriptions in that language. Those were rainy years, and with the flourishing of the rank undergrowth and the necessity of uncovering and cleaning every stone, progress was slow. I acknowledge the kind help given me by Miss Leacock (now Mrs. Carter), and her departure from Barbados during the early stages of the work was a great loss to me. The Barbados Museum and Historical Society was established in 1933, and the publication of a Quarterly Journal by the Society commenced in November in that year. It was then proposed to print the inscriptions by instalments with biographical details of the subjects of the memorials along with illustrations of the synagogue and its appointments. However, an appeal for donations towards the cost of printing and photographic work brought a few sympathetic letters but no other results, and the project had to be abandoned.

In 1938, during a visit to the United States, I made the acquaintance of Mr. Edward D. Coleman, Librarian of the American Jewish Historical Society, and showed him some of the transcripts. The encouragement which I received from him and Dr. D. de Sola Pool of Congregation Shearith Israel, Central Park West, New York City compelled me to acquire an elementary knowledge of Hebrew, and to undertake to copy the writing on the stones in that language. On my return to Barbados, I gave close application to the work, becoming far advanced in copying memorials in Section A of the graveyard when Mr. Coleman arrived at Barbados on a cruise ship. The ship stopped at Barbados over the week-end and Mr. Coleman spent several hours in deciphering obscure inscriptions and checking my copy. Being apparently satisfied with the progress already made, Mr. Coleman urged me to continue on the same lines with every promise of assistance on his part in supervising and checking the results. From time to time I sent Mr. Coleman portions of the manuscript to which he must have given considerable time and labour in correcting errors. I received word that the Publications Committee would consider the inclusion of my compilation in their Publications if it should be presented in complete form, which was a great impetus to the work.

In the spring of 1939, Mr. Coleman again visited Barbados and remained about a fortnight, examining the transcripts and checking them with the writing on the stones. I suggested that we should complete the compilation together and publication should be made in our joint names, a proposition which he very magnanimously rejected. A bare acknowledgement of the assistance he had given me in deciphering difficult inscriptions and checking my notes was all he expected or desired. I was then on my third and final tour of the graveyard. First, I had copied only English and Spanish-Portuguese inscriptions: on the second tour I added all the Hebrew writings decipherable, and on the final tour every inscription was checked and others included which had been discovered later by my own efforts as well as through changes made by the owners in certain features of the graveyard.

VIII

The first step towards the publication of the transcripts was the typewriting of the Hebrew characters from my manuscript, which was done under Mr. Coleman's supervision in New York. Shortly afterwards, to my profound sorrow and amazement, I learnt of Mr. Coleman's sudden and unexpected death. With the advent of the war and other considerations the publication of the compilation was postponed. For my part, I cared not whether it was produced or not. The death of my friend, Mr. Coleman, to whom I owed so much for his assistance and encouragement in the course of the labours which I had undertaken, dulled the edge of all former zeal to see the manuscript in print. Now that it is to be published, in my heart and mind, it is dedicated to his memory.

As one gazes upon the present scene of desolation in the graveyard of the synagogue, with features so vastly and deplorably changed since I first began to copy the memorials, it is with feelings of thankfulness and satisfaction that I can regard as fulfilled the self-imposed obligation of preserving for all time the fading records carved upon the tombstones, seeing that the original stones for the most part, are no longer visible.

Such is the reward for the hours of work in the quiet surroundings and peaceful shadow of the ancient buildings, and some solace at least for the poignant loss of the memorials themselves.

In regard to the character of the tombstones and their inscriptions, it may be noted that every stone is of imported material - marble, or limestone of Purbeck or similar variety, and usually of the full length and width of the grave it covers. The quality of workmanship in the carving of the inscriptions and design varies considerably. The excellence of the work in many instances indicates an English origin; others are obviously the work of local stonemasons. Errors in the Hebrew lettering lead to the supposition that the sculptor was not familiar with their proper form. Here and there the efforts of a maladroit workman leave one in doubt as to the characters intended.

In the transcripts, no attempt has been made to improve on the written words of the memorial; a faithful representation of the original is intended, and attention has been given to the reproduction of errors in the text. It will be seen that the corresponding date in Hebrew is often erroneously stated. It may be inferred that the compiler of the epitaph merely guessed at the Hebrew date, otherwise he failed to consult some authority on the point.

The publication of this work in England has been sponsored by the Records Committee of the Spanish and Portuguese Jews' Congregation in London, in which they have had the assistance of the Jewish Historical Society of England, the Spanish and Portuguese Jews' Congregation (Shearith Israel) of New York, and American Jewish Archives of Cincinnati besides that of private individuals in Brazil and Curaçao, who have since contributed to the publications fund. The American Edition of the book has been undertaken by the American Jewish Historical Society, who with the aid of the Elias and Mina Baron Fund, have arranged for the publication of that Edition in New York, including a Preface to be written by Professor Salo W. Baron, under whose Presidency the American Society agreed to assist in the project. I gratefully acknowledge with deep appreciation my indebtedness to these generous organizations and friends who have thus made it possible for the book to be printed and published, and special thanks are accorded to Professor Baron for his active interest in the American publication.

I also wish to record my debt of gratitude to the late Mr. Albert M. Hyamson, O.B.E., F.R.Hist.S., a now deceased member of the Records Committee of the London Congregation, through whose vision and keen interest, in co-operation with Rabbi Isidore S. Meyer, Librarian of the American Jewish Historical Society, the sponsors were encouraged to undertake the project.

With great happiness special acknowledgement is made to Mr. Wilfred S. Samuel, F.S.A., F.R. Hist. S., F.S.G. for his Foreword to the book and for having given so generously of his advice in stages of its publication. To Mr. Richard Barnett, M.A., F.S.A., Honorary Archivist of the Spanish and Portuguese Congregation, London, I tender my warmest thanks and deepest gratitude for his careful and painstaking editing of the MS and the difficult task of seeing it through the press and correcting the proofs, besides the inclusion of additional material gathered from Barbados Burial Records now deposited in London.

And finally to Mr. David Mellows, the Secretary of the Spanish and Portuguese Jews' Congregation in London, and to many others who have helped in the preparation and publication of this work I pay tribute and offer my sincere thanks for their kind and valued assistance.

FOOTNOTES

(TO INTRODUCTION)

1. March 29, 1833.

2. For the most part, this account of the ceremony is quoted from the *Barbados Globe* newspaper of April 1, 1833.

3. This fountain and the coloured glass window are now in the passession of the Barbados Museum and Historical Society.

4. The Ark now adorns the walls of a bathing pool in a private residence in Barbados.

5. Now used as one of the appointments of a chapel or "mission house" in Bridgetown, which had borne various names, "The Christian Mission" and "The Anchor Mission" are among them.

6. Since removed, and a floor laid, dividing the building into two storeys.

7. The lighting fixtures are in Washington, D.C., in a private house.

8. Published in the *Journal of the Barbados Museum and Historical Society.* Vol XV, part 2, February 1948.

9. *The History of Barbados,* by Sir Robert Schomburgk, Ph. D., London; Longman, Brown, Green and Longman, 1848.

10. See Page 94 of Vol. 1 of *Calendar of State Papers* (Colonial Series), years 1574 — 1660, preserved in the state paper department of H. M. Public Record Office, London, (Edited by Noel Saintsbury), London: Longman, Green, Longman and Roberts, 1860, quoting extracts from Domestic Correspondence, Car. I. (i.e. King Charles the First) Vol. CXVII, No. 53, Cal. p. 335. Abr. Jacob, farmer of customs in London in 1622, was a west-countryman who established himself as a merchant in Lisbon and achieved knighthood. Despite the deceptive name, he was a non-Jew.

11. The Minutes of Council from which quotations are made in the text are in original manuscript volumes preserved in the Government Registry at Bridgetown. They are mostly not paged, and they have never been printed. Copies of

11. *(Cont'd)*

these Minutes were regularly forwarded to England and extracts from a large number appear in the Calendar of State Papers (Colonial Series) referred to in Note 10.

12. The "presentment" of the Grand Jury was referred to in Minutes for 1656. The actual document or "presentment" is not preserved.

13. At page 42 of the second edition of the History quoted in *Additional Notes on the History of the Jews in Barbados.* N. Darnell Davis. A.J.H.S. Publications No. 18 173-76.

14. A.J.H.S. Publications No. 18, p.9 *et seq.*

15. *Calendar of State Papers,* Dom. Series, (1655) p.583.

16. On 16th December 1873 the Petition of Edward Samuel Daniels, Warden of the Hebrew Community, was presented to the House of Assembly by Mr. W. Brandford Griffith (afterwards Sir Brandford Griffith, Governor of the Gold Coast), member for the parish of St. Joseph, praying that the Community be relieved from parochial taxation on the property belonging to the Synagogue congregation.

The Petition (afterwards printed as a Document of the House in the Official Gazette of December 18, 1873) is as follows: —

BARBADOS. To His Honour the Speaker and other Members of the Honourable House of Assembly.

THE HUMBLE PETITION of Edward Samuel Daniels, Warden of the Hebrew Community of this Island, on their behalf, sheweth: —

1. That for over two centuries there has been a Congregation of his Co-religionists in this Island, and that for the whole period they have never applied to the country for pecuniary aid, nor been a burden to it in any manner.

2. That they have been always ready and willing to assist to the utmost of their power their brethren of other religious denominations.

3. That they formerly assisted their poor from voluntary contributions, but that their community having so much diminished they are no longer able to do so. That some money having been left for the Synagogue by some of their richer brethren, they purchased with it house property in this Island, the rental of which is kept solely for the purpose of defraying expenses towards the keeping of the Synagogue and its outbuildings in proper order, and maintaining their poor.

4. That at present they have not many poor members, but frequently poor Jews arrive here and apply for relief, and rather than permit them to go upon the parish, the Jewish Community maintain them until they can obtain some employment; in the case of their non success they give them pecuniary aid and pay their passage to some other place where their endeavours to earn a livelihood may be more successful.

5. That the Legislature has acted with great liberality towards all religious denominations who have sought aid from the public, but the Jewish Community have refrained from preferring any petition for assistance hitherto.

16. *(Cont'd)*

6.   That as already stated, with the exception of such contributions as they are able to make from their private sources, the fabric of their Synagogue and sundry matters in connection therewith are kept in order and maintained out of the funds arising from the property belonging to the Synagogue.

7.   That they are yearly taxed by the Vestry from £20 to £22 on the above mentioned property.

8.   That they have lately been refused by the Vestry (although the above facts were stated to them) remission of such taxes, and Your Petitioner therefore, on the behalf stated, now prays Your Honourable House to be relieved by legislation, of this taxation on the property belonging to the Synagogue, or to grant him such relief as to your honourable House may seem meet.

> And Your Petitioner, as in duty bound, will ever pray. etc., etc., etc.,
>
> E. S. Daniel,
>
> Warden of the Hebrew Community of Barbados.

Similar Petitions were presented to the Governor Sir Rawson W. Rawson, and to the Legislative Council by one of its members, Hon. Francis Goding.

An Act to give effect to the Petition was passed by the House of Assembly on 20 January 1874, by the Legislative Council on the 17 February 1874 and assented to by the Governor on 18 February 1874 which is the effective date of the Act.

The Act declared that the House property in the City of Bridgetown then belonging to the Synagogue, should be free of taxation for parochial or other purposes by the Vestry of St. Michael in so far as regards any tax to be laid in respect of ownership of property, and that the same should be free also from police and highway taxes.

17.   Although it is contrary to Jewish Law, one occasionally encounters synagogues surrounded by graveyards. There is one at Chatham (Kent).

18.   This graveyard within a small area between the backyards of the houses fronting on Swan Street, White's Alley, and James Street respectively, was mentioned in deeds of 1813 and 1814 which are recorded in the Deeds Registry in Bridgetown, viz:-

9 April 1813.   Isaac Parris of St. Michael, but then in colony of Surinam, by Thomas Pierrepont of St. Michael, Barbados, his attorney, for £1500, sells Moses Mendez Da-Costa of St. Michael, merchant, a house and 3270 sq. ft. of land, bounding on lands of Abraham Lindo, on an alley called Morris's Street, and on the burying ground of the Hebrew nation and on Swan Street.

24 May 1814.   Thomas Pierrepont of St. Michael, merchant, to Thomas Sampson of same parish, merchant, for £3500, sells house and land in Swan Street, bounding on lands of Rachael Pinheiro, David Lindo, Jael Pinheiro, and the burial ground belonging to the Jews, and on Swan Street.

19. The Document is entered at length in the Deeds Registry at Bridgetown, Vol. 337, folio 895 *et seq.*

20. Dated 22 July 1905, recorded in the Deeds Registry.

21. Recorded in Vol. 106 of Powers, folio 420 *et seq.*

22. Recorded in the Deeds Registry in Vol. 513, folio 294.

23. The first approach to this strange proposal was made by Mr. Yearwood during the preliminary negotiations for the sale and purchase of the synagogue and graveyard, and was reported in a letter from Mr. Baeza to the Secretary of the Bevis Marks Congregation dated 28 July 1927.

24. 16 September 1927.   Letter in reply from Secretary of Bevis Marks to E. I. Baeza.

25. Ibid.

26. 12th January 1928.   Letter E. I. Baeza to Secretary of Bevis Marks.

27. 7 February 1928.   Letter from Secretary of Bevis Marks to E. I. Baeza.

28. 14th February 1929.   Letter from Secretary of Bevis Marks to E. I. Baeza.

29. 20 March 1929.   Letter E. I. Baeza to Secretary of Bevis Marks.

30. Ibid.

31. 9 May 1929.   Letter H. G. Yearwood to E. I. Baeza.

32. The synagogue building is now (1953) occupied as offices by the Barbados Turf Club.

BURIAL GROUND ENCLOSURE A.

1.   Commencing at the angle of the enclosure wall near
the south-eastern corner of the Synagogue, under a genip
tree, there are four ledgers in a row.

הילודים למות והמתים להחיות

S.ᴬ

DA BEM AVENTURADA / PIA Y DEVOTA DEBORAH /
MULHER QUE FOY DO / HAZAN MEHIR A COHEN /
BELINFANTI Fᵒ FAI / TEBETH Aᵒ (flaked) / S A G
D G

*Burial Register: 5503 4 Tebet Deborah widow of Hazan
Mehir A. Cohen Belinfe.*

   'Widow' is incorrect.   Her husband survived her and
died in 1752.   See M.I. no 324.

2.   Da Bem Aventurada Ester / Abigail Mulher Que Foy /
de ABRAHAM BRANDAO Jᵒ / Em Sabath 3 de Yiar / 5503

     S A G D G

*Burial Register: 5503 3 Yiar (1743) / Ester Abigail widow
of Abraham Brandao.*

   'Widow' is incorrect.   She predeceased her husband.
See M.I. 337.

1

3. The first (arched) line of Hebrew is hidden by the low wall of the court-yard. Only two characters in the first line are visible, namely ל ר

תחת זאת עניה הדסה

אסתר בת אביחיל

נעלמה מעיני אישה

כיום שנקראת אביגיל

Around the sides and under the Hebrew inscription -

Here lyeth the Body of Mrs Hester Aigaill (sic) late wife of Benjamin Gomez who Departed this Life 25 of Sepr. 1743 Aged 20 Years.

S^{A.}

Da Yncurtada Evirtuoza / Pia Y temeroza de D^s Ester Abigail Mulher que foy de Binjamin Gomez a / Recolheo D^s para Sy em / 18 Tisry 5504 que / Corresponde a 25 Sep^o. 1743 / de Idade de 20 Annos

S . B . A . G . D .

Below in a sunken oval is an arm from the clouds felling a tree. This device frequently occurs in the stones of all ages.

Burial Register: 5504 18 Tisri - 1743 25 September Hester Abigail wife of Benjamin Gomez aged 20 years.

4. Broken at left bottom corner

SEPULTURA

De Bien Aventurada Virtuosa / Y Caritativa ABIGAIL Mulher / que Foy de MOSSEH NUNEZ / Faleceo em 8 de Ab 5502 que / Corresponde 28 de Julio 1742. S B A G D G.

Burial Register: 5502 8 Ab-1742 28 July, Abigail widow of Moses Nunes.

5.

Do bem Aventurado Honrado he / Temme de D:S Abraham
Baruh / Henriq:S qual en sua vida Sus / tentou Esta Sª
Esnoga de Nidhe / Ysrael Y a de Fendeu Con todo seu / Poder
en Fazer Sustentar heteve / Forsas nos poses actos athe- /
de sua y a zida Contra Osque / As quy xerom ut Tagar
faleceu / em 15 de Adar Primeuro 5461 A / que corresponde
a 12 de Feber⁰ 1700. / Sua alma goza da gloria.

תנצבה

*Burial Register: 5461 15 Adar-1700 12 February, Abraham
Baruch Henriques*

6. Broken across the middle.

DO BEM AVENTURADO / VENERAVEL VEHO HON / RADO
DAVID NAHAMIAS / QUE FALECEO EM Ð / NISAN A° 5462 /

SUA ALMA GOZE DA GLORIA

ת׳נ׳צ׳ב׳ה׳

וישכב דוד עם אבותיו
כבן שמונים [sic] וששים שנה
משכיל יהי בכל שנותיו
ועמוד תתענג לקץ ימין

Burial Register: 5462 23 Nisan (1702) David Nahamias.

7.
S^A

DA BEM AVENTURADA LUNA / VIRTUOZA MULLER Ð
FONSADO / COMSORTE QUE FOI DE DAVID / NAHAMIAS
FELISE EM ESTA / VIDA YA RECOLHEV DEOS / PARA
MILLOR MUNDO EM / 21 DE MENAHEM ANNO Ð / 5468

SUA ALMA GOZE DA GLORIA

תנצבה

Burial Register: 5468 21 Ab Luna wife of David Nahamias.

3

8.

Do Bem Aventurado / Jacob Da Fonseca Me / Q Faleceo
em 16 D / Sebat 5462 /

תנצבה

Burial Register: 5462 16 Sebat Jacob de Fonseca.

8a & 8b. Two ledgers lying between the first and second
rows.in this corner of the enclosure.

8a.   Around the sides and top :-

HERE LYETH INTERR'D THE BODY OF MR IMANUEL
ABOAB FURTADO WHO DEPARTED THIS LIFE THE 15th OF
JUNE 1767 AGED 43 YEARS.

מצבת

קבורת הגביר הנעלה נעים זמירית
ישראל עמנואל אבוהב פורטאדו
נ׳ל׳ע׳ יום יד לחודש סיון שנת התקכז
ויהיו ימי חייו שלשה וארבעים שנה

ת׳נ׳צ׳ב׳ה׳

S.^A

Del Bienaventurado / YMANUEL ABOAB FURTADO / que
fue Dios Servido / Recojer para su Santa Gloria / en 18
del mez Sivan Año / 5527 que corresponde a 15 / Juno 1767
de la Edad de / 43 Años.

S B A G D L E G.

*Burial Register: 5527 18 Sevan 1767 15 June Emanuel Aboab
Furtado aged 43 years.*

8b.   Around the sides and top :-

HERE LYETH INTERR'D THE BODY OF MR SAMUEL MOSES
MASSIAH LATE MERCHANT WHO DEPARTED THIS LIFE THE
25th OF APRIL 1751 AGED 45 YEARS.

וילך שמואל הרמתה

שמואל בן ארבעים וחמש שנה

איש בחור וענו אמת וכושר

במשה שמו בחולי נשתנה

וקראו צור תמים פועל בישע

ולדוע נשמתו בגבוהים

ויעל משה אל הר האל הים

SEPULTURA

Del Bienaventurado / Semuel Massiah que fue / mudado
Su nombre en / Mosseh que falecio de / edad de 45 años en
11 de / Yiar del año de 5511 que / Corresponde de 25 de
Abril / de 1751.

ת׳ נ׳ צ׳ ב׳ ה׳

*Burial Register: 5511 11 Yiar 25 April 1751 Samuel
Moses Massiah aged 45 years.*

Carving: Tree chopped down.

9   Commencing at boundary wall on left :-

Around the sides and top :-

Here Lyeth interr'd Ye Body of the Charitable & Pious
Anjelah Da Costa de Andrade late wife of David Hiŝ DaCosta
de Andrade who departed yˢ life ye 18 of Ap¹ 1848   Aged 50
years and 6 months.

בלע המות לנצח לפק

1   כ נועת [?] בעברת בנים אנגלה

2   למנוחה עלית מבור מצולה

3   בלב נשבר נתפרדה וכבילה

4   תהיה נשמתך ברום זבולה

5   קרבה נש ען במשפט גאולה

6   בעולם אשר ברא בהמלה

5

Da Bemaventurda / Devotta y Pia ANJELAH - Mr Que Foy Do
Bemav^{do}. / Hazan R. DAVID HIŚ / DA COSTA DE ANDRADE /
Fa.^u em Prime^{ro}. Hiar 5508 / Corresponde a 18 Abril / 1748
da Ydade de 50 Annos / y 6 Mezes.

תנצבה׳׳׳׳

*Burial Register: 5508 1 Yiar - 1748 18 April ---- wife of David
Hisquiau Da Costa D'Andrade aged 50 years.and 6 mos.*

10.

בשנת ואתה לך - לקץ ותנוח ותעמוד
לפק
דניאל איש חמודות אתה
על כן אודך סעשיך עתה
צדקה ומעשים טובים פזרת
לשמי ערבות בערב הסתרת
סשוח ופרנם תלמוד תורה
אשר על זה זכית לאורה
אור הצדיקים היא שכרה
להולכי דרך תמימות וישרה

Do Bemaventurado pio Y temerozo / de Deos Venerado
Velho DANIEL / MASSIAH o Recolher Deos para / Sua
Eterna Gloria em 5ª Feyra as 2 / oras da tarde da Ydade
de 66 Años / Sendo 7 Hilul A^o 5502 corresponde / 26
Agosto 1742 / S B A G D G

תכצבה

Carving: Tree chopped down.

*Burial Register: 5502 7 Elul   1742 26 August Daniel
Massiah aged 66 years.*

11.   Around the sides and top :-

    HERE LYETH INTERR'D YE BODY OF YE CHARITABLE /
ESTER SARAH LATE WIFE OF AARON BARUH LOUZADA / WHO
DEPARTED THIS LIFE THE 20 OF OCT.ʳ 1744 AGED 36
YEARS AND 7 MONˢ.

לסספֿד לשרה ולבכ׳ת׳ה׳
אשת נעורים פה טמונה
שמה אסתֿר ונשתנית שרה
ברוכֿה היא במקום השכֿונה
ובגן עדן נפשה קשורה
במר בוכים היא נפרדה
שהיתה ענוה ולא זדֿה

Sᴬ

    Da Bemaventurada Y / Virtuoza Pia Y Devota - Ester
Sarah Mulher que Foy de Aharon Baruh / Louzada Fᵒ em 26
Hes -/van Aᵒ 5505 Corresponde / a 20 de Outubre 1744 de /
Ydade de 36 Anos Y 7 / Mezes /

תנצבה

*Burial Register: 5505 26 Hesvan 1744 20 October Sarah wife
of Aaron Baruch Louzado aged 36 years.*

12.

מצבת
קבורת הישיש הנכבד אהרן ברוך
לוזאדה נלע׳ ביום ה׳ ו׳ לחודש ניסן
שנת התקבח ליציר׳ ויהיו ימיו ס׳ד
שנים י׳א חדשים ועשרים ימים

ת נ צ ב ה

Sᴬ

Do.B.A.De AARON BARUH / LOUZADA que foy Dˢ Servido /

7

Recolher p^a sy em 5^a: f^a: 6 de / Nisan 5528 que Corresponde / 24 Marco 1768 de Idade de / 64 Annos 11 Mezes and
20 Dias. / S A G D E G A

*Burial Register: 5528 6 Nisan 1768 24 March Aaron Baruch
Louzade aged 64 yrs 11 mos. & 20 days.*

13.   Recently broken in two pieces and sunk into ground.

Around the sides and top :-

HERE LYETH INTERR'D THE BODY OF THE CHARI-
TABLE SARAH LATE WIFE OF MORDECAY MASSIAH WHO
DEPARTED THIS LIFE THE 30th DECEMBER 1746 AGED
34 YEARS 10M^s AND 15 DAYS.

כי שרה שמה

שרה הצנועה טובה גברת

אבי מלך שלח ולו הביאוה

אשת חיל לביָלה עטרת

ובשנים לה׳ סמנו לקחוה

נשמתה גנוזה בעליות

עם בנות ישראל חסדניות

Sepultura.

De la Bienaventurada / Honesta y Charitativa / S^{ra}.
D^a. Sarah Massiah / que passo este mundo / al mejor alos
34 An'os / 10 Meses y 15 Dias de su edad / en 28 de Tebat
5507 / que Corresponde a 30 / de Diziembre 1746.

תנצבה

*Burial Register: 5507 28 Tebet 1746 30 December Sarah
wife of Mordechay Massiah aged 34 years 10 mos & 15 days.*

14.   Around the sides and top :-

Here lyeth interr'd Ye body of Ye Charitable Rachel
late wife of Abraham Massiah Senr who departed this life

ye 6th of April 1749 aged 25 years.

רחל חמש ועשרים היו שניה
ושלמה חוקה בתום וכושר
עזבה בעלה ושני בניה
להלוך להתעדן בטוב האושר
לכן להיות זכרון בישראל
היא מצבת קברת רחל

SEPULTURA

De la Bienaventurada / honesta y Charitativa S^{ra}. /
D^a. RACHAEL MASSIAH / que alos 25 Años de / su Edad Fue
Cortada / de esta para la Mejor / vida en 29 de Nisen Año /
a 6 de Abril de 1749 / .

תכצבה

*Burial Register: 5509 29 Nisan 1749 6 April Rachel
wife of Abraham Massiah Snr. aged 25 years.*

Carving: Tree chopped down.

15.   Hebrew inscription in faint letters :-

ויגוֹע יצחק וימת ויאסף אל עמיו לפק̃
קבורת
הנביר טוב וישר הלא הוא יצחק
מסיח עלה למנוחתו ערב שבת כו
לחדש חשון שנת התק̃ג

S^A

Do Bemaventurado varao / Pio y Recto Ishac Massiah /
Faleceo em 26 Hesvan 5503 / Corresponde a 18 Novembro /
1742.

ת"נ"צ"ב"ה"

*Burial Register: 5503 26 Hesvan 1742 18 November
Isaac Massiah.*

9

16.   In seven pieces, recently broken.

S^A

S^A

Del Angel Rachel Filha / de Jacob e Deborah Da /
Fonseca Faleceu em 27 / Sebat 5503 que Corresp / onde a
10 de Febreiro / 174$\frac{2}{3}$ / de Idade de 9 Annos / e 3 Mezes.

S B A G D G

Burial Register: 5503   27 Sebat   1743   10 February Racel
de Fonseca child of Jacob & Deborah aged 9 yrs and 3 mos.

17.

מעונה ועונה לאיש תם וישר
שמו אהרן חי בכנפי שכינה
מעוטר בחכמה מנוחה נכונה
ויקיץ ויחיה וישבע וידשן

S^A

DO BEM AVENTURADO VENE / RAVEL E VIRTUOZO
VARAO / AHARON BARUH LOVZADA / DOTADO DA CIENCIA
DA LEY / DIVINA SUA ALMA GOZE DA / GLORIA FALECEV
EM 17 DE / TISRY ANO 5456.

תֹנֹעֹבֹה

Burial Register: 5456   17   1695   10 October Aaron
Baruch Louzada aged 25 years.

18.

קבורת רחל אלמנת הֹה אהרן ברוך לוייזאדה זֹל אשר
נאספה לגן עדנה בשנת גֹנ...ּ חייה ביום חמישי לחדש
כסלו שנת תֹנֹוֹח היא התסד ליצירה

ראו ציון הלז ופקדוה   : בני עמה יזכרז במוובתה
לזאת אשת חיל ידעוה   : גדולה בנשים בצדקתה
יתומי אב ואם ילדוה   כבניה גדלו בצלתה

10

כבת גֹן לנוה בנוחה   ובשנת תנוח קראוה

ושם יאמרו שלום מנוחתה   בצל כנפי סרום יקרבוה

ת׳נ׳צ׳ב׳ה׳

Da Bem Aventurada Temeroza de / Dᵃ Rachel Viuva de
Aaron Baruh / Louzada que Dˢ tem que Foy DŜ / Servido
Recolher para su em 5 de / Kisleu Aº 5464 / que Corres-
ponde A 2 de Novembro de / 1703 de ydade de 53 anos / Sua
Alma Goze da Gloria / Amen / Tem asua Cabeseim sua Primᵃ
Netta / de 13 Mezes que Recolheu el dio 6 dias / depois
do seu Falecim.

*Burial Register: 5464 5 Kislev 1703 2 November Rachel
widow of Aaron Baruch Louzado aged 53 years.*

      Third row commencing at enclosure wall: four in a
row.

19.   Around the sides and top :-

HERE LYETH INTERR'D THE BODY OF THE CHARI-
TABLE RACHᴸ VALVERDE WIFE OF Yᴱ LATE DAVID VAL-
VERDE JUNʳ DECEᴰ WHO DEPARTED THIS LIFE THE 29ᵗʰ
DAY OF NOVᴿ 1745 AGED 28 YEARS.

היא מצבת קבורת רחל

בצאת ישראל לבוא אל תוך עמיו

רחל היא נשארה בהריונה

ותקו בו מאל רוב תנחומיו

ותקש בלדתה את בת אונה

מדוד מנעה צור ישראל

אז והיא נתנה לעדרי אל

SEPULTURA

De la Bienaventurada y / Honesta Sʳᵃ Dᵃ RACHEL /
Vᵃ Del Bienaventurado / DAVID YSRAEL VALVERDE / que
Fallecio de parto alos / 28 Añs de su Edad en 16 / de
Kislev Año de 5506 /.

תנצבה

Carving: Tree chopped down.

Burial Register: 5506 16 Kisler 1745 29 November Rachel widow of Israel Valverde Jnr. 28 years.

20.   Around the sides and top :-

HERE LYETH INTERR'D THE BODY OF THE CHARI-
TABLE ABR^M IS^L. HIZ^A VALVERDE LATE MERCH. WHO
DEPARTED THIS LIFE THE 17th day of JULY 1746 AGED
34 YEARS.

ויקרא אבי סלך לאברהם

אבהם ישראל וחזקיה
שמות שנשתנו בזה הגבר
נשמתו פרחה לעליה
וינוח גופו בזה הקבר
כמוהר סלות בריתותיו
זוכרות לפני אל זכיותיו

SEPULTURA

Del Bienaventurado / ABRAHAM VALVERDE / que fue
Mudado su Nombre / en Ysrael y Despues en / Hisquija que
Fallecio a los / 34 Anos de su Edad en 11 / de Menahem
Ano de 5506.

תנצבה

Carving: Tree chopped down.

Burial Register: 5506 11 Ab. 1746 17 July. Abraham Israel Hisquiau Valverde aged 34 years.

21.   Recently broken across the centre.

Around the sides and top :-

HERE LIES INTERR'D YE BODY OF MRS. ESTHER

12

YE WIDOW OF ABRAHAM HISQUIAU VALVERDE WHO DIED
ON SATURDAY YE 26 TAMUZ 5515 or 5TH JULY 1755
SHE WAS A GOOD WIFE A TENDER MOTHER & VERY CHARI-
TABLE.

מצבת

קבורת הכבודה הצנועה והנכבדת
מרת אסתר אלמנת הגביר הנעלה
אברהם חזקיהו באלוירדי נלע׳ יום שבת
קודש ששה ועשרים יום לחדש תמוז שנת
התקטו ליצירה בת מ׳ד שנים

ת׳נ׳צ׳ב׳ה׳

S^A

Da Bemaventurada D^a ESTHER / Viuva de ABRAHAM
HISQUIAU / VALVERDE Faleceo Dia de Sabath / 26 Dias
do Mes de Tamuz Ano / 5515 que Corresponde a 5 de /
Julho 1755 de Idade de / 44 Annos.

רבות בנות עשו חיל   מות ..ארצה ראש׳ן
אסתר עלתה על כולנה   כי כבתה מאור שמש׳ן
מחמד עין אלי בעלה   ולבניה העריב דב׳ן
לאביונים פזר נתנה   לא חדלה את תירוש׳ן
וזכותה תעמד לעד   תהיה לה פרח שוש׳ן

נפשה תעלה לשמי מרום להיות רועה בגן דיש׳ן

Burial Register: 5515 26 Tamus 1755 5 July Ester
widow of Abraham Hisquiau Valverde aged 44 years.

4th from wall in 3rd row.

22.   Around the sides and top :-

HERE LYETH INTERR'D Y^E BODY OF JACOB VALVERDE
LATE MERCH^T OF THIS ISLAND WHO DEPARTED THIS LIFE

13

JULY 12TH 1756 AGED 43 YEARS

מצבת

קבורת הנביר הנעלה כהר יעקב
יהושע וואלוירדי נלע׳ יום שני ארבעה
ועשר יום לחדש תמוז שנת התקי׳ו ליצירה

תנצבה

S^A

Do Bemaventurado JAHACOB / JEOSUAH VALVERDE
faleceo / Segunda Feyra 14 Dias do / Mez de Tamuz 5516
que / Corresponde a 12 de Jul / -ho 1756. / S BAGDEG.

Debaxo de esta Lossa eh Peregrina Valverde Yaze en
Censsa .... Irrevocables Leyes del Destino / que nuestro
Humano Lei quiso...../ Solo vive enel Cielo y Se hizo
Dig ... / Pues quanto esta humanidad enc.... / Convertido
se vera en po ... tien... (Letters on the right of each
line indistinct.)

Carving: Tree chopped down.

*Burial Register: 5516 14 Tamus 1756 12 July Jacob
Valverde aged 43 years.*

Three ledgers in a row.

23. Recently broken in six pieces. Around the sides
and top :-

HERE LYETH INTERR'D YE BODY OF M^{RS} SIMHA
SARAH WIFE OF MR JACOB VALVERDE JUN^R WHO DEPARTED
THIS LIFE Y^e 25th OF DE ⌊broken⌋ AGED 29 YEARS &
2 MONTHS.

תוחלתו צדיקים שמחה
קול שמחה מכופל להקשיב דמינו
על שמחה ופריה בעת לדתה
קול צעקה כיולדה פעָנו
שערבה שמחה וגיל בר ...
שתים בבת אחת יקונן פינו
ויבשר יש שכר לפעולתה
לכן סנעו עינים סלהורייד מים
ששמהרד   שמחה על השמים

Dela bienaventurada / Charitative y Honesta / S^{ra} D^aSimha
Sarah / Valverde q̃ alos 30 Anos / Fallecio de parto y fue /
Sepultada Con Su hija en / 20 de Tebet del ano 5504 / que
Corresponde a 25 de / Diziembre 1743.

תנצבה

*Burial Register: 5504 20 Tebet 1743 25 December Simha
Sarah wife of Jacob Valverde aged 29 yrs. and 2 mos.*

24. Recently broken in four pieces.

Around the sides and top :-

HERE LYETH INTERR'D THE BODY OF Mr ISAAC HAIM
VALVERDE MERCH^T WHO DEPARTED THIS LIFE THE 3RD:
DAY OF AUGUST 1743 AGED 33 YEARS.

ויקרא אבי־סלך ליצחק

בהיר בשחקים לקח ביושר
לחיים זה האיש קודם חצות
החסד וצדקה הנם העושר
שלוה וקיים כדי רצות
בדין הלך בצדק לפניך
והוא הדרך לחזות פני

15

DEL CHARITATIVO Y /Encortado YSHAAC / HAIM VALVERDE
que / Fallecio alos 33 Años de / Su edad en 24 de / Menachem
del Año 5503.

תנצבה

*Burial Register: 5503 24 Ab. 1743 3 August Isaac Haim
Valverde aged 33 years.*

25. Broken in seven pieces.

Around the sides and top :-

Here Lyeth interr'd the Body of the Pious & Charitable
Mr JACOB FRANCO NUNES of Barbadoes Merch[t] who departed
this life on the 8th of Hesvan 5487 of ye Creation of ye
WORLD, which is ye 22d of October 1726 aged 80 years.

מצבת

קבורת הישיש הנכבד ונומל
חסדים יעקב פראנקו נוניס
ויעקב הלך לדרכו ויפנעו בו
מלאכי אלדים בן שמנים שנה
ביום שבת קדש שמנה לחדש
מרחשון ׳ התׁׁ״פז

ת׳נ׳צ׳ב׳ה׳

Do Bemaventurado & / Caritativo JAHACOB / FRANCO NUNES
que foy / Deos servido recolher para / sua Santa Gloria em
Sabat / 8 Hesvan 5487 de Annos / 80 / SBAGDG.

Carving: Tree chopped down.

*Burial Register: 5487 8 Hesvan 1726 27 October Jacob
Franco Nunes aged 80 years.*

26. Two ledgers together.

S^{A}

Da Bem Aventurada / Y virtuoza de Luna Mulher/De JACOB FRANCO NUNES / que foy deos Seruido / Recolher para Sy em 6 / De Yiar 5466 / que Compresponde A 9 / De Abril 1706. / Sua Alma Goze de Gloria /.

Burial Register: 5466 6 Yiar 1706 9 April Lunah wife of Jacob Franco Nunes.

27. Cherub's Head.

DA MALLOGRADA VIRTVOZA /etemeroza mulher as^{ra} Ester / mulher de Moseh Espinoza / que foi noso senhor Seruido / chamar para Si em 21 de / tamus 5470 que corresponde / a 8 de Julho 1710. / SUA ALMA GOZE DA GLORIA.

Burial Register: 5470 21 Tamus 1710 8 July Ester wife of Moses Espinoza.

28.

מצבת

קבורת הישיש הנכבד יוסף
ישורון מנדיש נפטר לבית
עולמו בט״ו בטבת התס
תנצב״ה

S^{A}

DO BEM AVENTURADO & TEMEROZO / DE D^{s} OS^{or} JOSEPH JESSURUN MENDEZ / QUE FALECEV DE 83 ANNOS FUNDOU A / EZNOGA DA NIDHE ISRAEL A DEFENDEU / & PROTEJEU ATE SUA JAZIDA COM SEUS / PAES QUE FOY EM 15 TEBETT 5460.

Here is burried the Body / of Mr LEWIS DIAS who was
beloved & / Respected by all men in his time / he died on
the 27 of December A° / 1699 Being 83 yeares of age.

Burial Register: 5460 15 Tebet 1690 [*sic*] *27 December*
Joseph Jeshurum Mendes aged 83 years. [*Lewis Dias was his*
alias.]

28a Actually between Nos. 28 and 29, but not visible at
first, and later copied as 165.

29 Recently broken from top to bottom.

S^A

Da bem aventurada de / bem Venida Gomes Hen- / -riques
Vivua de Isaque / Gomes Henriques que / faleceo Em 31 de
Agosto / 1701 que Conresponde / a 6 de Elul 5461.

Sua alma Goze da gloria.

תֹנׅצׅבֹה

Burial Register: 5461 6 Elul 1701 31 August Venida
widow of Isaac Gomes Henriques.

30 Flaked, and Hebrew inscription indecipherable.

DO Y[..] CURTADO EVIRTVOZO / MANCEBO A[.....]
AIM BVRGOS / Q FOI APANA ...VOS / EM DIA DE BVOTO
DE .....AN / A° 5.6.

תֹנׅצׅבֹה

Burial Register: 5462 Tisri 1702 Aaron Haim Burgoss

31 Inscription illegible.

18

Da Bem Aventurada Honesta / Devota E Caritativa Donha
Sarah / Abigail Mendes Mulher que foy / da Mosseh de
Selomoh Mendes / que foy arrebatada desta para / melhor
vida na flor de sua idade / Em 27 Adar 5474 que Corresponde / a 3 Marco 17$\frac{13}{14}$.

S. B. A. G. D. G.

מצבת

קבורת הכבודה והצנועה גדולה בצדקה
ובגמלות חמדים אשת חיל עמרת בעלה
אשה יראת ה״ היא תתהלל מרת שרה
אביגיל אשת הנביר כה״ר מסה בכר שלמה
מינד״יש ז׳לע בת כ״ה שנים ביום כ״ו אדר התעד

תנצ״ב״ה

Carving: Tree chopped down.

Burial Register: 5474 27 Adar 1713/4   3 March   Sarah
Abigail wife of Moses de Solomon Mendes.

Do bem auenturado Mosseh / Haim Coutinho que faleceo
em 10 / de Siuan 5466 que Corresponde a 12 / Mayo 1706,
S.V /

Sua Alma Goze da gloria.

Skull and cross-bones incised.

מצבת קבורת הנביר כה״ר מסה חיים קויפיני[ו]
נלע יום א׳י לחדש סיון שנת התסו
תנצבה

Burial Register: 5466   10 Seuan   1706   12 May   Moses
Haia Coutinho.

DA . BEM . AVENTURADA / JVENERABLE VELLA S^{RA} /
RIBCA MVLLER q^e FOY DOS^R / DAVID VLLOA q^e D^s TEM
Q FOY / D^s SERVIDO RECOLLER DEST^E / MAV MVNDO P^A
OVTRO / MELLOR EM 23 DE ROSHODES / NISAN 5470 -q^e
CONRES PONDE / EM 11 DE - ABRILL 1709 SUA ALMA /
GOZE DE GLORIA.

תנצבה

*Burial Register: 5470 23 Nisan 1709 April Ribca wife
of David Villoa.*

35 De bem Aventurada de / Sarah Mulher de Danell Jeosuah /
de Leao que foy D.S[....] / Recolh[..] seos Povos em ..
de / Tebet 5456 que Conresponde / a 19 Decem^{bro} 1695 Emais
aseos / pez.... Enterada huma sua / C...ca (p nome Rachell
que faleseu / Em 30 de Sebat 5456 Seos / Seija perda de /
Se pacado.

*Burial Register: 5456 22 Tebet 1695 9 December Sarah
wife of Daniel Jeshurun de Leao.*

36.   Flaked and illegible.

Four together in a row

37 Da bem Aventurada / Evertuoza Senhora Lea / Mulher
de Pinhas Abarbarel / faleceo en 22 de Sebath / Anno
5473 / que Ccrresponde 6 de / Fevrerro $17\frac{12}{13}$ de Idade de /
44 Annos Sua vendita alma / goze de eterne gloria.

*Burial Register: 5473 22 Sebat 1712/13 6 February Leah
wife of Pinhas Abarbanel, aged 44 years.*

מצבת

קבורת הצנועה והנכבדת מרת
רבקה ואלוירדי נלע ביום א
שלשה ימים לחדש סיון התסו

תנצבה

DA BEM AVENTURADA EMODESTA / VIUVA RIBCAH
VALVERDE Q / FALECEO EM 3 DE SIVAN 5466 /
S A D G.

Burial Register: 5465   3 Sevan   Mrs Rebecca Valverde.

מצבת קבורת הכבודה והצנועה מרת
שרה זונתו של הגביר כהר בנימין פירירא
די ליאון נלע יום ב יב לחדש ניסן התסה

תנצבה

S^A

DE BEM AVENTURADA E VERTUOZA / SENHORA SARAH
MULHER DE BENJAMIN PEREYRA DE LEAO que / FOY D^s
SERVIDO RECOLHER ASEOS   / POVOS PARA PLANTALA NO
LUGAR / DAS JUSTAS Y TEMEROSAS DE DEUS / SEGUNDA
FEYRA EM 12 NISSAN / 5465 que CORRESPONDE A 26
DE / MARCO 1705 S.V. / S A G D G.

*Burial Register: 5465   12 Nisan   1705   26 March   Sarah
wife of Benjamin Peyra De Leo.*

40. Flaked and broken.

Do Bem Aventurad..... / Vertuozo Honesta ... Benja.
Pereira..... / faleceo 13 de .... / 5474 que corr.... / 16

41   Around the sides and top :-

HERE LYETH INTERR'D THE BODY OF THE WORTHY .
GENEROUS AND CHARITABLE JOSEPH MENDES WHO DEPART-
ED THIS LIFE THE 17 DAY OF JULY 1707.

מצבת קבורת הגביר הנכבד
נשא ונעלה זקן ונשוא פנים
הוא הראש הקצין כהר יוסף
סינדיש נפטר לבית עולמו
יום ה׳ כ׳ח לחדש תמוז התסז

ת׳נ׳צ׳ב׳ה׳

DO BEMAVENTURADO DOM / JOSEPH MENDES QUE FOY
DEOS / SERVIDO RECOLHER PARA SY / DESTE MUNDO
PARA OUTRO / MELHOR EM QUINTA / FEYRA 28 / TAMUS
5467 QUE CORRESPONDE / A 17 JULLIO 1707 S.V.
SUA / ALMA GOZE DO MAIS SUBLIME / DA DIVINA
GLORIA.

Burial Register: 5467 28 Tamus 1707 17 July Joseph
Mendes.

42   Small stone, with carving in relief of a child and a
rose-bush.

Around the sides and top :-

Here lyeth interr'd the body of Elias y[e] son of David
& Simha Abigaill Valverde who departed this life ye 22nd
of August 1725 Aged 37 Months.

Do Anjo ELIAV Filho / de DAVID & SIMHA / ABIGAIL
VALVERDE / que Falleceu em do / mingo 24 de Elul / Ano
5485 / de Idade de 37 Mezes.

*Burial Register: 5485 24 Elul 1725 22 August Elias
son of Daniel (sic) & Simcha Abigail Valverde aged 3 years
& 1 month.*

43   Around the sides and top :-

Here lyeth interred the body of Abr. Valverde Junr.
late Mercht. of this Island who departed this life Oct.
19th 1739 Aged 26 years.

מצבת

קבורת הנביר הנכבד אברהם
ידידיה ואלוירדי נפטר לבית עולמו
יום שבת קדש כט לחדש תשרי שנת
ה״ת״ק״

ת״נ״צ״ב״ה״

Do Bemaventurado y / Honrado ABM. JEDIDJAH /
VALVERDE q̄ Faleceo Em / Sabath 29 de Tisry Anno /
5500. / S A G D E G

Carving: Hand from clouds felling tree.

*Burial Register: 5500 29 Tisri 1739 20 October
Abraham Valverde jnr aged 26 years.*

44   מצבת

קבורת הבתולה שרה רודריניש
פיריירה נפטרה ביח חשון שנת
התרף

תנצבה

23

Da Bemaventurada / Donzella Sarah Rodriges / Pereira
F^o em 18 de / Hesvan A^o 5480. / S.A.G.D.G.

45   Around the sides and top :-

HERE LYETH INTERR'D THE BODY OF M^{RS}. IAEL

VALVERDE WHO DEPARTED THIS LIFE THE 13TH DAY OF

AUGUST ANNO (blank) 1721 AGED 56 YEARS.

מצבת

קבורת המאושרת הצנועה והנכב־
דת מרת יצל אשת הנביר
כמ׳ אברהם ואלוירדי נ״ע שנאספ [ה]
אל עמה עם צדקניות וחסדניות
נל׳ע במוצאי שבת יום ראשון לחדש
אלול בשנת ת״בורך סנשיב י״ה״ל

א״שת   לפק

תנצבה

SA / Da Bemaventurada Virtuoza / S^{ra} Jael mulher que
foy Do / Bemaventurado Sor Abraham / Valverde que D^s Faleceo / em Sa liente Sabath 1° Elul 5481 / SUA ALMA GOZE
da GLORIA

Carving: Hand from clouds felling tree.

Burial Register: 5481   1 Elul   1721   13 August   Mrs Jail
Valverde aged 56 years.

קבורת רחל אשת הגביר משה פראנקו נוניש
בת ששה עשר שנים וחצי אחר שילדה בת נפטרה
ביום י"ם לחדש אדר הראשון שנת התעח

תנצבה

עם אשכלות עוב ובק־צירה	גפן להתפאר אשר בורתה
תזעק אהה כי נהפכו צירה	רחל עלי משבר ובת המלימה
אכן לאכר נהפכו שיריה	משתה שמנים ק־וההה יולדת
סות תשלח לה הסון צירה	רחל בריה ראתה צלסות
בעל כדל תמוב עלי צירה	רחל במר לבה ידיד עזבה
	בת שש עשר שנים ועוד החצי יום בו לאבל והפכו שיריה

S   SA / Dela Bienavenurada Senora Rachel / Muger de
Moseh Franco Nunes que / F^{o} de sobre Parto de Edad de 16
Anos / Y medio en 19 de Adar primero que / Corresponde a
9 de Febrero de 171$\frac{7}{8}$. S.A.G.D.L.G.

Carving: Hand from clouds felling tree.

Burial Register: 5478 19 Adar 1717/8, 9 February
Rachel wife of Moses Franco Nunes aged 16 years.

47   Around the sides and top :-

HERE LYETH INTERR'D THE BODY OF M^{RS} RACHEL THE
WIFE OF JACOB VALVERDE WHO DEPARTED THIS LIFE THE
13TH DAY OF JUNE 1722 AGED 37 YEARS.

מצבת

קבורת האשה המאושרת
הצנועה והנכבדת סרת רחל אשת
של הנביר כהר יעקוב ואלוירדי
שנאסף [ה] אל עסה עם צדקניות
וחסדניות נל'ע ביום ד: תשעה יסים
לחודש תמוז בשנת ויצב: יעקב
מצבה על קברתה הוא מצבת
קברת רחל לפק

תנצבה

SA / Da Bemaventurada Virtuoza Sa. / Rachel mulher
que foy do S^{or} / Jacob Valverde que foy Ds Servido /
Recolher para sy 16 dias Depois / De seu Parto em Dia de
quarta / Feira 9 do mez de Tamuz 5482 / SUA ALMA GOZE
DA GLORIA.

Carving: Hand from the clouds felling tree.

*Burial Register: 5482 9 Tamus 1722 13 June Rachel
wife of Jacob Valverde aged 37 years.*

48   Around the sides and top :-

HERE LYETH INTERR'D THE BODY OF JAEL HANA Y
DAUGHTER OF DAVID AND SIMHA VALVERDE WHO DEPARTED
THIS LIFE Y 21st DAY OF OCT^{R}. 1742 AGED 26 YEARS
AND 2 MONT.

כי את חנה אהב

יעל יעלת חן בצור חנה
אהובה בין בנות לעת בואנה
סבנות לבעלה   אלקנה

26

ועלתה מן ארץ על כלנה
דלנה בהרי קדש חלולים
הרים הנבהים ליעלים

Sepultura / Dela Bienaventurada Prudente / Honesta y
Virtuosa S^{ra} Don- / -zella Dª JAEL HANA VALVERDE /que
Fallecio enlos 26 Años / de Su Vida paso ala Mejor / en 5
del Mes de Hesvan del / Año de 5503.

Carving: Hand from clouds felling tree.

Burial Register: 5503 5 Hesvan 1742 21 October Jail
Hana of David & Simcha Valverde aged 26 years and 2 mos.

48a Stone lying south of No. 48 and north of No. 15.

Around the sides and top :-

HERE LYETH INTERR'D THE BODY OF SIMHA / ABI-
GAIL THE WIFE OF DAVID VALVERDE / WHO DEPARTED
THIS LIFE THE 20TH DAY OF JUNE / 1750 AGED 58
YEARS.

ושבחתי אני את השמחד [ה]

שמחה בלא שמחה יומם וליל
אשה ידועת חולי ומכאבות
גם כן בלי גילה שמה אביגיל
והמות חובתה בא לנבית
פרחה לגן עדן נשמתה
להכין שמה מקום מנוחה

SEPULTURA

Da Demaventurada S^a / D^a Simha Abigail Valverde / que
paso de esta vida a / Milhor em quarta Feira / 27 de Sivan
/ A o de 5510.

ת״נ״צ״ב״ה״

Burial Register: 5510 27 Sevan 1756 20 June Simha
Abigail wife of David Valverde aged 58 years.

49   S^A / Da Bemaventurada & / Virtuoza Ester Mulher / q'
foy de Ishac Aboab / Furtado q' foy D^s servido / recolher
p^a. sy em 4 de / Kislev, A^o 5481 q- corresponde / a 23 de
Novembro 1720 / S A G D G

   Carving: Hand from clouds felling tree.

Burial Register: 5481 4 Kislev 1720 23 November
Esther wife of Isaac Abab [!] Furtado.

50.   סצבת

         קבורת המאושרה הצנועה
        והנכבדת מרת רחל אשת הגביר
      משה לופיז נפטרה ב״כ לחדש תמוז
                    שנת התפג

                    תנצבה

                      S^A

   Bemaventurada Virtuoza / & Honesta RACHEL LOPEZ Mr.
q' / foy de MOSSEH LOPEZ, Falleceo / em 20 de Tamuz
A^o. 5483 q' / Corresponde a $\frac{12}{23}$ de Julho 1723 / S A G D G
/ Mortal que de un tumba te desvias / Sin reparar que es
tu vida un vient^o / Mira que muerte cruel y tirana / Smo
vinere oq vendra mañana.

Burial Register: 5483 20 Tamus 1723 12 January [!]
Rachel Lopez.

51   S^A

       Da Bemaventurada Pia / Devota Caritativa e Virtuoza /

                        28

S.^{ra} DONA ESTER M^R DE / ABRAHAM NUNES, Faleceo / em
Sesta feira 6 de Dez:^{bro} / Corresponde a 13 de Tebeth /
Anno 5478. S A G D G.

מצבת קבורת המאושרה
הצדקת הצנועה והנכבדה
מרת אסתר אשת הנביר
אברהם נונים נפטרה לבית
עולמה בערב שבת קדש
י״ג לחדש טבת בשנת ותלקח
אסתר אל המלך לפׄק

תִנׄצׄבׄהׄ

Carving: **Tree chopped down.**

*Burial Register: 5478 13 Tebet 16 December Ester wife
of Abraham Nunes.*

Three ledgers east of wall.

52

מצבת קבורת המאושרת הצדקת
הצנועה והנכבדת מרת אסתר אשת
המאושר הנביר ירמיה בורגוש נׄעׄ
נפטרה לבית עולמה בי״ט לחדש
טבת בשנת ותלקח אסתר אל המלך

לׄפׄקׄי

תנצבה

S^A / Da Bemaventurada Pia Devota / Caritativa Ê Virtuoza S^{ra} DONA / ESTER q' foy Mr. de YRMIAHU / BURGOS
faleceo em 12 de Dez:^{bro} / corresponde a 19 de Tebeth/ A°
5478 / S A G D G

Carving: Hand from the clouds felling tree.

Burial Register: 5478 9 Tebet 12 December (no year)
Ester de Jereмiah Burgos.

53   Around the sides and top:-

HERE LIES INTERR'D Y BODY OF Y MOST CHARITABLE
PIOUS & WELL-BELOVED YOUTH ISAAC HAIM SON OF JACOB
& DEBORAH DA FONSECA VALLE WHO DEPARTED THIS LIFE
Y 11th MARCH 1759 AGED 26 YEARS 4 MO^S. & WAS LA-
MENTED & WELL RESPECTED BY ALL THAT KNEW HIM.

מצבת

קבורת הבחור הנחמד ירא ה' אוהב צדק ורודף
שלום בן חשוב ורע אהוב יצחק חיים בן הנגיר
הנעלה וסרת יעקב ודבורה דא פונסיקא ואליו
אשר נתבקש בישיבה של מעלה ביום א י"ב לחדש
אדר שנת התקיט בן [כו] שנים
תנצבה

מופתר בשם טוב עלה יצחק
להשתעשע ברום שחק
ובעדן גן מעדניו
ללקוט פרי מעלליו
להתעלץ בתוך ברים
ולהתחבר עם כוכבים
להתענג מזיו ההוד
עם סובבי כסא כבוד

S^A / Do Bemaventurado Humilde E / Virtuozo mancebo
ISHAC HAIM filho / de JAHACOB E DEBORA DA FONSECA /
Valhe que foy D^s Servido Recolherlo / Para sua Santa Gloria
em domingo / 12 de RHadar entre as 3 & 4 da tarde / 5519

30

que Corresponde a 11 de Marco de / 1759 de Idade de 26
Annos e 4 Mezes / S A G D E G A

Carving: Hand from the clouds felling tree.

Burial Register: 5519   12 Adar   1759   11 March   Isaac
Haim son of Jacob and Deborah Da Fonseca Valle aged 26
years & 4 months.

54   מצבת קבורת הישיש הנכבד המשכיל
                 ' ונבון ירא אלקים וסר מרע כה"ר
        ירמיהו עמנואל בורנוש נ"לע יום א ד" ניסן
                   התע"ה   תנצ"בה

        Sa / Do bem aventurado entendi / do etemente de Deus
Irmiahu / Himanuel Burgos falleceu de / idade de 80 annos
em 4 Nissan / 5475 que corresponde a 27 Marco 1715 / S A G
D G

Burial Register: 5475   4 Nisan   1715   27 March   Jeremiah
Imanuel Burgos aged 80 years.

Two ledgers

54a   Inscription indecipherable.

54b   Hebrew decipherable in part only :-

                   קבורת... .. ביר ריער
                   יע קב דימירע ...
                   עולמו בים מ לחדש...
                   הרבד

                        תנצבה

                         31

S^A

Da Bemaventurada e / Virtuoza Pia E Farta de / Annos
Lunah M^r que / Foy de Is^k de la Penha / F^o Em 1 hilul A^o
5500 Sua / Bendita Alma Goze Da / Eterna Gloria./

תנצבה

*Burial Register: 5500   1 Elul - September   Lunah wife of
Isaac la Pinha.*

56.

S^A

Da Bemaventurada (broken) Est .... / Nunes que foy
(broken) / ... ido recolher para (broken) / .... de Adar
54... q[ue cor]responde a $1\frac{7}{18}$ de / Febreiro $17\frac{21}{22}$ / S A G
D G.

*Burial Register: 5480   1 Adar   1721/22   17/18 February
Isaac Nunes. [but the text of epitaph seems to refer to
a female].*

57

סצבת

קבורת הגביר הנעלה כה״ר יעקב
רודריגש סארקיש נפטר לבית עולמו
יום שלישי כ״ט לחדש אלול ה׳ת״פ״ה׳
ת׳נ׳צ׳ב׳ה׳

SA / Do Bem Aventurado YAHACOB / RODRIGUES MAR-
QUES que foy / Deos Servido Recolher para Sua / Santa
Gloria em 3^a f.^{ra} 9 Ellul / 5485 / S B A G D G

58

סצבת

קבורת האשה הנכבדה סרת רבקה

אשת הגביר יעקב בוהנו פרנסם נ׳ל׳ע׳
יום ב׳ לחדש טבת שנת התפט
ת׳נ׳צ׳ב׳ה׳

SA / Da Bemaventurada RIBCAH / BUENA FRANCEZA
Mulher que / foy de IACOB BUENA FRANCES / Faleceu em
2 de Tebet Anno / 5489 / S A G D G

Burial Register: 5489   2 Tebet   Rebecca wife of Jacob
Bueno   Frances.

59   Flaked and broken across the centre.

מצבת

קבורת הגביר הנכבד בנימין דא
[פ] נשקא [ואלי?], נלע יום ה לחדש
אלול שנת ה׳ת׳צ׳א׳   ׀

תנצבה

S^A / ......ado Beniamin / ......Falleceu em / ...q^e
Corresponde / ... Agusto de 1731 / .... A G D G

60   In the border :-

HERE LYETH INTERR'D THE BODY OF THE MOST
FAMOUS DOCTOR DANIEL HAIM AGUILA WHO DEPARTED
THIS LIFE YE 2^d OF SEP^R 1733.

מצבת

קבורת הרופא המובהק דניאל
חיים די אניליא שנפטר לבית
עולמו ביום כ ה לחדש תשרי
שנת התצ׳ר׳
תנצבה

33

SA

Do Bemaventurado / Honrado y Virtuozo / Doctor Famozo
Daniel / Haim de Aguila que / Faleceo em 2^d Feyra 5 / de
Mez de Tisry ano. 5494 / q Corresponde a 2 de / Settembro
1733. / S A G D G.

Burial Register: 5494 2 Tisri 1733 2 September
Dr Daniel Haim de Aguila.

Four large ledgers east of wall.

61   מצבת

קבורת האשה הכבודה מרת שרה
אשת הנביר דניאל מסיח נ׳ל׳ע׳
יום א לחדש אלול שנת התצ

ת׳נ׳צ׳ב׳ה׳

SA

Da Bemaventurada SARAH / Mulher q^e foy de DANIEL
MASSIAH / Falleceu em p^{ro} de Elul do Anno / 5490 q^e
Corresponde a 3 de / Agosto / S B A G D G.

Burial Register: 1 Elul 1730 3 August Sarah wife of
Daniel Massiah.

62   Broken in three pieces.

מצבת

קבורת חכבודה והצנועה והצדקת
מרת שרה אשת חזקיהו פאניקו נ׳ל׳ע׳
ביום איב שבט התפא   ת׳נ׳צ׳ב׳ה׳

34

Da Bemaventurada Devo... / Caritativa e Virtuoza
SARAH / Mulher que foy de HISQUIAH / PACHECO recolheu
Deos para / sua Santa Gloria em Domingo / 12 Sevat 5481
que Corresponde / a 29 Janeiro 1721 / S B A G D G.

Carving: Tree Chopped Down.

*Burial Register: 5481 12 Sebat 1721 29 January Sarah
wife of Hisquiau Pacheco.*

63   Around sides and top :-

HERE LYETH Y^e BODY OF MR. DAVID HEZEKIAH DA
COSTA DE ANDRADE AGED 63 YEARS & 3 MONTHS WHO
DEPARTED THIS LIFE YE 13 APRL 1740 BEING READER
TO THIS CONGREGATION OF BRIDGETOWN 26 YEARS.

וילך דוד הלוך וגדול

מצבת

קבורת הישיש הנכבד הגביר הנעלה
נעים זמירות ישראל כבוד רבי דוד
חזקיהו דא קושטא די אנדראדי
איש חי ס״ג שנה ונפטר לבית עולמו
ביום כ״ז לחדש ניסן שנת ה״ת״ק

Eight more lines of Hebrew, very worn, deciphered by Mr. Edward
Coleman as follows:

דוד בעת דודים לוקח ביושר
לכן עזב סדור התחתונים
נכבד בשם הטוב אסתי עושר
שהנחיל כעטרה לראש בנים
זאת היא לדוד תפארת ואושר
ואלה דברי דוד האחרונים
הגבר הוקם על בקהילת אל
ונעים זמירותיו בישראל

35

Falecio alos 63 Anos de Su / Edad en 27 de Nisan Ano de / 5500

תנצבה

Burial Register: 5500 27 Nisan 1740 13 April Hazan David Hizekiah De Andrade aged 63 years and 3 months.

64   Broken across centre and left corner.

In the border :-

HERE LYETH INTERR'D THE BODY OF THE PIOUS AND CHARITABLE MR. SIMEON MASSIAH WHO DEPARTED THIS LIFE THE 15th DAY OF JANUARY 1746 AGED 73 YEARS.

הושיע׳ י״י מסיחו

שמעון שהוא גביר הנעלה
הישיש הנכבד ונשוא פנים
רוחו ונשמתו לרום עלה
להתענג בדודים הצפונים
נפטר בשם הטוב ונם תהלה
היא עטרת תפארת לבנים
משיח כנויו עסקו סוהל
ונעים זמירות אל בישראל

Sepultura

Del Bienaventurado y / Venerable Ansiano / Simon Massiah que Alos / 73 Años de Su vida passo / a la mejor en 15 de Sebat / Año 5507 que Corresponde / a 15 de Henero 1746.

תנצבה

Carving: Tree chopped down.

Burial Register: 5507 15 Sebat 1747 [!] *15 January Simeon Massiah aged 73 years.*

36

Seven large ledgers in a row.

65   Indecipherable.

66   Around the sides and top :-

HERE LYETH INTERR'D THE BODY OF MR. DAVID
ISRAEL VALVERDE WHO DEPARTED THIS LIFE THE 16th
DAY OF OCTOBER 1745 AGED 35 YEARS.

ישראל נושע בְּיִיֽ

דוד בשם אביו ישראל שמו :
כשהתחיל היום אורו לזרוח:
הלך ואץ לבוא בחצי יומו :
ונקרא לעלות לחיי נוח
נמצא בעת החן והשלמות
אז ויקרבו ימי דוד למות

SEPULTURA

Del Bemaventurado y / Charitativo DAVID / ISRAEL
VALVERDE que / Fallecio a los 35 Años / de Su Edad y
Fue / Sepultado en Roshodes / Hesvan Año de 5506.

תנצבה

Carving: Tree chopped down.

Burial Register: 5506 1 *Hesvan* 1745 16 *October* *David
Israel Valverde 35 years.*

67   מצבת

קבורת הישיש הנכבד הנעלה כה״ר אברהם
נונים נפטר לחיי העולם הבא יום י״ח לחדש

תנצבה

S^A

Del Bemaventurado Caritativo / y Temiente de D.^s
ABRAHAM / NUNES falecio en 18 del Mez / Hesvan A° 5497
que Corresponde / a $\frac{13}{24}$ Outobre 1736 / S B A G ח L G.

Carving: design of rose bush in bloom.

O.^s Tu que me Estas miriando Mira Bien / que Bives
bien por que no Sabes la horam quando / Te Veras a Sy
tambien.

*Burial Register: 5495 [!] 18 Sevan 1736 23/24 October
Abraham Nunes.*

68   Broken across the centre.

מצבת

קבורת הישיש הנכבד שלמה רפאל
ברוך לואיסדא נל׳׳ע יום ד׳ לחדש
כסליו שנת ה׳ת׳ק׳ד׳ ויהיו ימי חייו ס׳׳ד שנה

ת׳נ׳צ׳ב׳ה׳

SA / Do Bemaventurado / Selomoh Rephael Baruh /
Louzada que Foy Deos / Servido Recolher para / sua Santa
Gloria em 5 de / Kislev A.° 5504 que Cor- / responde a 10
Novem- / bro 1743 de Ydade de / 65 Annos / S B A G D E G

*Burial Register: 5504 5 Kislev 1743 10 Novembre
Solomon Raphael Baruch Louzada aged 65 years. (The
Hebrew epitaph, above, however, has 4th Kislev.)*

קבורת האשה הכבודה מרת
יעל אשת הנביר שלמה ברוך
לוזדה נ׳לע יום י״ז חשון שנת
ה׳ת׳צ׳א׳

תנצבה

SA / Da Bemaventurada YAEL / Mulher q^e Foy de
SELOMOH / BARUH LOUZADA Falleceo em / 17 hesvan Anno
5491 Correspo- / nde a 17 8bre Anno 1730 / S A G D G

*Burial Register: 5491 17 Hesvan 1730 17 October Jail
wife of Solomon Baruch Louzada.*

70 SA / Da Bemaventurada y / Virtuoza a Sta RACHEL /
Mulher que Foy Do Bem / aventurado Sr MOSEH / BRANDAÕ
que D^s. tem / Faleceo em 23 de Kisleu / 5493 que Corresponde / a 29 de Novr 1732 / S A G D G

*Burial Register: 5497 [!] 23 Kislev 1736 [!] 29 Nov
Rachel wife of Moses Brandao.*

קבורת הצנועה והנכבדה אשה יראת ה׳
שרת אסתר רחל אשת הנביר בנימין גומיש
נפטרה לבע עשק/כ/לחדש כסליו שנת
התצד ליצירה

Carving: Tree bearing fruit, with words DANDO FRUTO
MURIO FLOR, in the circumference.

תנצבה

SA / Dela Malograda Honesta y Virtuoza / ESTER
RACHEL Muger que Fue de / BENIAMIN GOMEZ Fallesio de
Edad de / 16 Annos en Viernes 20 Kisleu 5495 / que Cor-
responde a 15 Novembro 1733 / S B A G D G

יציר חומר אסיר יצר   כמו נחש יסיתך
זכור מות וצלמות   ביום שוהם יהתך
התתפאר ואחז ושאר   בתוך קבר ישיתך
וחזניחם ותניחם   ותפר את בריתך
... חצי ימים   ותעזוב מהציתך
... אנוש נכאה   וכזאת אחריתך

Burial Register: 5494 20 Kislev 1733 15 Nov Ester
Rachel wife of Benjamin Gomes aged 16 years.

72   Child's small stone.

Sa/ Do Anjo Aaron / Filho de Benjamin / & Ester Nunes
que / D.ˢ Foy Servido Re- / colher para sy em / 5 f.ʳᵃ 13 de
Yiar 5509 / que Corresponde a 20 Abril 1749 de / Idade de
15 Mezes / & 8 Dias.

Burial Register: 5509 13 Yiar 1749 20 April Aaron
child of Benjamin & Ester Nunes aged 1 yr 3 mos & 8 days.

East of Wall, five large ledgers.

73   Broken in three parts and almost illegible

מצבת

קבורת המאושרה הצנועה והנכבדה
אשת הנביר
לחדש תשרי שנת

תנצבה

Da Bemaventur../ S.ᴿᴬ Angela M.... / Jahacob Massiah /

40

4 de Tisri.... / Correspon......

Burial Register: 5484 4 Tisri 1723 20 September,
Angel wife of Jacob Massiah.

74   סצבת

קבורת הכבודה והצנועה סרת
אסתר זוגתו של הנביר כהיר דוד
אבוהב פורטאדו נלע״ יום כ לחדש
תשרי התפח

SA / Da Bemaventurada & / Virtuosa ESTER Mulher que /
foy de DAVID ABOAD fURTADO / que Recolheu Deos para /
Sua Santa Gloria Em 20 / Tisry 5488: que são 21 Setemb /
re 1727: de Idade de 33 Annos / S B A G D G

Burial Register: 5488 20 Tisri 1728 24 September
Ester wife of David Aboab Furtado aged 33 years.

75   Around the sides and top :-

HERE LYETH INTERR'D THE BODY OF MR. DAVID ABOAB
FURTADO MERCHANT WHO DEPARTED THIS LIFE Y^e 27 OF
JUNE 1742.

בשנת ויקרבו ימי דוד למות לפק.

פרח דודי לעדן סוכנה
לאבואב אנשי אסונה
פורת בנים בסתנה שכינה
דום כי נסעת לעם נאסונה

SA / Do Bemaventurado y / Honrado S^r. DAVID /
ADOAD FURTADO q / Recolheo D^s Fm Sua / Gloria Em 14
Sivan / 5502 Corresponde 27 / Junio 1742.

תנצבה

Burial Register: *5502* *14 Sevan* *1742* *27 June* *David*
Aboab Furtado.

76   Around the sides and top :-

     HERE LYETH INTERR'D THE BODY OF MOSES HAIM
NUNES CASTELLO WHO DEPARTED THIS LIFE APRIL Y 17TH
1799 AGED 33 YEARS & 4 MONTHS.

מצבת

קבורת הגביר הנכבד משה
חיים נוניש קאשטילו שנפטר
לבית עולמו ביום ה כט לחדש
ניסן שנת   והאיש משה ענו

     SA / Do Bemaventurado / Honrado y Virtuozo S.^{r} /
MOSES HAIM NUNES / CASTELLO que Faleceo / em 5 feira
29 de Nisan / Anno 5559 [sic] / S A G D G

Burial Register: *5489* *29 Nisan* *1729* *17 April* *Moses*
Haim Nunes Castello aged 33 yrs & 4 mos.

77   Around the sides and top :-

     HERE LYETH THE BODY OF YE CHARITABLE & PIOUS
JUDITH NUNES CASTELLO LATE WIDOW OF MOSES H.^{M}
NUNES CASTELLO WHO DIED SEP.^{R} 23^D 1759 AGED 64.

     SA / Da Bemaventurada y / Virtuoza Pia y Devota /
JEUDITH Viuva que foy / do Bemaventurado MOSEH H.^{A} NUNES
CASTELLO f.^{o} / 2.do de Tisry 5520 Correspon- / de
a 23 Septembro 1759 / Ydade 64 Annos / Q S B A G D G

Burial Register: *5520* *2 Tisri* *1759* *23 Septembr* *Judith*
widow of Moses Haim Nunes Castello aged 64 years.

42

78 HERE LYETH INTERR'D THE BODY OF IACOB VALVERDE
WHO DEPARTED THIS LIFE ON TUESDAY THE FIRST DAY OF
JULY 1729 AGED 14 [?44] YEARS.

מצבת

קבורת הגביר הנכבד יעקב
ואלוירדי שנפטר לבית עולמו
יום נ מ״ו לחדש תמוז שנת
ויעקב הלך לדרכו ויפגעו בו
מלאכי אלהים

תנצבה

S A / Do Bemaventurado y Temerozo / de D.ᔆ IACOB VAL-
VERDE q / Falleceo em 3.ᵈ Feira 15 do / Tamus Anno 5489 /
S A G D G.

*Burial Register: 5489 15 Tamus 1729 1 July Jacob Val-
verde aged 44 years.*

79   In left and right top corners - a dove.   Beneath the
inscription a woman standing, holding a child.

Around the sides and top :-

Here lieth interr'd y Body of Ester Franco Nunes late
wife of Moses Franco Nunes Merchant who departed this life
Oct the 29th 1729 Aged 26 years.

מצבת

קבורת האשה הצנועה והנכבדת
מרת אסתר אשת הגביר משה פראנקו
נוניש שילדה בן זכיר נפטרה עם בנה ביום
... לחדש מרחשון שנת ותלקח אשור
ביד המלך

43

Da Bemaventurada Honrada y Caritativa / ESTER Mulher
q foy do S͟ᴿ MOSEH / FRANCO NUNES faleceo do parto em/
4ª feira 17 de Marhesvan Anno 5490 / S A G D L G

*Burial Register: 5489 Tisri 1729 29 October Ester
Franco wife of Moses Nunes aged 20 [!] years.*

80   מצבת

קבורת הנביר הנכבד והישר
משה פראנקו נוניש שנפטר
לבית עולמו ביום ו׳ י״א לחדש
אייר שנת֗ ומשה עֹלה עֹל
האֹלהים
תנצב״ה

Around the sides and top : -

Here lyeth interr'd the body of MR MOSES FRANCO
NUNES late Mercht. of this ISLAND who departed this
life on the 17th of April 1730 aged 38 years.

SA / Do bemaventurado Honrado / Recto y Caritativo
S͟ᴼᴿ / MOSEH FRANCO NUNES / que faleceo em Sexta Feira
/ onze de Iyar Anno 5490 / S A G D E G

*Burial Register: 11 Yiar 1730 17 April Moses Franco
Nunes aged 38 years.*

81   Around the sides and top:-

HERE LYETH INTERR'D THE BODY OF ISHAC HAIM
ISRAEL NUNES WHOM DEPARTED THIS LIFE THE 29TH
DAY OF JULY 1733 AGED 14 YEARS

מצבת

קבורת הבחור הנחמד יצחק
חיים ישראל נוניש שנפטר
לבית עולמו ביום א כ״ח לחדש אב
שנת וי׳ע׳ל׳ מ׳מ׳ט׳ באר שבע
ת׳נ׳צ׳ב׳ה׳

SA / Do Mancebo Virtuozo / ISHAC HAIM ISRAEL
NUNES / q^e Faleceo em Domingo 28 / de Ab a 5493 de Idade /
do 14 Anos / S A G D G

*Burial Register: 5493 28 Ab 1733 29 July Isaac Haim
Israel Nunes aged 14 years.*

82   Around the sides and top :-

HERE LYETH INTERR'D THE BODY OF JAEL NUNES
WIFE OF DAVID NUNES MERCHT. WHO DEPARTED THIS
LIFE Y 2^D. OF APRIL 1742 AGED 45 YEARS.

תבורך מנשים יעל

SEPULTURA

De la Bienaventurada Pia / y Virtuosa S^{ra}.. D^a. JAEL /
RACHEL NUNES que paso / de esta amejor vida en Vier- /
nes 9 de Nisan de 5502 que / Corresponde a 2 de Abril de /
1742 en los 45 Anos de / Su Edad.

Script letters :-

Jael es de su esposo la Corona / Como Senora Justa y
Virtuosa / Jael Nunes sin par digna Matrona / Rachel se
muda para Ser Gloriosa / Levantense sus Hijos y esto abona /
Eloqios que la aclameri mas dichosa / Rachel en la Ramah
triumphante habita / Jael mas que Mugeres see Bendita.

45

היא מצבת קבורת רחל

תנצב״ה

Burial Register: 5502 9 Nisan 1742 2 April Jael wife
of David Nunes aged 45 years.

83 Child's grave; stone facing in reverse direction:
broken in many places.

S^A

Do Anjo David Filho / de Ishac Israel de / Piza
Faleceu em 17 de / Tamuz 5497▪... / ponde a 5 de Julho
.... / de Idade de 11 Mezes e... / 25 Dias que foy Nacido /
em 18 de Julho 1736.

Burial Register: 5497 17 Tamus 1737 5 July David son
of Isaac Israel De Piza aged 11 mos. & 25 days.

84 Large Ledger. In the border :-

HERE LYETH INTERR'D THE BODY OF DAVID NUNES
SON OF MOSES & LEAH NUNES WHO DEPARTED THIS LIFE
Y 27TH DAY OF MAY 1746 AGED TWENTY MONTHS.

מצבת

קבורת הילד הנעים דוד רפאל
נונים נל״ע יום ג׳ י״ט לחדש סיון
שנת התק״ו

תנצבה

S^A

Do Anjo DAVID REPHAEL / NUNES Filho de MOSEH /
y LEAH NUNES Faleceu / em 3ª Feira 19 de Sivan / 5506

q Corresponde a 27 / Mayo 1746 de Ydade de / 20 Mezes.

Burial Register: 5506 13 [!] Sivan 1746 27 May David Raphael child of Moses & Leah Nunes aged 1 yr and 8 mons.

85 HERE LIES INTERR'D THE BODY OF JAEL HANAH NUNES
LATE WIFE OF ABRAHAM ISRAEL NUNES WHO DEPARTED
THIS LIFE JANUARY THE 16.th 1733/4.

מצבת

קבורת האשה הכבודה הצנועה
והנכבדת סרת יעל חנה אשת הנביר
אברהם ישראל נוניש שנפטרה ביום ד̄
כ"ג לחדש שבט שנת תב̄ורך מנשים יע̄ל
אשת חב̄ר

תֹנֹצֹבֹה

S A

Da Bemaventurada Honrada / y Virtuoza JAEL HANAH /
NUNES qᵉ Faleceo em quartᵃ / Feira 23 do mez de Sebat /
a 5494 qᵉ Corresponde a 16 / de Janeiro 1733/4 / S A G D
E G .

Carving: Tree chopped down.

Burial Register: 5494 23 Sebat 1734 16 January Jail Hanah wife of Abraham Israel Nunes.

86 Broken in many pieces, some missing.

S A / Dabemaventurada Rebca / Francez que Faleceu /
de Adar primero 54.... /
Here Lyeth the Bo.. / ... Mᴿˢ REBEKAH ..... / was
well Belove.... / & departed th .... / of February ....

Burial Register: 5494 1 Adar Mrs Rebecca Frances aged 70 years.

Three small ledgers east of sea-grape tree.

87. Broken. Around the side and top :-

Isaac Haim Nunes Son of MOSES & LUNA NUNES who departed this life July ye 13 178[0].

Centre :-

SA / Do Anjo ISHAC / HAIM NUNES / Filho de MOSEH / & LUNAH NUNES / que otomou D.ᵃ p.ᵃ /sy em 10 de Menahem / [1780] de Idade de / ..Mezes & 12 Dias.

Burial Register: 5490 10 Ab. 1730[!] 13 July Isaac Haim child of Moses & Luna Nunes.

88 Broken. Around the sides and top :-

..... lyeth the Body of Moses son of Isaac & Deborah Gomez Who Departed this Life the 28 April 1743 Aged 26 Mon.ˢ

ה״ נתן וה״ לקח יהי שם ה׳ מברך

S. / Do Anjo / Moseh Filho de Ishac & / Deborah Gomez q foy / D.ˢ Servido Recolher / para Sy Em 15 (?) de Yiar 5503 que Corresponde / a 28 Abril 1743 de / Idade de 26 Mezes / y 10 Dias

Carving :- Panel with arms: three dolphins.

Burial Register: 5503 15 Yiar 1743 28 April Moses son of Isaac & Deborah Gomez aged 2 years 2 mos and 10 days.

89 מצבת

קבורת הילדה דבורה בת הנביר דוד
נוניש נ׳ל׳ע׳ ביום ב׳ כ״ב לחדש טבת
שנת ה׳ת׳צ׳ד׳

SA / Da Deborah Filha de / David Nunes q̃ Faleceo / en 2ᵃ Feira 22 de Tebeth / q Corresponde a 17 de / Dezembro 1733 de Idade de / 10 A.ˢ SAGDG

90   Around the sides and top :-

HERE LYETH THE BODY OF MRS. DEBORAH LATE WIFE
OF MR. JACOB DE FONSECA VALLE WHO DEPARTED THIS
LIFE 23 OF OCTO.ʳ 1764. AGED 55 YE.

Centre :-

מצבת

קבורת האשה הצנועה
והנכבדה מרת דבורה אשת
הישיש והנכבד יעקב דה
פונסיקא ואלי נלע יום שני
כו לחדש תשרי שנת תקכה
בת נה שנה

תנצבה

De la bienaventurada / Y Caratativa Deborah / Muger
que fue de Iahacob / Da Fonseca Valle que fue / Dios servido Recojer / para su santa / Gloria en / 26 de Tisry
5525 que cor / responde a 25 de Octub / 1764 de Edad de
55 An / S B A G D G

91   מצבת

קבורת הגביר כה״ר מתתיה רפאל
פרירא די ליאון נלע יום ד׳ שני של
פסח שנת ה״ת״צ״ו

ת״נ״צ״ב״ה״

49

SA / Do Bemaventurado Honesto / Mathatias Rephael
Pereira / de Leao Faleseu ho Segundo / dia da Pesah 4 Fr.ª
16 Nisan 5496 que Corresponde a 15 / de Marco 1735/6
S B A G D L E G

Burial Register: 5496 16 Nisan 1736 15 March Raphail
Pereira de Leao.

92   SA / Da Bemaventurada Sarah / Mulher que foy de
Abraham / Brandon qual fo em 5 de RH / Hesvan 5518 que
corresponde / a 12 de Juno 1758 da Idade de 57 / Annos
S A G D G

Burial Register: 5518 5 Hesvan 1758 12 June Sarah
wife of Abraham Brandon aged 57 years.

93   מצבת

קבורת האשה הכבודה והצנועה מרת רחל
חנה אשת הנביר יצחק די קםפוש נ׳ל׳ע׳ יום ו
לחדש אייר   בת כ״ז שנה שנת ה׳ת׳צ׳ו׳

ת״נ״צ״ב״ה״

    SA / Da Bemaventurada virtuoza y ca- / retativa Rahel
Hanah mulher qᵉ foy / de Yshac de Campos qᵉ falheceo em /
6 de Yiar 5496 qᵉ corresponde a 6 de / abril de 1736 de
Idade de 27 annos S B A G D E G. / flor qᵉ desejo la parca /
en la hedad mas primorosa / cortando por la rais / una tan
perfecta rosa.

Carving: Hand from clouds felling tree.

Burial Register: 5496 6 Yiar 1736 6 April Rachel Hanah
wife of Isaac Campos aged 27.

94   מצבת

קבורת האשה הכבודה והצנועה מרת שרה

לאה אשת הגביר יצחק די קמפוש פרירא
נ׳ל׳ע׳ יום ח לחדש סיון בת כב שנה שנת
ה׳ת׳צ׳ו׳   ת׳נ׳צ׳ב׳ה׳

SA / Da Bemaventurada virtuoza y ca- / retativa Sarah
mulher q.ᵉ foy / de Yshac de Campos Pereira qᵉ falhe- / ceo em 8
de Sivan 5496 q.ᵉ corespon- / de a 7 Mayo 1736 de Idade de 22 Annos /
S B A G D E G / Asusena desojada / Ytu fraganca perdida /
mas tu olor es premanente / en la Eterna Vida.

Carving: Hand fron clouds' felling tree.

*Burial Register: 5496 8 Sevan 1736 7 May Sarah Leah
wife of Isaac de Campos Pereira.*

95   Much worn.

.... de Campos / ..... de junio / que Corresponde a 27 de / Sivan .... sua.....

Possibly identical with *Burial Register 5505 27 Sevan
16 June Abraham Hisquiau De Capes.*

96   Right top corner of stone and part of Hebrew inscription obscured by roots of cabbage palm.

]סצ[בת ...

והצנועה סרת אסתר
משה לופש נל׳ע׳ יום

התצו׳

SA / Da Bemaventurada e Honesta / ESTER HANAH Mulher
/ de MOSEH / LOPEZ que foy Deos Servido / Recolher para
sy em 10 de Sivan / do Anno 5496 que corresponde / a 9* de
Mayo 1736 / S A G D.

Carving: Hand from clouds felling tree.

* 10 Sivan 5496 was 20 May 1736.

*Burial Register: 5496   10 Sivan   1736   9 May Ester Hannah
wife of Moses Lopez.*

97   Top of stone and most of Hebrew inscription obscured
by roots of cabbage palm.

Around the sides and top :-

HERE LYETH INTERR'D YE BODY OF M..... DEPARTED
THIS LIFE YE 28TH AUGT. 1747 AGED 70 YEARS.

Centre :- (portion only visible)

פירירא ...

ד' תצרי ...

SA / Da Bemaventurda / Caritativa y Temente / de D^s.
D^{na}. LEBANAH / Mulher de MATATIA / PEREIRA de LEAÕ /
Faleceu em 6^a f^a 4 de Tisri / 5508 que Corresponde / a 28*
Agosto 1747 de 70 / Annos de Idade / S B A G D G

* If the Hebrew date, 4 Tisri, is correct, the corresponding civil date should be September 8.

*Burial Register: 5508   6 Tisri   1747   28 August   Lebanah
wife of Matatia Pereira de Leao aged 70 years. [She was
then his widow: he had died in 1736.]*

98   Around the sides and top :-

HERE LYETH YE BODY OF YE BELOVED MORDECAY
BURGOS DE PIZA WHO DEPARTED THIS WORLD YE 22^d of
JULY 1749 AGED 11 YEARS 8 MONTHS & 3 DAYS & WAS
LAMENTED BY YE PUBLICK.

ויעל מלאך י"י

מרדכי נער טוב יפה תמים
מירא דכיא בריה סדותיו
גדול בדעת צעיר הוא בימים

52

לשנים עשר לא הגיעו שנותיו
והודיע דעתו שהיא שלמה
בחפץ הלסוד והחכמה
קודם קיצור חליו חש מתתו
נפטר סן אביו באלה סלות
יצו השם אתך את ברכתו
וסאחי ואחיותי תראה גילות
ועזבם בוכים וצועקים
והוא שמח עלה לשחקים

SEPULTURA / Del Bienaventurado y / dichoso Angel
Mordechai / Burgos Israel de Pisa / que alos 11 Años 8
Meses / y tres dias de su Vida / paso ala mejor en Sabat /
18 de Menachem Año de / 5509 que Corresponde / a 22 Julio
de 1749.

נצבה

Burial Register: 5509 18 Ab. 1749 22 July Mordechay
Burgoss Israel de Peiza aged 11 yrs & 8 mos.

99   Elaborate stone, with Cherubim in four corners and
the lettering in relief.   Broken in upper right corner.

Around the sides and top :-

HERE LYETH INTERR'D THE BODY OF THE CHARITABLE
LUNA BURGOS WHO DEPARTED THIS LIFE JUNE THE NINE-
TEENTH 1756 AGED 73 YEARS.

מצבת

קבורת הזקנה הכבודה והצנועה
סרת לונה בורנום אלסנת הגביר
הנעלה סרדכי בורנום נלע ליל שבת
כא יום לחדש סיון שנת התקיו ליצירה
בת ע״נ שנים
ת׳נ׳צ׳ב׳ה׳

53

Da Bemaventurada Dona LUNA / BURGOS Viuva de MORDECHAY / BURGOS falleceo Noite de Sebat / vinte e hum do mez de Sivan / 5516 que Corresponde a Des / e nove de Junho 1756 de / Idade de 73 Annos / S B A G D E G. /

Esta Lossa que Ves oh Caminante / Senisas della que animeidas Viste / De la Necessidad ser digno Atlante / Alivio al Pobre ser consuelo al Triste / Luna en la Virtud firme y Constante / Luze en el Empireo donde esiste / Alma Feliz que con Devoto Zelo / Escala se labro para Subir al Cielo.

Carving: Hand from clouds felling tree,

Burial Register: 5516 21 Sevan 1756 19 June, Luna widow of Mordechay Burgos aged 73 years.

100 Around the sides and top :-

HERE LYETH INTERR'D THE BODY OF THE PIOUS WORTHY & CHARITABLE MR. ABRAHAM DE PIZA WHO DEPARTED THIS LIFE THE 3^D NOVEMBER 1766 AGED TWENTY-THREE YEARS 6 MONTHS & 16 DAYS.

מצבת

קבורת הגביר הנעלה החסיד ועניו אברהם
ישראל די פיזה נ״ל״ע״ באחד לחדש כסליו שנת
ה״ת״ק״כ״ז״ בן שלשה ועשרים שנה ושבעה
הדשים איש גומל חסד ורחמן אהוב מכל
קרוביו אוהביו ומיודעיו ישר נאמן בכל מעשיו
ירא שמים במעבדיו בן שכיבד אבותיו ושלם
בכל מידותיו

תנצבה

SA / Del Bien Aventurado Virtuozo / Devoto y humilde

Abraham Israel / De Piza que fue Dios Servido llamar / desta vida transitoria al Glorioza / y Eterna en el primer dia del Mes / de Kisleu Ano 5527 que Corresponde / a 3 Noviembre de 1766 de Edad / de 23 Añõs y 7 Meses fue bene- volo / y caretativo Estimado de todos / sus Parientes Amigos y Conosidos / Recto y Verdadero en sus Acciones / Temeroso de Dios en sus Obras / hijo Obediente a sus Padres y / complecto de todas heroicas / Virtudes / S A G L E G.

Burial Register: 5527 1 Kislev 1766 3 Novr Abrahaa De Piza aged 23 yrs 6 aos & 16 days.

101   מצבת

קבורת הזכנה [sic!] הנכבדת שרה
מסיח נלע יום מד לחדש
ניסן שנת התקכא

תנצבה

S A.

Da bemaventurada Anciana / Sarah Massiah que f⁰ em 13 de / Nisan 5521 que Corresponde / a 17 de Abrill 1761 de Idade / de 80 Annos / S A G D G.

Carving: Tree chopped down.

Burial Register: 5521 13 Nisan 1761 17 April Ananna Sarah Massiah aged 80 yrs.

102   Small stone alone.

Sacred to the Memory / of ISAAC JOSEPH.DAVID LINDO and BENJAMIN Infant Sons of / MOZLEY ELKIN.

Burial Register: 5584 Adar 1824 1 March Isaac Joseph child of Mozeley Elkin.

Burial Register: 5590 18 Tisri 1829 16 October David Lindo child of Mozeley Elkin.

Burial Register: 5595 18 Hesvan 1834 20 November
Benjamin child of Mozeley Elkin.

Three large ledgers in a line, east of wall.

103

SACRED TO THE MEMORY OF / ESTHER / WIFE OF
Mr. M. ELKIN OF THIS ISLAND, MERCHANT, / WHO DE-
PARTED THIS LIFE THE 13TH SEPTEMBER / A.M. 5584 /
AGED 31 YEARS.

Burial Register: 5584 9 Tisri 1823 14 Sepr Esther
wife of Mozely Elkin aged 31 years.

104

SACRED / TO THE MEMORY OF / ALFRED BENJAMIN
ELKIN / WHO DEPARTED THIS LIFE / 7TH OCTOBER 1834/
CORRESPONDING WITH 4TH TISRI 5595 / AGED 20 YEARS
5 MONTHS / AND 21 DAYS.

Burial Register: 5595 4 Tisri 1834 7 October Alfred
son of Benjamin Elkin.

105

SACRED / TO THE MEMORY OF / MOZLEY ELKIN /
WHO DIED AUGUST 25TH 1856 / AGED 70 YEARS.

Burial Register: 5616 24 Ab 1856 25 Aug Parnas
Mozeley son of Isaac Elkin aged 70 years.

[Mozeley of Isaac Elkin married Sarah of David Lindo 9th
March 1825.]

106 Small stone.

SACRED / TO THE MEMORY OF / ROSE SARAH / DAUGHTER OF / MOZLEY & ESTHER ELKIN / WHO DEPART- ED THIS LIFE / THE 19TH DAY OF SEBAT / A.M. 5598/ CORRESPONDING WITH / THE 14TH OF FEBRUARY 1838 / AGED 16 YEARS / AND SIX MONTHS.

Burial Register: 5598 19 Sebat 1838 14 Feby Rose Sarah daughter of Moseley & Esther Elkin aged 16 years & 6 mos.

107

SACRED TO THE MEMORY OF / SARAH / WIFE OF MOZLEY ELKIN / who departed this life / on 15th day of Tebet 5599 / or 1st January 1839 aged 42 Years. / Her Virtues need no epitaph, her name will / ever excite a tear from the poor, the unfortunate, the / afflicted, her exemplary piety will outlive the life / of man and leadeth her gentle spirit on to Heaven; / there may it rest in peace ! Amen.

Burial Register: 5599 15 Tebet 1839 1 January Sarah wife of Mozeley Elkin aged 43 years.

Three in a row at N.W. corner adjoining boundary wall of Department of Public Works.

108 Raised tomb with large granite slab.

In Memory of / EDWARD SAMUEL DANIELS / BORN 27 SEPTEMBER 1838 / DIED 29 JUNE 1905 / 'OUR LOVED ONE' / ALSO HIS WIFE / MARY ELIZABETH / BORN 22ND AUGUST 1840 / DIED 16TH JANY. 1907. / 'OUR DEAR MOTHER'.

Burial Register: 5665 26 Sivan 1905 29 June 2 p.m. Edward Samuel Daniels son of Samuel Elias and Sophia

57

Daniels aged 66 yrs and 9 mos and 2 days.

Burial Register: 5667 Shebat 1. 1907 16 Janry 3 p.m. Sophia Mary (otherwise called Mary Elizabeth Clarke) Hebrew Zipporah Miriam Daniels, widow of Samuel Edward Daniels, late Parnaz of this congregation aged 65 years and 25 days buried by C. S. Baeza.

109 Raised tomb with upright white marble tombstone: carved figure of infant sleeping.

ANNIE MARIE / CHILD OF / EDWARD SAMUEL / & MARY DANIELS / BORN JUNE 1 1882 / DIED NOV. 27. 1885.

Burial Register: 5646 19 Kisliv 1885 27 Nov 2 A.M. Annie Marie child of Edward and Sohpia (? Daniels) 3 years 5 mos and 27 days.

110

כי עמך מקור חיים באורך נראה אור

[A crown]

פנ

SACRED / TO THE MEMORY OF / ISAAC BABER ISAACS, / WHO DIED / IN THE ISLAND OF TOBAGO / 20TH TAMUS 5624 / (24TH JULY 1864) / AND WAS INTERRED HERE 29TH IDEM / AGED 38 YEARS.

Samuel, Sidney St. Mile End, London.

Burial Register:

1st Entry: 5624 20 Tamus 1864 24 July Isaac Baber son of Judah Baber Isaacs aged 38 years.

2nd Entry: 20 Tamus 5624 24 July 1864 Isaac Baber Isaacs aged 38 years. Died in Tobago, his remains brot here in the Schr 'May Queen' & buried in the reserve land belonging to the Elkin family which is not laid down in the Carera book.

111. Paving square let into boundary wall.

B.E. / M.E. / J.H.

112 Small paving square let into slab of concrete, equi-distant between boundary Wall, Magazine Lane, and wall of courtyard.

PERLA LINDO / DIED 9 MAY 1904 / AGED 70.

Burial Register: 5664 24 Iyar 1904 9 May 10 p.m.
Perla Lindo daughter of Jacob & Esther Abarbanel Lindo.
Aged 70 years 8 mos 12 days buried by E.S. Daniels.

113 Square of Bath stone with letters in lead.

REBECCA / DAUGHTER OF / JOSHUAH & JUDITH / LEVI. / BORN 20 MARCH 1828, / DIED 10 OCT. 1891 - TISHRY 5652.

Burial Register: 5652 8 Tisri 1891 10 Oct. 4.15 a.m.
Rebecca Levi daughter of Joshua & Judith (Jane) Levi
aged 63 years 6 months & 20 days.

114 Square of stone with letters in lead as No. 113.

SARAH / DAUGHTER OF / JOSHUAH & JUDITH / LEVI, / BORN 20 NOV. 1815 / DIED 21 DEC. 1887 - 6 TEBET 5648.

Burial Register: 5648 6 Tebet 1887 21 Dec. Sarah Levi
daughter of Joshuah and Judith (Jane) Levi aged 72 years
one month and one day.

115 Gothic stone.

IN MEMORY / OF / JACOB LINDO / BORN IN LONDON / IN THE YEAR OF 1804, / DIED IN BARBADOES /

OCTOBER 24TH IN HIS 85TH YEAR / 1887.

Into His hands my spirit I consign.

Burial Register: 5648, 6 Hesvan 1887 24 October, 4.15 p.m. Jacob son of David & Sarah Abarbanel Lindo of London aged 82 years and 6 days.

116 Sacred to the memory of / JOSHUAH LEVI, / who died 14 Oct. 1870, / corresponding with / 19 Tisri 5631.

Burial Register: 19 Tisri 5631 Octr 14 1870 Joshuah Levi aged 88 yrs.

Small stone attached to above: letters in lead

JOSHUAH LEVI, / DIED 19 Tisri 5631 - 14 Oct. 1870.

117
מצבת

Here lies Interred the / Body of SARAH / Wife of P. RUBINS who / departed this life / the 14th August 186.. / corresponding with 27 Adar / 5628 / aged 50 years.

תנצבה

Burial Register: 5628 26 Ab 1868 14 August Sarah wife of Phillip Rubins aged 50 years.

118 ISAAC ELIAZER SOESMAN, / Geboren te Suriname / 3 July 1806 / Overleden te Barbadoes / 1 October 1864.

Burial Register: 1 Tisri 5625 1 Oct 1864 Isaac Eleazar Soesman aged 58 years and three months (from Surinam).

119 In Memory / of / SAMPSON SHANNON / who Died / Sep. 26th 1860 / Kipur day 5621 / Aged 60 Years.

Burial Register: 10 Tisri 5621 26th Sept 1860 Sampson Shannon aged 62 years.

פ׳נ

כ׳ פנחם בר שמעון

נפטר יום ב׳ ט״ז תמוז

שנת התר״ט״ו׳ לפ״ק

ת״נ״צ״ב״ה״

In Memory of /ALEXANDER SAMUEL / SON OF / JAMES
SAMUEL / OF LONDON / WHO DEPARTED THIS LIFE / 4
MONTHS AFTER / HIS ARRIVING IN THIS ISLAND / JULY
2nd 1855 - 5615 / aged 28 YEARS / TO THE INEXPRES-
SIBLE GRIEF / OF HIS WIFE AND FAMILY / MAY HIS
SOUL REST IN PEACE.

*Burial Register: 16 Tamus 5615. 2 July 1855 Alexander
Samuel aged 28 years.*

121 Small stone originally upright, now lying flat, in
excellent preservation.

Sacred to the Memory of / BENJAMIN C. D'AZEVEDO /
Born 2 Nov. 1815, / corresponding with / 29 Tisri, 5576, /
Died at St. Pierre, / Martinique, / 26 May, 1878, Corres-
ponding with / 23 Iyar, 5638

*Burial Register: 5638 23 Yiar 1878 26 May Benjamin
son Moses & Hannah Cohen D'Azevedo died at St. Pierre,
Martinique at 2 of a.m. aged 62 years 6 mos & ....
(bound up).*

121(a) Another stone lying at the foot of No.121.

Benjamin / son of / Moses and Hannah Cohen / D'Azevedo
/ died 23 Yiar 5638-26 May 1878 / Aged 62 yrs 6 mos & 24
dys.

West of No.120.

122 SACRED / to the Memory of / SAMUEL ELIAS DANIELS /
who departed this life / at the age of 48 years / on the
9th of May 1853, / Corresponding with the 1st Yiar 5613. /
This is a small tribute of affection / from a loving wife
and children. / May his Soul rest in Peace.

*Burial Register: 1 Iyar 5613 9 May 1853 Hazan Saml
Elias Daniels aged 48 years.*

123 At base of sugar-apple tree.

כי מלאכיו יצוה לך

In Memory of / MR. MOSES PINHEIRO / who departed
this life / on the 22 Novr 1831 / corresponding / with the
the 17 Kislev 5592 / Aged 56 Years.

*Burial Register: 5592 17 Kislev 1831 22 Nov Moses son
of David Pinheiro aged 56 years.*

124 Small square stone.

Ester de Jacob da Costa Gomez / d. 12 Sep. 1833 /
corr. 28 Elul 5593.

*Burial Register: 5593 28 Elul 1833 Sep 12 Esther de
Jacob DaCosta Gomez.*

125 Broken across the middle.

Sacred to the memory / of / RACHEL / wife of / DAVID
M.C. Baeza / who departed this life / on the 22 September
1833, / Corresponding / with the 9th Tisry 5594 / Aged 27
years 8 months & 22 days.

*Burial Register: 5594 9 Tisri 1833 22 September Rachel
wife of David Moses Cordoza Baeza aged 27 years 8 mos &
22 days.*

[David Moses Cardoza m. 25 May 1831 Rachel of David Lobo]

126 To / the memory of / MOSES BELASCO, / late reader
of this / congregation, / who departed this life / on the
10th Hesvan 5595, / corresponding with / 12th November
1843; / Aged 52 years, 11 months and 26 days / This tomb
is erected as / a tribute of / respect.

Burial Register: 5595   10 Hesvan   1834   12 Novemb.   Hazan
Moses son of Abraham Belasco aged 52 years 11 mos & 26 days.

127 Small square stone let into cement.

Under this tomb lies the body / of RACHEL, wife of /
Jacob Frores Demeza / who departed this life / 11th May
1835, Corresponding / to the 12 th Iyar 5595 / Aged 44
years & 10 days.

Burial Register: 5595   12 Yiar   1835   11 May   Rachel wife
of Jacob Frois de Meiza aged 44 yrs & 10 days.

128 Small square stone, leaded letters.

MENESSAH / SON OF / BENJ^{N}. AND JUDITH COHEN /
D'AZEVEDO / DIED 3 YIAR 5596 - 20 April 1836 / AGED
33 YRS.

Burial Register: 5596   3 Yiar   1836   20 April   Menasseh
Cohen son of Benjamin Cohen D'Azevedo aged 33 years.

129 RACHEL FINZI / died 8th Janry. 1838 / coresponding
to 11th Tebet 5598 / Aged 78 Yrs. & 6 mos.

Burial Register: 5598   11 Tebet   1838   8 January   Rachel
widow of Samuel Isaac Finzi aged 78 years & 6 mos.

130 Sacred to the memory of / SARAH NUNES, / and BEN-
JAMIN NUNES, / children of / DAVID and SARAH NUNES
CARVALHO, / who departed this life / on the 10th Kislev
5603, / (13th Nov. 1842) / and 5th Sebat 5603,. (7th Jan.
1843) / aged 19 years / and 15 years.

A. Cary Fecit, Boston.

Burial Register: 5603 10 Kislev 1842 13 Nov. Sarah Nunes of David & Sarah Nunes Carvalho aged 19 years.

Burial Register: 5603 5 Sebat 1843 7 January Benjamin Nunes son of David and Sarah Nunes Carvalho aged 15 years.

Commencing east of wall.

131

רחל בעת רצון נקראת ביושר
ללכת לישיבת העליונים
אשר שם תענוג ונועם אושר
ונפשה נפרדה מתחתונים
פה לגופה מקום מנוחתה
ולרחל זה מצב קבורתה

Sa / Dela bienaventurada / Doncella Rachel Baruh / Henriquez que f? en 26 / De Adar 5502 que corres- / ponde a 19 Febrero 1741 / de Edad de 60 Annos / S A G D G

Burial Register: 5502 26 Adar 1742 19 Febry Rachel Baruh Henriques aged 60 years.

Three in a line, near tree stump.

132 Around the sides and top :-

HERE LYETH INTERRED THE BODY OF MOSES VALVERDE WHO DEPARTED THIS LIFE THE 25 DAY OF APRIL 1739 AGED 22 YEARS AND FOUR MONTHS.

מצבת

קבורת הבחור הנחמד משה ואלוירדי
נלע ביום ד כב לניסן שנת
ה״תצ״ט.

64

SA / Do Bemaventurado y Virtuoso / Mancebo Moseh
Valverde / faleceu em 4.ª feira 28 de / Nisan 5499 que
Corresponde / a 25 de Abrill 1739 de / Ydade de 22 A y 4
Mezes. / S A G D E G.

*Burial Register: 5499 28 Nisan 1739 25 April Moses
Valverde aged 22 years & 4 mos. [Hebrew epitaph above,
however, reads '22nd Nisan'.]*

133 Broken in three pieces; inscription undecipherable.

134

מצבת

קבורת הכבודה הצנועה והנכבדת
מרת שרה לאה זוגתו של דוד לופיש
נלע כח לחדש טבת שנת התצט

תנצבה

SA / Da Bemaventurada Honesta y / Temenite de D.ª
Sarah Leah / Mulher que foy de David / Lopez faleceu en
28 de Tebet / 5499 [sic!] que corresponde a 27 de / Decembro 1738 / S A G D G.

*Burial Register: 5489[!] 28 Tebet 1728[!] 27 December
Sarah Leah wife of David Lopez.*

South of last row.

135

מצבת

קבורת הישיש הנכבד אהרן חזקיהו
פירירא נפטר לבית עולמו כב לשבט
שנת התקא

ת׳ נ׳ צ׳ ב׳ ה׳

SA / Do Bemaventurado y / Honrado Aaron Hisquiau /
Pereira Faleceu em 22 de / Sebat A? 5501 q̃. Correspon- /
de a 29 de Janeiro 174$^0_1$ / S A G D E G.

*Burial Register: 5501 22 Sebat 1741 29 January Aaron
Hisquiau Pereira.*

136   סצבת

קבורת הבחור הנחמד
אברהם חזקיהו
סנדים בליסאריו נלע בן
י׳׳ם שנה ומ׳ חודשים ביום ה׳
י׳׳מֶ לחדש כסלו שנת ה׳ת׳צ׳ח׳

תנצבה

SA / Do Bemaventurado mancebo / Abraham Hisquiyau
Mendes / Belisario q^e foy D^s servido / Recolher para sy
desta p^a / melhor vida de Ydade do / 19 Annos y 9 m^s em
5$^{ta}_{..}$ f$^{ra}_{..}$ / y 19 Kisleu do Anno 5498 / S B A G D E G

*Burial Register: 5498 19 Kislev   Abrah. Hisquiau Mendes
Belisario aged 19 years & 9 mos.*

Near the wall.

137   סצבת

קבורת הבחור הנחמד יצחק חזקיהו
בן פינחם הלוי לונדיריש נפטר בכם
בתשרי שנת ה׳ת׳ק

תנצבה

SA / Do Bemaventurado Ishac / Hisquiyahu Filho de
Pinhas / Aleuy de Londres Faleceo / em 29 de Tisry anno

5500 que / Corresponde a 20 de Outubro / anno 1739 de
Edade de 28 anno / e quatro mezes. / S B A G D E G

Burial Register: 5500   29 Tisri   1739   20 October   Isaac
Hisquiau son of Pinehas Alevy aged 28.

Two ledgers near a saman or inga tree.

138   Much broken.

סצבת

קבורת הגביר הנכבד בניסין דא
...גנ   יום ד לחדש
אלול שנת התצא

תנצבה

...ado BENJAMIN / ...... Falheceu em / ...qᵉ Corresponde / . .. Agusto de 1731 / ..... D G.

139   SA / Da Bem Aventurada RACHEL / SARAH CARVALLO
que falaceo / Em 3 de Tamus Anno 5478 / S A G D G

Burial Register: 5478   3 Tamus   Rachel Sarah Carvalla.

140   Around the sides and top :-

HERE LYETH INTERR'D THE BODY OF REBECCA WIFE
OF SAMUEL RAPHAEL DE CAMPOS (broken) THE 19 DAY OF
AUGUST 1772 AGED 105 YEARS.

סצבת

... הצנועה הנכבדת והצדקת
... רבקה אשת הגביר שמואל רפאל
די קמפוש נל״ע יום רביעי כ״ מנחם
תקל״ב״ בת ק״ה שנה
ת״נ״צ״ב״ה״

SA / Da Bienaventurada Caritativa / y Temente de Dˢ.
Dⁿᵃ Ribkah / Mulhere de Samuel Rapael / de Campos Falecue
em 4ᵃ / fᵃ 20 de Minahim 5532 que / Corresponde a 19
Agosto / 1772 de 105 Annos de Idade / S A B A G D G.

Burial Register: 5532 20 Ab, 1772 19 August Rebecca
widow of Samuel Raphael Campos aged 105 years.

141 SA / Do Bem Aventurado, / Y virtuozo Varão O Sᷓ /
Semuel Rephael de Campos / Que Foi Dˢ, Servido / Recol-
her Para Si Em 11 / De sebatt Aᵒ, 5480 que / Corresponde
A 10 De / Janeiro 1719

ת״נ ״צ ״ב ״ה ״

Burial Register: 5480 11 Sebat 1719 10 Jany Samuel
Raphail Campos.

Three stones together.

142

מצבת קבורת הבחור הנחמד כה״ר
משה חיים בן הגביר כה״ר אברהם
נונים נלעֶ י״ח לחדש חשון שנת התעֶן
תנצבה

S ᴬ

Do bemaventurado Mosseh / Haim Filho de Abraham /
Nunez felleceo em 18 / Hesvan 5473 que Corresponde / a 7
Novembro 1712 SV. / S A G D G .

Carving : Hand from cloud felling tree.

Burial Register: 5473 18 Hesvan 1712 7 November
Moses Haim son of Abraham Nunes.

בשנת ותקרא שמו בֶּן אוני

מצבת

קבורת האשה שמתה בחבלי ילדה
נכבדת וצנועה בבית בעלה זמנה ותיקנה
לדרכה צידה   נשמתה תלך למערת
המכפלה הלא היא שמה רחל חנה אשת
הנביר ירסיהו ברוך לויזאדה לגן עדן
נקראת ביום כ"ט לחדש חשון בשנת היא
מֶצבת קבורת רחל לֶפֶּק

תנצבה

Around the sides and top :-

Here lyeth interr'd the body of the ingenious and
charitable Rachel Hanah late wife of Jeremiah Baruh Louzada who departed this life the 28th of Oct[r.] 1741 aged
31 years and 6 months.

SA / Da Bemaventurada Honesta Pia / Devota Caritativa
y Temeroza de / D[s.] RACHEL HANAH Mulher q[e] / Foy de
IRMEYAU BARUH LOUZADA / q[e] foy D[s] Servido Recolher la /
para Sua Eterna Gloria 5 Dias / Despois de Seo Parto de
Idade / de 31 Annos y Meyo F[o.] em 4[a.] feyra / 29 do Mes
Hesvan 5502 Corresponde / a 28 Outobro 1741 Sua Malugra-
mento / Seia Expiacão de Seos Pecados Amen / S B A G D G.

Carving : Tree chopped down.

144

מצבת

קבורת התלמיד הנחמד פינחם חזקיהו
אבארבאניל נפטר לבית עולמו יום א
י"ז בטבת שנת התקל"ב

תנצבה

S^A.

Do Anjo Pinhas Hizqa. Filho de / Joseph & Sarah Abarbanel / Faleceo em Domingo 17 de Tebet / 5502 q^e Corresponde a 13 Dez-/ -embre 1741 de Ydade de 11 Añõs / y 6
Mezes / S A G D G.

*Burial Register: 5502 17 Tebet 13 December Pinhas
Hisquiau son of Joseph & Sarah Abarbanel 11 years and 6
mos.*

145 S^A

Do Bem Aventurado / Ytemerozo De Deus O S $^R_{\underline{a}}$ / Yacob
Bueno Frances que / Faleseo Em 6 De Tamus A^o / 5479 /

/ תנצבה

Que Corresponde a 12 De / Junho 1719.

*Burial Register: 5479 6 Tamus 1719 12 June Jacob
Bueno Franco.*

146 S^A.

DA BEMAVENTURADA Y / VERTVOZA S.$^{RA}_{\cdot\cdot}$ RACHELL /
MULLER Q^e FOY DE YACOB / BARVH LOVZADA Q FOY /
D$^S_{\cdot}$ SERVIDO RECOLHER / P^A. SY EM 13 DE NISAN /
5470 SUA ALMA GOZE DA / GLORIA.

תנצבה

*Burial Register: 5470 13 Nisan Rachel wife of Jacob
Baruch Louzado.*

147 Broken across diagonally.

SA / Da bem Aventurada De D$^{na}_{\cdot\cdot}$ / Rachell Buena Henriques mulher / q^e foy de Ab$^m_{\cdot}$ Buena Henriques / faleceu

en 10 de Sivan 5476 q.ᵉ / Corresponde a 21 de Mayo 1716 /
S A G D G.

*Burial Register: 5476 10 Sevan 1716 21 May Rachel
wife of Abraham Bueno Henriques.*

148 Badly broken and piece missing.

SA / Da Bem Aventurada Evirtuoza / Ribcah de Andrade
que Faleseo / en Rochodes Tebett 5468 que / Corresponde a
13 Decembro 1707 / Sua Alma Goze da Gloria.

Burial Register: 5468 1 Tebet 1703 [!] *13 December
Rebecca De Andrada.*

149 Around the sides and top :-

Here Lyeth Interr'd the Body of David Nunes Castello
Late of this Island Merchant who Departed this life the 22
of January 17$\frac{11}{12}$ Aged 54 years.

הנה מצבת קבורת זאת נאמן

בברית האיש נפטר שמו דוד

יהיה נזכר בתוך מלאכי צבאות

תהי נפשו תסיד לפני האלהים

האיש אשר נפטר לעולמים שמו

יהיה נזכר לרחמים לפני מלך מלכי

המלכים.

SA / Do Bem Aventurado de / David Nunes Castello que /
Faleceo Em 25 de Sebatt / do Anno 5472 Sua Alma / Goze da
Gloria.

תנצבה

*Burial Register: 5472 25 Sebat 1711/12 22 January
David Nunes Castello.*

150 Around the sides and top :-

Da Malograda Encurtada Caritativa Virtuoza Etemeroza
de Deus Ass.ra Debora Sarah Cahanet Mulher que foy de
Mosseh Cohen Peyxoto que achamou D.s pera si em 16 de
Sivan 5469 Anos תנצבה

הנה זאת מצבת קבורת
מרת דבורה שרה כהנת
סבת שבע עשרה להילדת
ישבה על משבר סבתה מתה
ולא גמר שנה לחפה בביתה
כי לחמשה ימים ליולדתה
ביום שבת בעלות המנחה
נפטרה לשמים נשמתה
תהיה זאת לזכרון ולרחמים
לפני סלך מלכי המלכים

Deserto esta he a Estatua da Sepultura. / Da Senhora
Debora Sarah Cahanet. / Deidade de Dezasete Anos Aser
nacida. / Esteve de Parto de Sua Filha Morta. / Enão
Cumpiro Ano Ao talemo Em Sua Casa. / Que ao quinto Dia
de Seu Parir. / Em Dia de Sabat aoras de Minha. / Parri-
une aos Ceos Sua Alma. / Seyga ysto por memoria Epiedades.
/ Diante de Rey do Reyes Dos Reyes. / Acabesa fica d.a sua
filha y. / dos peis oitra filha qe fa.o no @ / 5472 Com sua
segunda. / Mulher /

Burial Register: 5469 16 Sevan Debora Sarah Cahanet wife
of Moses Cohen Peyxoto.

151 Marble slab, near to No. 48.

Around the sides and top :-

HERE LYETH INTERR'D THE REMAINS OF MR. MOSES
LOPEZ SENIOR WHO DEPARTED THIS LIFE THE, 17TH OF
APRIL 1762 AGED 69 YEARS.

ויקרא אל משה ביום השביעי ומשה עלה אל
האלהים ויקרא אליו הי
מצבת
קבורת הישיש ונכבד איש צדיק תמים
כבוד נה"ר משה לופיץ אבי יתומים עוזר
דלים מרחם עניים חונן אביונים חסיד
ישר ונאמן זקן ונשוא פנים בשבת כ"ך
לניסן לפ"ק שנה בש"כר נפטר לב"ע וזכרו
לברכה תמיד נזכר נשמתו בעדן ה" כנן רצוב
ורוחו [?] נפשו תלין בטוב

ת'נ'צ'ב'ה'

SA / Del B.A. Horado Hu- / milde Caritative y / Virtuozo el S.r MOSEH / LOPEZ qui en passo. / desta amejor
vida para / gozar el fruto de sus / buenas obras en 27 de /
Nissan 5522 que Cor- / responde a 17 de Abril / 1762 de
Edad de 69 Annos / S B A G D E G

*Burial Register: 5522 27 Nisan 1762 17 April Moses
Lopez Snr aged 69 years.*

Three together in a row :-

152 Flaked and illegible.

153 Broken across the top.

SA / Da bem Aventurada / Evirtuosa Mulher de fonsado /
as.ra Leha Mulher que foy / de Jacob Baruh Loizada aqual /
Recolheu os Ds para Muilhor / mundo seu filho Primo- /
jenito de Ydade de 38 annos / faleceu em 15 De Sebatt /
5462 que Corresponde a / 2 de Feub.ro de 170½. / Sua alma
goze da gloria.

תנצבה

*Burial Register: 5462 15 Sebat 170½ 2 February Leah
wife of Jacob Baruch Louzado.*

73

154 Long narrow stone, broken on one side, almost illegible.

.... rade de sa / en 27 de....

155 Very old stone, flaked and lettering partley indecipherable :-

....DA / .... MUL / ... LEAC. / ... 29

156 S.ᴬ

Da Bemaventurada Ester / Mulher que foy de Daniel / Hᵐ. Vllao faleceu en 21 de / Tebet 5504 que Correspo/ -nde a 26 de Dezembro / 1743 / S B A G D G.

Burial Register: 5504 20 [!] Tebet 1743 26 December Ester wife of Daniel Haim Villao.

157 Broken in two places :-

Sᴬ

Do bem aventurado Varao / Dancel haim Vlloa que Recolheu / deos a seus povos Em 16 de / Tebett Anno 5474 de Ydade / de 47 Anos Sua Alma .. (Broken) / Gloria Eterna Com seus pais.

תנצבה

Burial Register: 5474 16 Tebet Daniel Haim Villao aged 47 years.

158 Beside a cocoa-nut tree (since felled).

Sᴬ

Da Bemaventurada E Virtuoza / Sʳᵃ muller de fonsa do Yndick / muller qve foy de Yshack / Gabai Ritson, que

recollev / deos a sevs povos em 18 de / Kislev do anno
5472 a criasaum / Sua alma Goze da Gloria / Com as Yustas
de ysrael.

תֻּ נֻ צֻ בֻ הֻ

Burial Register: 5472   18 Kislev - de Isaac Gabai Risson.

Two together.

159   S^A

DO BEM AVENTURADO E / ONRADO VARAÕ YAHACOB /
LVIZ QUE FOY APANHADO / A SEUS POVOS EM PRIMEYRO
DE / ROSHODES AB 5461

ת׳ נ׳ צ׳ ב׳ ה׳

עד פה יבוא האיש והחכמה
משכיל ונבון תם וישר
סולם לעלות אל זיו עליונה
... ויעקב בעדן מעונה

Burial Register: 5461   1 Ab   Jacob Luiz.

160   Cherubim in top corners.   In the border :-

HERE LYETH INTERR'D Y BODY OF (broken) SARAH
DAUGHTER OF MORDECAY AND SARAH MASSIAH WHO DE-
PARTED THIS LIFE Y 8TH OF APRIL 1746 AGED 9 MONTHS
& 21 DAYS.

ה נתן וה לקח

SA / Do Anjo Angla Sarah / Massiah Filla de Mordecay /
& Sarah Massiah quo / (broken) .. / colher para sy en 29 /
de Nisan 5506 que Cor- / responde a 8 de Abril 1746 / de
Idade de 9 Mezes / & 21 Dias.

75

Carving: Two birds in oval plaque.

*Burial Register: 5506   29 Nisan   1746   8 April   Sarah
daughter of Mordecai & Sarah Massiah aged 9 mos. and 21
days.*

Two ledgers together.

161 SA / DO BEM AVENTURADO / EVIRTUOSO VARAO
DANIEL / BUENO HENRIQUEZ QUE / FOI APAÑADO ASEUS
POVOS / EM 5 DE TAMUS A° 5459 / SUA ALMA GOZE DA
GLORIA.

תנצבה

Burial Register: 5 Tamus   Daniel Bueno Henriques.

162 SA / DO BEM AVENTURADO / EHONRADO VARAO /
DAVID SUAREZ QUE / FALECEU EM 9 DE / NISAN A°
5459.

תנצבה
[2 lines of Hebrew indecipherable.]

Burial Register: 5459   9 Nisan   David Suares.

163
מצבת

קבורת האשה הכבודה הצנועה
והנכבדת אשת חיל עטרת בעלה
רבקה אשת יעקב לוזאדה אשר
הלכה לבית עולמה ושבה אל בית
אביה כנעוריה בכד סנחם שנת החנז
סדר ופנית בבקר, והלכת לאהליך
ת׳נ׳צ׳ב׳ה׳

76

רבקה ברוכה היא ונם לוווזאדה
תפרח כשושנה ונם שורשה
תישיר תל־פיה והיא הורשה
בנן אלהים היא הלא צעדה

Da bem aventurada Evirtuoza / Ribcah Mulher de Jacob
Baruh / LOUZADA que foy Deos servido / Recolher a Milhor
Mundo na / flor de sua Ydade em 24 de / Menahem Anno 5457
que / Corresponde a primeiro de / Agosto 1697 / SUA ALMA
GOZE da GLORIA /

*Burial Register: 5457 24 Ab 1797 1 Aug Rebecca wife
of Jacob Baruh Louzado.*

A Stone lying between Nos. 28 and 29 which had been
omitted.

164 De bem Aventurada onesta / Evertuoza Ester Antunes
que / faleseu de ydade de 84 annos / em 16 de Sebat do
Anno 5463 / de Criacao do mundo que Com- / -responde em
22 Janeiro $1703\frac{2}{3}$ que Sua B$^{\underline{ta}}$ Alma GOZE da / Gloria.

תנצבה

*Burial Register: 5463 16 Sebat 1702/3 22 January
Ester Antunes aged 84 years.*

165 Da bem Aventurada Evertuosa / Molher de fonsado A Sta
Ribca / Molher que foy de David Gabay / Letob Aqual Recolheu os^{r} / Deus para millor Mundo / faleseu em 22 de Sivan
5463 / que Comresponde a 27 de / Mayo Anno 1703 Que sua /
Bendita alma goze da devina / gloria.

תנצבה

*Burial Register: 5463 22 Sivan 1703 27 May Ribca
wife of David Gabay Letob.*

166 Da S^{ra} Rachell de Meza / Que falleceu Sendo VV /
dos^{or}: Ishak de Meza em / 17 Nissan 5459 / SUA ALMA
GOZE da GLORIA.

*Burial Register: 5459 17 Nisan Rachel widow of Isaac
de Meiza.*

167 Very flaked and illegible.

168 Flaked :-

   D.... Burgos / .... / 5467

Working west from boundary wall at Magazine Lane.

169 Single tomb.

   DA VIRTVOZA DONZELLA / SARAH FILHA DE YMANVEL
/ ISRAEL DIAS FALECEO EM / 5 DE ADAR RISON 5464.

תנצבה

*Burial Register: 5464 14 Adar Sarah daughter of Emanuel
Israel. [Dias]*

170 Skull and crossbones below :-

   DO BEM. AVENTURA- / DO DAVID CHILLAO / QUE
FALECEV EM 14 / DE TEBET A° 5458.

תנצבה

Burial Register: 5458 14 Tebet David Chillao.

172 Very small child's grave.

   De DANIEL Filho / De SIMHON E SARA / MASSIAH q
faleceo / Em 29 de Tebet / 5466.

172 S^A / DO BEM AVENTURADO / YSHAK DE MEZA QUE / FALECEO EM 21 DE HESUAN / 5457.

תנצבה

Burial Register: 5457 21 Hesvan Isaac de Meiza.

173 Around the sides and top :-

HERE LYETH INTERRED THE BODY OF ISAAC MENDEZ SON OF JOSEPH MENDEZ WHO DEPARTED THIS LIFE ON THE 3 DECEMBER AGED XXI YEARES.

מצבת

קבורת האדם [?] הנכבד יצחק סינדיש נ"ע
עלה לסרום בשבעה במבת שנת התנו

בואו אחי בכו אותי	זאת מצבת קבורתי
כלה נאה קרובתי	ארסתי לי וקדשתי
לא זכיתי לחופתי	לא ראיתי ארוסתי
זיין מבת שנת סותי	יום בו היתה פקודתי
ותהי גן בית סנוחתי	רחום כפר לאשמתי

תנצבה

Do bem aventurado de Isaque / Mendez fillo de Joseph Mendez / que foy D^s servido recoller na flor / de sua Idade p^a Plantarlo em .an (crack) / Eden Lugar dos J... Evir- / -tuosos adonde su. muita / Gloria supra a.. alta de sua / Idade falleseo em 7 de Tebet / 5456 que corresponde a 3 de / Dec^{bro} 1696 ã.

יי נתן ויי לקח
יהי שם יי סבורך

Burial Register: 5456 7 Tebet Isaac son of Joseph Mendes aged 21 years.

79

174   Do Bem aventurado de / Abraham de Leao fillio / de
Mosseh Perreira de Leao^s / q foy Ds Servido Recol- / -ler
a Seos Povos em 6 de / Hesvan ano 5453 q Cor- / -responde
a 6 de Octubro / 1692 / SUA ALMA GOZE da GLORIA .

תנצבה

*Burial Register: 5453   6 Hesvan   1692   October   Abraham
de Leao son of Moses Pereira de Leao.*

Two together near cabbage palm.

175 SA / DA BEM AVENTURADO / YAEL SERANA FALLECEV
/ EM 7 DE TISRI A° 5455.

תנצבה

Burial Register: 17 Tisri   Israel Seranafael [sic].

176   Broken and mended.

SA

DO BEM AVENTURADO DE / JOSEPH SENIOR SARAIVA
/ QVE FOI APANHADO A SEOS / POVOS EM. 26 DE /
MENAHEM A° / 5454.

תנצבה

Burial Register: 5454   26 Ab   Joseph Seraiva.

177   S^A

Do Bem Aventurado he / temeroso Varao ' Ymanuel /
Namias que foy Deus / Servido recolher para si / na flor
de Sua Idade de / 44 Annos para plantarlo / em Ganeden
lugar dos / Justos & Virtuosos Adonde / sua murta supra
afalta de / sua Idade, faleceo Em 22 / de Nisan anno 5474.
/ S B A G E G / AMEN.

178 Triangular stone.

HERE LYETH YE BODY OF / DAVID RAPHAEL DE MAR-
CADO / MERCHANT WHO DEPARTED / THIS WORLD YE 14TH
OF AUGUST / 1685.

SEPULTURA DO BEMAVENTURADO / DE DAVID RAPHAEL
DE MERCADO / QUE FALECEO EM 24 DE MENAHEM / AN⁰
5445 SUA ALMA GOZE DA GLORIA.

פה איש אשר נקבר לכל עינים
דוד רפאל הוא בקרית ספר
נפשו חיה גופו כמו גל אפר
נכח כנשר עף עדי שמים

*Burial Register: 5445 24 Ab 1685 August 14 David
Raphael de Mercado.*

179 Sᴬ /DE YSHAC DO / VALE FAº EM / 20 ADAR 5452.

Burial Register: 5452 25 Adar Isaac de Valle.

180 Illegible.

181 DE ESTER RODRI.... / QVE FALECEV / EM 11
TAMVS ... / 5451.

Burial Register: 5451 11 Tamus Ester Rodrigues.

182 Illegible.

183 DEL BIEN AVIENTVRADO / E VIRTUOZO ISHAC DE /
DAVID DA SILVA Qᴱ / RECOLLEO DEVS PARA SVA /

GLORIA EM 17 DE TAMZ / 5452 QVI / CONRESPONDE A
26 DE / JVLHO SVA ALMA GOZE / DA GLORIA / AMEN.

Carving: Tree chopped down.

Burial Register: 5452 17 Tamus Isaac de David Da Silva.

184 Very large lettering :-

ESTER DE / CASERES Q / AB -45-.

Burial Register: 5454 2 Ab Ester de Caseres.

185 DA BEM AVENTURADA / JUDICA ISRAEL DIAS F / EM
3 DE TEBET / A° 5451.

תנצבה

Burial Register: 5451 3 Tebet Judica Israel Dias.

186 DO ENCURTADO DE ABRAHAM / ARON F° DE JOSSEPH
MENDES / QUE FOY DS SERVIDO RECOLHER / A SEOS
POVOS EM 8 DE TISRY A° / 5452 / SUA ALMA GOZA DA
GLORIA.

תנצבה

*Burial Register: 5452 8 Tisry Abraham Aaron son of
Joseph Mendes.*

187 Inscription in raised letters :-

מצבת קבורת

האיש הנכבד פנדיאל
אבודיאינטי נפטר
לבית עולמו ביום
כז לירח אב שנת
החנא תנצבה

82

DO BEMAVENTURADO / PAGDIEL ABUDIENTE / QVE
FALESEO EM 27 DE / AB 5451 EM BARBADAS.

Carving: Skull and Cross bones, at bottom.
          Flowers on a stem at 2 top corners.

Burial Register: *5451   27 Ab   Rachel* [*sic*] *Abudiente.*

188   S^A

DO BEM AVENTURADO SELO / MOH ₿ MEDINA q FOI
DS / SERVIDO RECOLHER A SEOS / POVOS EM 24 DE
HESVAN / A° 5452.

תנצבה

Burial Register: 5452   24 Hesvan   Solomon Medina.

189   צדיק

 יפרח   (palm leaves)   כתסר

אברהם בן גדעון אבודיהנשי

איש תם ואיש ישר בארחותיו
הכין ברב כחו בחיתו
אוצר כל סחסד זכיותיו
להיות לסגן לו לנשסתו
דין אסת צדיק כסדותיו
גוסל לכל חסד אסונתו
יזכר ביום הדין והנדרם
ישרו וצדקתו לאברהם

      Do Bemaventurado & Tomerozo / De Ds os^{or} Abraham
Abudiente que / De 84 Annos passou desta Vida a / Da
Gloria Etterna Em 4 Tamuz / 5457 / Conresponde a Conta/

83

Vulgar Com 3 Julho / 1697. / Sua Alma Goze da Gloria.

*Burial Register: 5457 4 Tamuz 1697 3 July Abraham
Abudiente aged 84 years.* [*Hebrew text has Abraham Gideon
Abudiente.*]

190 S^A/ DA VERTVOZA & HONESTA / RACHEL MOTHER [sic]
QVE FOY / DE ABRAHAM ABVDIENTE / Q FALLECEV EM 22
HESVAN / A° 5456 / Q CONRESPONDE COM 21 / 8^{bro}
1695. / SVA B^{ta} ALMA GOZE / GLORIA.

*Burial Register: 5456 22 Hesvan 1695 21 October Rachel
wife of Abraham Abudiente.*

191 Two lines, very worn.

   S^A / JUD .. H...

192 S^A / DA BEM AVENTURADA / SARAH ...... / EM 15
DE NISAN 5462

תנצבה

     (Perhaps identical with *B.R. 5452   10 Nisan   Sarah
Turrs,*

193 DA BEM AVENTURADA / ABIGAIL DA FONSECA / MEZA
F° EM 19 YYAR / A° 5452.

תנצבה

Burial Register: 5452   19 Yiar   Abigail de Fonseca

194 Broken in four pieces.
     At top, cross-bones, pickaxe, and spade: at base,
hour-glass and skull.

S^A / DO BEM AVENTVRADO / S^{OR} JAHACOB MASSIAH /
FALLECEV / EM 11 DE TEBET A° 5453 . / SUA ALMA GOZE
DA GLORIA.

Burial Register: 5453   11 Tebet   Jacob Massiah.

195 At top, cross-bones, pickaxe and spade: at base,
skull and cross-bones.

S^A / DA BEM AVENTVRADA / S^{ra} DEBORAH MASSIAH /
FALLECEV / EM 6 DE ADAR DO A° 5453 . / SUA ALMA
GOZE DA GLORIA.

תנצבה

Burial Register: 5453   6 Adar   Deborah Massiah.

196   S^A

Da Bem Aventurada / e Virtuozã Rachell / Idanha Que
foy Ds / Servido Recolher a seos / Povos em 7 de Sivan /
de 5453 a Que Cor- / -responde a Pr° de Junio / de 1693 ã /
Sue Alma Goze da Gloria

ת׳נ׳צ׳ב׳ה׳

[Leaf]   [Leaf]

Burial Register: 5453   7 Sevan   Rachel Idanha.

197 DA LA BIEN A BENTURADA [!] DE / SARAH ROD-
RIGUES CIVDAD REAL / QUE RECOLLO DIOS EN 3 SIVAN
/ 5453 / ANOS QUE CON RESPONDE A 7 / IUNIO 1693
A NOS. / SUA ALMA GOZE DE LA GLORIA.

*Burial Register: 5453   3 Sevan   1693   17 June   Sarah
Rodrigues Cividad [sic].*

85

198 Tablet in boundary wall, Magazine Lane.

.... בחור כארזים

.. תורה ומצות כרם

כבוד שמו שמואל בן כהר

ירמיה בורגוש עלה אל

השמים ביום שח' כג תשרי

שנת התנד לכע תנצבה

... chosen as the cedars
the law and commandments...
his name Samuel son of
Jeremiah Burgos. He ascended to
heaven on the Sabbath Tishri 23
in the year 5454 (1694) since creation
May his soul be bound upon the bond of life

199 Returning to centre, between three cabbage palms.

S ᴬ

Do Encurtado de Abraham / de Yshac Ysrael de Piza /
Faleceu em 23 de Nisan / Anno 5466 Sua Bendita / Alma
Goze De Gloria

תנצבה

*Burial Register: 23 Nisan 543[!]6 Abraham son of Isaac
Israel de Peiza.*

200 Much flaked.

DA BEM AVE... / TVRADA HAIM ... / CARDOSO
QVE .... / F.... ECEV.... / DE HESVAN 5449 ...

תנצבה

Burial Register: 5449 15 Hesvan Haim Cordoza.

201   Very large and deep legtering :-

    Da Bem aven- / turada vertu- / oza mulher de / Fonsado
Rahael / namia qve foy / descans.r a seos / Povos Em 22 de
/ Roshodes ylull / Anno 5444.

*Burial Register: 5444, 22 Elul   Rachel wife of Namias
Fonsada.*[*sic*].

202 DO BEM AVENTURADO / DE AARON NAVARRO / QVE
FALECEO EM 23 / DE XLVL A° 5445.

תנצבה

Burial Register: 5445 23 Elul   Aaron Navarro.

203 .. / DA BEM AVENTVRADA / DE DYNAH PACHECO /
QVE FOR APANHADA / A SEUS POVOS EM 14 / DE NISAN
DE 5441. / Sua Alma Goze Da Glorya.

Burial Register: 5441   14 Nisan   Dynah Pacheco.

204

בו צוער רך שנים ממקומו
נז   חיש לחזות נועם זיו כבודך
קולו סתחנן בצרור מאודך
אלי קבל את נפש שלמה

    .. / DO YNCVRTADO / E VIRTVOSO MANCEBO /
SELOMOH RODRIGVES / SOAREZ QVE FOY / RECOLLIDO
AMILLOR / MVNDO EM 2 DE SIVAN / ANN° 5440 SUA
ALMA GOZE de AGLORIA /

Burial Register: 5440 2 Sevan.   Solomon Rodriguez Sorez.

87

205 S^A

De David Fillo De / Joseph E' Jael Ysvrvn / Mendes
Que Foy / Recollido A sev / Cria Dor Oultimo / Dia De
pesah do Anno / 5440 /

206 S^A

De Mose Filho / do Joseph E Jael / Iesurum Mendes /
Faleseo em 5 De / Kislev 5442

*Burial Register: 5442 5 Kislev 1682 Moses son of Joseph
& Jail Jesurun Mendes.*

207 S^A

De Abraham filho / De Joseph E Jael / Iesurum Mendes /
Faleseo em 22 de / Hesuan 5445.

*Burial Register: 5445 22 Hesvan Abraham son of Joseph
& Jail Jeshurun Mendes.*

208 Small stone.

S^A

De Eliau filho de / Jacob E Ribcah / Baruh Louzada /
que faleceo em / 21 DE SEBAT 5441

209 Small stone, touching No. 208.

De Yshac Filho / Jacob E Ribcah Ba- / ruh Louzada que
/ faleceo em 2 DE ADAR / A° 5446.

*Burial Register: 5446 2 Adar Isaac son of Jacob &
Rebecca Baruch Louzado.*

210   Small Stone toucing No. 200.

DE RACHEL FILHA DE / IOSEPH E JAEL YESVRVM /
MENDES FALECEV EM 28 / ... YIAR A° 5446.

*Burial Register: 5446   28 Yiar   Rachel daughter of Joseph
& Jail Jeshurun Mendes.*

211   S^A [Within three leaves.]

    De Yshac Baruh / Henriquez Fillo de / Abraham Baruh
Henri- / quez Falleceu em Prim^{ro} / de Hesvan Ano 5456.

*Burial Register: 5456   Hesvan   Isaac Baruch son of
Abraham Baruch Henriques.*

212   Square stone let into boundary wall.

                        S^A

DO BEM AVENTVRADA / HANAH ALVARES / FALECEO
EM 7 YIAR / 546- [5 or 6].

                    תנצבה

Working west from boundary wall.

213   S^A / DO BEM AVENTVRADO DE / YACOB PACHECO QUE
FALECEO / EM 28 DE ADAR RISON 5442 / SUA ALMA GOZE
DA GLORIA.

                    תׅנׅצׅבׅהׅ

Burial Register: 5442   28 Adar   Jacob Pacheco.

214   Broken in two pieces.

    DA BEM AVENTVRADA / RIBKA PACHEGO QVE /

89

FALECEV EM 10 DE AB / A° 5441.

תנ׳צ׳ב׳ה׳

Burial Register: 5441 10 Ab Rebecca Pacheco.

215.   S A

DA BEM AVENTVRADA / SARAH MVLHER DE / YEHOS-
VAH HAYAYA F° / EM 27 DE TAMVZ A° / 5439 SUA ALMA
GOZE/DA ETERNA GLORIA.

Burial Register: 5439 27 Tamuz Sarah Widow of Joshua
Hayaya.

216   S A

DO BEM AVENTVRADA / YEHOSVAH HAYAYA F° / EM
7 DE ELVL A° 5438 / SUA ALMA GOZE DA / ETERNA
GLORIA.

Burial Register: 5438 7 Elul Hoshua Hayaya.

217   S A

DE MOSEH BARVH / LOIZADA FALECEV / EM 9 ELVL
/ A 5437.

Burial Register: 5437 9 Elul Moses Baruch Louzado (child).

218 Inscription worn away and stone broken in two pieces.

219 Very worn.

S A [Within leaves.]

DO BEM AVENTVRADO / DAVID Y S DIAS / FALESEV

... / 27 NIS.. / 5436 SUA ALMA GOZE DA GLORIA.

Burial Register: *5436 27 Nisan David Dias* [*sic*].

220 Very Worn.

DO BEM AVEN / TURADO VARAO / Y MAHIL Y^S DIAS /
QUE FOY APANHADO / A SEUS POVOS / EM 29 DE YIAR /
545..

Burial Register: *5436 29 Yiar Jeremiah* [*sic*] *Dias.*

221 Skull deeply incised.

דוד שכב עם אבותיו
כבן תשעים שבע ימים
תמים היה בדורותיו
ישוב יעסוד לקץ ימים

S^A

DO BEM AVENTVRADO E / VIRTUOSO VARAO DAVID /
IESURUN MENDES QUE FOI / APANHADO A SEUS POVOS /
DE HIDADE DE 90 ANNOS / EM 5 DE NISAN ANNO 5435.

Burial Register: *5435 5 Nisan David Jeshurun Mendes.*
[*Died 90 years of age.*]

222   מצבת

קברת היׄקׄרׄ הרופא
אברהם אנריקש פלורץ
שנאסף אל עמיו נ"
לחדש שבת (!) שנת הׄתׄלׄׄנׄ

תׄנׄצׄבׄהׄ

91

S^A / DO BEM AVENTVRADA / DOVTOR ABRAHAM /
HENRIQVEZ FLO RES / QVE FOI APANHADO / A SEVS
POVOS EM 3 / DE SEBAT ANNO / 5433.

Burial Register: 5433 3 Sebat Abraham Henriques.

223 .. / DO BEM AVENTVRADE / DE MOSSEH HAYM /
NAHAMYAS QVE FOY / DEOS SERVIDO / RECOLLEIO A
SEOS / POVOS EM 28 DE ELVL / 5432.

Burial Register: 5432 28 Elul Moses Haim Nahamyas.

224 S^A / DO YNCVRTADO VIRTVOZO / EMANSO CORDEIRO
/ ABRAHAM LOPES PEREIRA / QVE FOY APANHADO A SEVS
POVOS / EM 19 DE SEBAT / ANNO 5431 / SVA ALMA
GOZE DA GLORIA.

תנצבה

ויגוע ויסת אברהם
על פני שרה אמו
ותשא עליו בכי
לה נהי וקינה

בנפש

נע נה ורוח

סרה

ובה אסרה

הה על זמן אורב כמו רוצח
נדע בחרון אף ופרץ פרץ
בחור כמו ארוז בעוד צומח
השכיב אלי עפר בקרב ארץ

Burial Register: 5431 19 Sebat (1671) Abraham Lopez Pereira.

225 S^A / DO BEM AVENTVRADO / DE YSHACK LEVYREZIO / FALECEV / EM 16 DE ADAR 5427.

תנצבה

Burial Register: 5427 16 Adar Isaac Levi Rizio.

226 Broken across the middle.

S^A / DO BEM AVENTVRADO / DE YACOB ABRAHAM / LEVEREZIO / QUE FOY / APANHADO / SEVS POVOS EM / 21 DE ADAR SENI / ANNO 5421 / SUA ALMA GOZE / DA GLORIA.

Burial Register: 5421 21 Adar Jacob Abraham Linerezio.
[*! for LEVI REZIO.*]

The S^A surrounded by 2 leaves.

227 S^A / DO . EMCVRTADO . ARON / DE MERCADO QVE / FALE.SEO EM 9 DE ADAR / 5420.

Burial Register: 5420 9 Adar (1660) Aaron de Mercado.

This stone would appear to be the second oldest in the cemetery.

Seven stones close together.

228 DE MOSEH FILHO DE / AB & JAEL VALVERD.. / FALECEO EM ... / TISRY A° 54..

229 Child's stone, indecipherable :-

A.5443 (?)

230 DO BEN.AVENTVRADO / ENCURTADO DE DIAS / ISHAK
GABAY RISSON / QVE FALECEO EM 15 / DE NISAN ANNO
54.. (flaked).

תנצבה

231   S A

DE YACOB FILLO DE / JOSEPH.E IAEL . YSVRVN /
MENDES FALESEV / EN 27 DE TAMVZ 5436.

232 White marble, broken in right bottom corner.

DE YOSIYAHV REPHAEL / FILHO DE DAVID CASTE /
LLO. QVE FOY DEVS SER / VIDO LEVALO PERA SI / EM
16 DE VEADAR ANO / 5459.

ת׳נ׳צ׳ב׳ה׳

י״י נתן וי״י לקח יהי שם י״י

מבורך

*Burial Register: 5459 16 Veadar Raphael child of David
Castello.*

233 S^A / De Sarah Gabay / Rison Falecev em / 13 de Nisan
5432 /

234 Illegible.

235 DE BEM AVENTVRADA / SARAH SIMHA. ISRAEL / DE
PIZA QVE FOY APA- / -NHADO. ASEOS POVOS / EM 7 DE
TAMVS . A°: 5438.

Burial Register: 5438 7 Tamuz Sarah Simcha Israel.

236 D SARAH ESTER PER^A / D LEAO M^R DE MOSEH
PER^A D LEAO QVE FALECEO / EM 16 D ELVL 5438.

Burial Register: 5438 16 Elul Sarah Ester de Moses Perdleao.

237 DA INCURTADA d' ESTER / MENDES FILHA d JOSEPH
/ MENDES QUE N... FOI / SERVIDO RECOLHER EM / 12
D TAMUS . D 5440.

Burial Register: 5440 12 Tamus (1680) Jòseph Mendes.
[Actually Ester, daughter of J.M.]

238 Illegible.

239 D ABRAHAM YDANA F$^{\underline{O}}$ / D YACOB YDANA QVE /
PARTYV DESTE MVNDO / EN 21 D HESVAN 5439.

Burial Register: 5439 21 Hesvan Abraham de Jacob Ydaño.

240 S^A / DE MOSEH HAMIS FALECEO / EM 10 DE NISAN
5440.

תנצבה

Burial Register: 5440 10 Nisan Moses Hamis.

241 S^A / DE MOSE F^O DE IOSEPH / MENDES FALESEV /
EM 12 MENAHEM / A^O

Burial Register: 5440 10 Ab Moses child of Joseph Mendes.

242 DE RIBCAH FILHA D / AB & JAEL VALVERDE /
FALECEO EM 22 D / MENAHEM 11 A^O 5447.

Burial Register: 5442[sic!]   22 Ab   Rebecca Valverde (child).

243 DE BEM. AUNTURADA / ESTER GAON QU .... / RE-
COLLYDA . AS.... / POUOS . EM. 21. DE ... Y /
ANO. 5427.

Burial Register: 5427   21 Tisri (1666)   Ester Gaon.

Working towards Magazine Lane :-

244 Small stone much flaked, inscription illegible.

245 Almost indecipherable.

- - Da Bemaventurada ..... . Don / zela DEBORAH
BURGOS Em 2....

*Possibly entered in Burial Register as 5448   23 Tisri
David Burgos.*

246 - - DO BEM AVENTVRA / DO VARAO SELOMOH /
TINOCO QVE FOY / APANHADO ASEVS / POVOS EM 24
DE / KISLEV A 5448.

Burial Register: 5448   24 Kislev   Soloman Tinoca.

247 - - DA YNCURTADA DONZELA / RAHEL ESTER HENRI-
QUES QVE / FALECV EM 11 DE SEBAT / ANNO 5448 /
SUA ALMA GOZE DA GLORIA. /   תנצב״ה

Burial Register: 5448   11 Sebat   Rachel Ester Henriques.

248 - - DE ARON GABAY RISSON QUE FALECEU EM 11
... 5448.

96

תנצבה

Burial Register: 5448 1 Yiar Aaron Gabay Risson.

249 Broken in two pieces, and very worn.

250 DO BEM. AVENTVRADO / VARAÕ DAVID YSRAEL Q̃ /
FALECEV EM 21 DE TANVS / ANNO 5449./ SVA ALMA
GOZE DA GLORIA.

תנצבה

Burial Register: 5449 21 Tamus, David Israel.

251 DO YLVSTRE / VARAÕ HONRADO / & SVBLYNE DN /
EPHAIM YESVRVN / HENRIQUES / FALECEO EM 19 / E
TISRY DO ANO / 5450 DA CRIACAO / DO MUNDO / SUA
ALMA GOZE / DA GLORIA.

*Burial Register: 5450 19 Tisri Ephraim Yeshurun Henri-
ques.*

252 S^A / Do yncurtado Eynsigne / mancebo Abraham de /
medina que Rendeu A alma / A seu Criador em 11 de / Nisan
anno 5452 / Sua Alma Goze de Gloria.

Burial Register: 5452 11 Nisan Abraham de Medina.

253 In angle of wall near warehouse :-

מצבת

קבורת הילדה אסתר
בת אברהם וררקה ...
ביום כד לחדש אייר
שנת התחה

97

254 S^A / DE HANAH F^A... JOSEPH / SENIOR FALESEO
EM ... / DE TEBET 5440.

*Burial Register: 5440   11 Tebet   Hannah child of Joseph
Ealeso.* [!*SENIOR*].

255 A large ledger lying on the surface of the ground and
out of alignment with the other tombstones, near the narrow
pathway which leads from Section A to Section B.   The
inscription records the burial of :-

    ABRAHAM ELIYAHU DA FONSECA VALLE, 14 Ellul
5418 [1658]

זאת מצבת קברת

היקר נכבד ... ונעלה
כבוד ... אברהם אליהו
דפונציקה והלי שנאסף
אל עמו   בארבעה
ועשר לחדש אלול
שנת   התיח

    Do Bemaventurado .... Varao AB^M / Eliav ... em 14....
Elvl / 54 ...

    *This stone is apparently the oldest in the
cemetery.   cf. No. 227.*

98

View of the exterior of the Synagogue. (1927).

BURIAL GROUND ENCLOSURE B

Commencing at north-western angle of boundary walls adjoining pathway, there are three ledgers :-

256 Broken in five pieces.

מצבה

קבורת החכם השלם הדין המצויין
הגביר תנעלה כמוהרר רפאל חיים יצחק
קאריגל אבד וסורה צדק בקק נדחי
ישראל בברבדאם יעא נלע בשני בשבת
יב יום לחדש אייר שנת התלז בן מח שנה
תנצבה

אל צור חסים פעלו   אודה ואצדיק דיניו

כי זן ישר ספעלו   וסאד עסקו רעיוניו

S^A

Do muy Docto Erudito & Insigne / H.H.R. Refael Haim Ishac Carigal / Ilustre Cabeca do K K de Nidhe / Israel en Barbadas que O' Soberano: / Jues chamo desta Transitoria Vida / em 2da F^{ra} 12 de Iyar 5537 que cor / responde a 19 de Mayo 1777 de / 48 Annos de Idade / S B A G D E G

Here lyeth the remains of the Learned / & Revd Rabbi Ralph Haim Isaac Carigal / Worthy Pastor of the Synagogue N Y / who departed this life on the 19 of May / 1777 Aged 48 Years.

Burial Register: 5537 12 Yiar 1777 19 May Haham Rephael Haim Isaac Carigal aged 48 years.

257 In the border :-

HERE LIETH INTERRED THE BODY OF ISAAC ISRAEL
DE PIZA ESQ^R WHO DEPARTED THIS LIFE THE 25 OF
ELUL 5540 WHICH CORRESPONDS TO THE 25 OF SEPR
1780 AGED 78 YEARS.

מצבת

קבורת איש ישיש ונשוא פנים
וירא אלהים הנביר הנעלה יצחק
ישראל די פיזה נלל̈ ביום כה לחדש
אלול שנת התקם ויהיו ימי יצחק
שמנה ושבעים שנה
תנצבה

Del bienaventurado Temiente / De Dios Isaac Israel De
Piza / que fue Dios servido recoger / para sy en 25 de
Elul 5540 / que corresponde a 25 de Setre / 1780 de Edad
de 78 Annos./ S A G L G.

Burial Register: 5540 25 Elul 1780 Sep 25 Isaac Israel De Peiza aged 78.

258 In the border :-

HERE LIES INTERRED THE BODY OF THAT PIOUS &
DEVOUT LADY MBS RACHEL DE PIZA LATE WIFE OF ISAAC
ISRAEL DE PIZA ESQ WHO DEPARTED THIS LIFE THE 28
OF ADAR 5539 WHICH CORRESPONDS TO THE 15 MARCH
1779 AGED 67 YEARS.

De la bein / Aventurada Devota y Pia / Sena BACHEL
DE PIZA Muger que fue de / ISAAC ISRAEL DE PIZA que

fue Dios / servido Recoger para si en 28 de / Adar 5539
que corresponde a / 15 de Marco 1779 de edad de / S B A G
D E G

*Burial Register: 5539 28 Adar 1779 15 March Rachel
wife of Isaac Israel De Peiza aged 67.*

There is a space between the third and fourth stones.

259 In the border :-

   HERE LIETH THE BODY OF JOSEPH JACOB LINDO WHO
DIED THE 21 OF OCTOBER 1793   AGED 3 YEA..
(broken at the right bottom corner.)

   Do Anjo Joseph Jacob / Lindo que fo em 15 de / Hesvan
5553 que cor / responde a 21 de Outu^{ro} / 1793 [!] de Idade
de 3 / Annos 6 Mezes y 4 Dias / S A G D ...

*Purial Register: 5553 5 Hesvan 1792   21 October
Jacob Joseph Lindo aged 3 yrs 6 mos & 4 days.*

Two ledgers.

260 HERE LYETH THE BODY OF MRS SARAH LATE WIFE OF
MR MOSES De PIZA WHO DEPARTED THIS LIFE ON THE 5
DAY OF MARCH 1773 IN THE 36 YEAR OF HER AGE.

מצבת

קבורת האשה הצנועה
והניכבדת מרת שרה אשת
הנביר הנעלה משה די פיזה
נלע ערב שבת עשרה לחדש
אדר שנת התקלג בת ל"ו שנים

תנצבה

De la bienaventurada / Honesta S.ª Sarah Muger / que
fue de Moseh d'PIZA / que fue Dˢ Servido recojer / para
su Santa Gloria en 10 / de Adar 5533 que corres / ponde a
5 de Marco 1773 / de Edad de 36 Anos / S B A G D G.

*Burial Register: 5533 10 Adar 1773 5 March Sarah wife
of Moses De Peiza aged 36 years.*

261   מצבת

הגביר הנעלה משה די יצחק
ישראל די פיזא נלע כמ כסליו
בשנת התקסא״״ פק
ויהיו כל ימיו חמשים ושמונה שנה

תנצבה

Here Lieth the Remains / of Mᴿ MOSES De ISAAC / De
PAZER who departed this Life / on the 29th of Keslev
5561 / which corresponds to the / 4ᵗʰ of December 1801 /
Aged 58 years.

*Burial Register: 5561 29 Kislev 1801 4 Decr Moses
son of Isaac Israel De Peiza aged 58 years.*

262 Fragment only, being the left bottom corner of a
stone.

In the border :-

HERE LYETH...

Portion of main inscription :-

... Me ..
.. respond ...
. de Idade de .. .
     .. .. & 27 Dias.
S B A G D

Space, and then five stones in a row :-

263 In the border :-

HERE LYETH THE BODY OF LUNAH WIFE OF MR VAL-
VERDE MERCHANT WHO DEPARTED THIS LIFE THE 31 OF
JULY 1782 AGED 40 YEARS & 4 MONTHS.

מצבת

קבורת האשה הכבודה
והצנועה מרת לונה אשת
הנביר הנעלה יעקב ואלוירדי
נלׄעׄ יום כ לחדש מנאחם שנת
התקמב

תנצבה

De la bienaventurada / Lunah muger que fue. de / Jacob
Valverde que fᵒ en / 20 de Menahem 5542 que / corresponde
a 31 de Julio / 1782 de Edad de 40 Anos / Y 4 Meses. S A
G L G.

*Burial Register: 5542 20 Ab. 1782 31 July. Luna wife
of Jacob Hisquiau Valverde aged 40 years and 4 mos.*

264 Large ledger broken in many places.

ותֿתֿפֿלל חֿנה ותאֿסֿר עלׄ לבי בה לפֿק

De la Incurtada honesta Virtuoza / Y Charitativa
mujer Hana de David / Robles de medina que fue llamada /
de Su Criador de la Edad de 23 anos / en 28 Agosto 1769 q:
corresponde / con 25 Ab 5529: / S A G D E G / Jaze de Bajo
de Aquesta Let.... / que en Su vida fue vixti ... /
...atria ala Estrang... (broken and missing).

*Burial Register: 25 Ab 1769 28 August Hanah of David
Robles aged 23 years.*

HERE LIE THE REMAINS OF MR HAIM BARROW LATE
MERCHANT OF THIS ISLAND WHO DEPARTED THIS LIFE
THE 31 OF OCTOBER 1789 AGED 45 YEARS.

(1 line of Hebrew in semi-circle :-)

והרוח תשוב אל האלקים אשר נתנה

פה תחת זאת המצבה
נגנז תיק נפש מרחבה
איש חסיד ישר ונאמן
לעניים כאב רחמן
לבני גילו רצוי ונאהב
ופרידתו היה נדאב
חיים שמו וברוך כנויו
מה שנים האיר יופיו
במ̅ק יא̅ חשון נסיעתו
שנת התקן לאומתו
בעדן תהיה נשמתו
ובקבורה תנוח גויתו
עדי יקיץ משנתו

S^A

Do bemaventurado Careta°. / e Devoto Haim Barrow que
/ foy D^s servido transmutar / desta Vida perecedeira p.^a /
a eterna em Sabado 11 de / Hesvan 5550 nos 45 Annos / de
sua Idade.

S A G D G

*Burial Register: 5550 11 Hesvan 1789 31 October Haim
Barrow aged 45 years.*

266 In the border :-

HERE LIE THE REMAINS OF MR ABRAHAM MASSIAH
LATE OF THIS ISLAND MERCHANT WHO DEPARTED THIS
LIFE THE 19 of OCTOBER 1792 AGED 72 YEARS.

ואברהם שב למקומו

מצבת

קבורת הגביר הנעלה הישיש
הנכבד זקן ונשוא פנים אברהם
מׁשיח נׁלׁעׁ גׁ לחדש חשון שנת
הׁתׁקׁנׁגׁ בסדר כי אותך ראיתי
צדיק לפני ויהיו ימי חייו שבעים
ושתים שנים וששה חדשים

תנצבה

Do. B.A. Venerado e / Caritativo Abraham Masiah /
foy trasmutado desta / Vida perecedeira para / a Abeterna
em 3 Hesvan / 5553 de Idade de 72 Annos / e 6 Meses. /
S B A G D E G /

His conjugal paternal & constant / affection rendered
Him a / Valuable pattern of Husband / Father & Friend the
rectitude / & Charity which biased his / actions endear
His Memory / to all who knew him.

*Burial Register: 5553 Hesvan 1792 19 October Abraham
Massiah aged 72 years & 6 mos.*

267 Broken across the centre.

Here Lieth the remains of / Mrs ESTER MASSIAH /
who departed this life on Monday / the 3 of Nisan 5562
corresponding / with the 5th of April 1802 / Aged 65 Years.

106

This brings us to the warehouse at the east of the enclosure.   South of and touching Nos. 266 and 267 are two
slabs :-

268 In the border :-

HERE LIES THE BODY OF MRS ABIGAIL WIDOW OF
MR ISRAEL ABADDY WHO DEPARTED THIS LIFE ON SUNDAY
24 ELLUL 5566 WHICH CORRESPONDS TO THE 7 SEPTEM-
BER 1806 AGED 75 YEARS.

Four lines of Hebrew :-

מצבת

קבורת האישה הכבודה והצנועה
מרת אביגיל די ישראל עבדי
נ̇ל̇ע̇ כ̇ד אלול שנת התק̇סו

SEPULTURA / de la Bienaventurada / ABIGAIL Viuda
del Señor / Hazan ISRAEL ABADDY / que fue Dios Bendito /
servido Recogerla Para / si en 24 Ilul 5566 / que corresponde a / 7ᵉ Septiembre Ano 1806 / de Edade de 75 Anos /
S A G D G .

Burial Register: 5566   24 Elul   1806   7 September   Abigail widow of Hazan Israel Abaddy aged 75 years.

269   מצבת

קבורת המשכיל ונבון הגביר הנעלה כה̇ר
משה חזקיהו רודריגים די ליאון שהיה
נעים זמירות ישראל בק̇ק נדחי ישראל
בברבאדאם יע̇א נל̇ע כ̇ו לחדש תמוז

107

בסדר ובשנת וֹהֹשִׁיבֹוֹ אֹתו העדֹה אל
עִיֹר סֹקֹלֹםֹוֹ והוא בן אחת וחמשים
שנה

תנצבה

S^A SᴬᴬA

Do Docto e Perito Moseh / Hisquiau Rodrigues de Leo[n]
/ q:e foy Hazan do Kaalkados / NIDHE ISRAEL em Barbadas
/ faleceu em 26 de Tamuz / Ano 5530 Corresponde a / 19
Julio 1770 de 51 Annos de / Idade. S A G D G.

Burial Register: 5530 26 Tamus 1770 19 July Hazan
Moses Hisquiau Rodrigues De Leon aged 51 years.

Returning to the west boundary wall of enclosure, five
stones in a row going east :-

270

ותקם רבקה בנערותיה
לנוח לעד םתה לראיה
בנות ישראל בכו על בנוליה
כי באה שמשה לא םלאו יםיה
נתבקשה בשם םוב לפנים ולפני
עם הצדקניות נשי נאסני
נחה שקםה בשמי םעוני
בשנת ותלך לֹדֹרֹשֹׁ את ד'

תנֹצבה

קבורת הבתולה הכבודה וחצנועה רבקה בת םאיר.
הבהן ביליפאנםי נעים זמירות ישראל נלבע יום שק ה
לאייר שנת הֹתֹקֹלֹבֹ ליצי' בת כב שנה תנצבה

This Mournful Tomb doth Inclose / A dutyful child a
faded Rose / Chaste modest peaceable & Good / Long

sufferings She patiently withstood / In life lived pitti'd,
in death lamented / In one Besign'd in the other contented
/ Tis the virtuous REBECA of happy Memory / daughter to
COHEN BELEFANTE late o' the Rectory / Departed this
life on Saturday being / the Fifth of Month Yeiar in
the Year 5534 / to the Creation which Corresponds / to the
16th April 1774 Aged 22 Years.

Device: Tree chopped down.

Burial Register: 5534   5 Nisan   1774   16 April   Rebecca
daughter of Meher a Cohen Belinfante aged 22 years.

271 In the border : -

The Earthly Remains of the late Mr Isaac Lindo who
was called from this transitory Life on the 10th October
1780 a true worthy & Pious Man.

מצבת

קבורת הגביר היקר ונעלה
יצחק בן הגביר דוד לינדו
נלע״ז בי״א לחדצ תצרי ינת
ויצא יצחק לצוח בשדה
לפנות ירב בן ארבעה
וחמציים צנה

תנצבה

Do Bemaventurado Inclito & devoto / Isaac Lindo que
O Soverano Iuiz / foy servido Chamar desta transitoria /
Vida Em 11 Dias do Mes de Tisry / Ano 5541 Corresponde
a 10 de / Outubre 1780 de 54 Anos de Idade. / S A G D G.

Burial Register: 5541   10 Tisri   1780   10 October   Isaac
Lindo aged 54 years.

109

272 Recently broken in nine pieces by falling tree and sunk into the ground.

Around the sides and top :-

מצבת קבורת

איש צדיק ירא אלהים תם וישר
בכל ענינ יו מהולל ומאושר
ויהי דויד בכל דרכיו תמים פעלו
משכיל ביראת שמים במוב שכלו
כקרא בינ ויו נונוב קאסטילו

• • •

• • •

• • •

אלה ... לנוח בגורלו
לקץ הימין בששי לששב יום שבת
שנת קֹהֹלֹת מבל מלאכתו בו שבת

תנצבה

מוב שם משמן מוב ויום המות מיום הולדו
יבוא שלום ינוחו על משכבותם הולך נכוחו
והיתה נפש אדוני צרורה בצרור החיים
הצדיק אבד ואין איש שם על לב
אין זה כי אם בית אלהים וזה שער השמים

Beneath this Tomb rests secure / From all evils, of happiness sure / One whose Morals were good / Whose principals [sic] temptations withstood / As a parent indulgent & Affectionate / As a Husband loving & dispassionate / As a Trader punctual & honest / As a Companion, Sincere & modest / Possessed of every virtue desirable / In every Station truly Amiable / *Tis David Nunes Castello of happy Memory / Whose pure life intitles his Soul to Eternal Glory* / Departed this life on Friday Night / the 6th of month Sebath 5535 which / corresponds to the 6th of

110

January / 1775 Aged 48 Years & 8 Months.

Carving: Under a tree, a castle attacked by skeleton with spear.

Burial Register: 5535 6 Sebat 1775 6 January David Nunes Castello aged 48 years & 8 months.

273 Fragment only. In the border :-

HERE LIETH THE BODY ..... RY 1794 Aged 70 Years.

Probably Judith, widow of Isaac Lindo.

Burial Register: 5554 20 Adar 1794 20 February Judith widow of Isaac Lindo aged 70 years.

274 Right top corner of stone broken and missing.

In the border :-

HERE LYETH THE BODY OF MRS ANGEL WIFE OF THE LATE MR EPHRAIM NUNES CASTELLO WHO DEPARTED THIS LIFE THE 23 DAY OF] AUGUST 1777 AGED 80 YEARS.

In the centre :-

מצבת

קבורת הצנועה והנכ[ב]דת
סרת אנגילה זונתו הנביר
הנעלה אפרים נונים קסתילו

נׄלׄעׄ כ סנחם שנת הׄתׄקׄלׄזׄ

תנצבה

Da Bemaventurada / Angela Viuva que foy do / B A Ephraim Nunes / Castello que f° em 20 de / Menahem 5538[!] que corresponde / a 23 de Agosto 1777 de Idade de 80 Annos. S A G D D.

111

Burial Register: 5538 20 Ab. 1778 [sic] *23 August Angel widow of Ephraim Nunes Castello aged 80 years.*

Commencing at west wall enclosure, third row, there are two stones together :-

275 In the border:-

HERE LIETH THE BODY OF MRS ESTHER LATE WIFE OF BENJAMIN DE CRASTO WHO DEPARTED THIS LIFE THE 5TH OF MAY 1769 AGED 21 YEARS 11 MONTHS AND 5 DAYS.

S^A / De la Bienaventuraday Virtuosa / Ester de Benjamin De crasto / que fue Dios Bendito Servito / de Recojer parasy de Edad de / Veinte y Un Ano Onze Mezes / y Cinco Dias en 26 de Jyar Anno / 5529 Que Conresponde a Veinte / y Cinco [sic] de Mayo 1769 Amadora / de hazer bien Querida y Estimada / de Todos sus Parientes Amigas / y Conosidas Obedientissima a / Sus genitores y Complecta en / Todas Suerte de Eroicas y / Illustres Acciones. S B A G D E G.

Burial Register: 5529 26 Yiar 1769 5 May Ester wife of Benjamin de Crasto aged 21 years 11 mos & 5 days.

276 Large ledger broken at top right corner.

In the border :-

UNDER THIS STONE LYES INTERRED GABRIEL DE CRASTO JUNIOR WHO DEPARTED THIS LIFE THE 7TH OF APRIL 1788 AGED 43 YEARS BEING A LOVING HUSBAND AFFECTIONATE BROTHER AND SINCERE FRIEND.

Centre :-

Debaxo de esta Estatua / esta depositado Gabriel de / Crasto que faleceio para ir gozar / de la Eterna Gloria

en 22d Adar / 5548 de Edad de 43 Annos / sendo amoroso
Marido Aficiona^{do} / Hermano y Affable & Intimisimo / Amigo
y pronto de render sus / Servicios a todo el Mundo.

מצבת

קבורת הגביר הנעלה גאבריאל
די כראסתו נׄלׄעׄ יום כ"ב לחדׄשׄ
אדר שׄנת הׄתׄקׄמׄחׄ בן שׄלׄושׄה

וארבעים שנה

תנצבה

Carving: Hand from the clouds felling tree.

*Burial Register: 5548 22 Adar 1788 1 April Gabriel
de Crasto Jnr. aged 43 years.*

277 Touching a royal palm tree, a large ledger broken in
three pieces across middle and diagonally :-

In the border :-

HERE LYETH INTERRED THE BODY OF MR JACOB
JOSEPH WHO DEPARTED THIS LIFE THE 17 AUG. 1770
AGED 73 YEARS WHO WAS BELOVED BY HIS FRIENDS
NEIGHBOURS AND ACQUAINTANCE.

מצבת

קבורת הישיש איש חיל רב פעלים
ירא אלהים כולו מהללים במצותיו
חפץ כאשר מצווה   איש תם וישר
לגן עדן ילוה כהׄהׄרׄ יעקב [?]
תׄנׄצׄבׄה כאשר היה מקוה נפטר לׄעׄ
יום שׄקׄׄוד כז לחו [לחדש] מנחם שנת תׄקׄל
לפׄק בן עׄג שנים

113

Burial Register: 5530 27 Ab. 1770 17 August Jacob Joseph aged 73 years.

Returning to the west boundary wall, five large ledgers in a row.

278 Broken in many places, flaked, and almost indecipherable.

In the border :-

HERE LYETH THE BODY OF MR BENJAMIN ISRAEL NUNES WHO .... (illegible).

In the centre :-

Do .... enturado..... Benjamin Israel Nunes / que f^o em 29..... / 5533 que cor.... / 19 de Augosto 17.. / de Ida...52.

S A ....D.

Burial Register: 5533 29 Ab. 1773 19 August, Benjamin Israel Nunes, aged 52 years.

279 Stone in fine state of preservation.

In the border :-

HERE RESTS THE REMAINS OF MRS DEBORAH WIDOW OF MR BENJAMIN ISRAEL NUNES WHO DEPARTED THIS LIFE ON TUESDAY 26 ' KISLEV 5566 WHICH CORRESPONDS TO 17 DECR 1805 AGED 80 YEARS.

מצבת

קבורת האשה הכבודה יהצנועה
מרת דבורה די בנימין ישרא[ל] נונים
נ̇ל̇ע̈ כ"ו בכסליו

בשנת

עוֹרִי עוֹרִי דְבֹורה

SEPULTURA / de la Bienaventurada / Señora DEBORAH
Viuda / de Señor BENJAMIN / ISRAEL NUNES que fue /
Dios Bendito Servido / Recoger la para si en 26 / Kislev
5566 que corresponde / a 17 de Deciembre 1805 / de Edad
de 80 Anos / S A G D G.

*Burial Register: 5566 26 Kislev 1805 17 Decr. Deborah
widow of Benjamin Israel Nunes aged 80 years.*

280   In the border :-

Sepultura do Bemaventurado Virtuoso e Humilde Senhor
Simhon Barrow que o Soberano Jues Chamo desta Transitoria
Vida em 6ta F^{ra} 25° de Iyar 5561 que Corresponde a 8° de
Mayo de 92 Annos de Idade.

Centre: twelve lines of Hebrew.

שׁוֹמר מצוה לא ידע רע ועת ומשפט ידע לב חכם

מצבת

קבורת החסיד וענֿיו המשכיל

ונבון הישיש הנכבד הנביר

הנעלה שמעון ברוך איש

ישר בכל דרכיו רודֿף צדקה וחסד

עושה ומעשה בכל כחו נפטר בשם טוב

ונתבקש בישיבה של מעלה בשיבה טובה

כה אייר בשנת ברוך מֿבֿגֿיֿם אֿשׁר

יהי רֿצֿוֿי אחֿיֿו ויחיו כל ימי חייו שנים

ותשעים שנה

תנצבה

Underneath this tomb / are deposited the Earthly
remains / of Mr SIMON BARROW / Aged 92 Years / His

115

moral and religious virtues added / to an unsullied &
exemplary conduct / through so long a period rendered /
him in life respected in death / regretted & no doubt
will secure / him Mercy from an All Blessed / Creator
and eternal Felicity / in his Heavenly Mansion / Ob. 8th
May 1801.

*Burial Register: 5561 25 Yiar 1801 May 8 Simon Barrow
aged 92 years.*

281 Around the sides and top :-

אשת חיל סי יםצא ורחוק מפנינים מכרה בטח בה לב
בעלה גמלתהו טוב ולא רע כל יםי הייה כפה פרשה
לעני וידיה שלחה לאביון עוז והדר לבושה ותצחק ליום
אחרון רבות בנות עשו חיל
ואת עלית על כלנה שקר החן והבל היופי אשה
יראת ה היא תתהלל.

In the centre :-

אשת חיל עטרת בעלה
בניה יאשרוה והוא יהללה
צדקת פעולותיה היא גמולה
בשערים מעשיה הם הילולה
מלאכי שלום יצאו למולה
מפרי ידיה שכרה יתנו לה
נפטרה בשם טוב למנוחה נכונה
ביום טוב ראשון סוכת מעונה
שנת ותלך לדרש את ה עם חנה
והצדקניות תחת כנפי השכינה
מצבת
קבורת האשה הכבודה והצנועה סרת בלהה אשת שמעון
בר ברוך נלבע יום שבת קדש ראשון של חג סוכות שנת
התקלד
ליצ בת גן שנים עלתה לעדן תנצבה

116

Script letters :-

Here rests, in hope of a better Life / A tender Parent
and a loving Wife / Honour was her standard, religion her
guide / A Friend to all and free from Pride / Relief to the
distressed, truly Charitable, / Sincere, Generous, and
Hospitable, / 'Tis the Virtuous BELLA late wife of SIMON
BARROW / Whome lived every Day as if to Die tomorrow /
She departed this life on ... 15 / of Tisre 5534 which
Corresponds to the 1st / of October 1773 Aged 53 Years /
The Lord receive her Soul in the glory of Heaven.

Carvings :-

At bottom - Under a tree, the figure of a woman
            rising from a coffin. Thunder-bolt
            issuing from clouds.

In two upper corners - Two Cherubims.

*Burial Register: 5534 15 Tisri 1773 1 October Bella
wife of Simeon Barrow aged 53 years.*

282 In the border :-

Here lies the Body of Mr SAMUEL HART Merch who
died on the 29th day of Tisry which corresponds with the
15th Day of October 1773 Aged 53 Years 9 months and 2 days
of a Putrid Fever in Bridgetown Barbadoes.

Six line of Hebrew :-

מצבת

קבורת הבחור הנחמד שמואל בר משה
נפטר ביום שבת קודש בתשעה ועשרים
לחדש תשרי שנת התקלד ליצירה ימי
היי ששה וחמשים

תנצבה

Aguy yaze el Señor Samuel / Hart dela Ciuda de

117

Newyork / Mercador quien havia / Nuevamente Arrivado de
New / Port en la Colonia de Rhode - / Island en Nueva
Ingalaterra / America del Norte Fallecio / en 29 de Tisry
A M 5534 / que corresponde a 15 d / Octubre 1773 de Edad
/ de 55 Anos 9 Mezes Y.. Dias / S B A G D L G

Burial Register: 5534 [*1773*] *20 Tisri   5 October   Samuel*
Hart aged 53* years, 9 mos, 2 days.
* Hebrew has 56.

Fifth row, near west wall.   Two stones together.

283   Six lines of Hebrew :-

מצבת

קבורת האשה הכבודה והצנועה אשת שם ואשת
חיל מרת חוה אלמנת יעקב בר יוסף נֹעֹ נֹלֹבֹעֹ יום ד
בשבת כז להדש אב יחל שנת הׄתׄקׄלׄוׄ ליצירה בת
לג   שנים
תנצבה

Script letters :-

    Beneath this marble fair not gay
    Lays beauty turnd into clay
    Once admired in ery [!] state of Life
    As friend Relation parent or Wife
    Traveler here stop and View
    Virtue Matched by very few
    Levelled low in humble dust
    To rise gloriously we trust
    Cropt early in full bloom
    Unhappy lot oh cruel doom
    Here tribute pay where most due
    With tears of sorrow this tomb bedew
    Yet mixd with comfort if not joy
    At the felicity her soul enjoy.

Burial Register: 5535   27 Ab.   1775   22 August   Eve
widow of Jacob Joseph aged 33 years.

118

HERE LIETH THE BODY [OF] SIMHA WIFE OF MR
ABRAHAM BUZAGLO WHO DEPARTED THIS LIFE THE 7 OF
OCTOBER 1789 AGED 41 YEARS & [blank] MONTHS

Six lines of Hebrew :-

מצבת

קבורת האשה הכבודה והצנועה

סרת שסחה אשת הגביר הנעלה

אברהם בוזאנלו נלע יום יז לחדש

תשרי שנת התקן

תנצבה

Da bemaventurada e / Honrada Simha mulher que foy de
Abra^m Buzaglo / que f⁰ em 17 de Tisry 5550 / que corres-
ponde a 7 de / Octubro 1789 de Idade / de 41 Anno /
S A G D G

*Burial Register: 5550 17 Tisri 1789 7 October Simha
wife of Abraham Buzaglo aged 41 years.*

285 Lying at the foot of the above is a stone covering a
child's tomb, the surface flaked and only an occasional
letter visible.

Two ledgers close together.

286 In the Border :-

HERE LYETH THE BODY OF ESTER LATE WIFE OF MR
EMANUEL BARUCH LOUZADA WHO DEPARTED THIS LIFE
OCTOBER THE 20 1775 IN THE 43 YEAR OF HER AGE.

מצבת

קבורת האשה הצנועה

והנכבדה סרת אסתר זוגתו

119

של הנביר הנעלה עימאנואל
ברוך לויזאדא נלּעּ יום ו׳ כ״ו
לחדש תשרי שנת הֵתֵקֵלֵוֹ
תנצבה

S^A / Da bemaventurada / Honesta Y Virtuoza / Ester
Mulher que foy d' / Emanuel Baruch Louzada / que foy D^s.
servido recol^{er} / para sy em 6^a. f^a 26 de / Tisry 5536 que
corresponde / a 20 de Outubro 1775 / da Idade 43 Annos /
S B A G D E G.

Burial Register: 5536 26 Tisri 1775 20 October Ester
wife of Emanuel Baruch Louzado aged 43.

287　　　　וישב העפר אל הארץ כשהיה

Then shall the dust return to ye Earth as it was.

תחת זאת המצבה נטמן נוף איש חסיד ישר
ונאמן נטע נעמן ואב רחמן אהוב לשמים
ולבריות ה״ה עמנואל ברוך לוזאדה נפטר
בשם טוב לבית עולמו שבעה לחדש כסלו
שנת התקנג ויהיו ימי חייו חמשה וחמשים שנה
תנצבה

　　Underneath this Tomb rests Secure / the last Remains
of / MR EMANUEL BARUH LOUZADA / who was universally
known / To be Religious & Honest / a loving Husband & a
tender Parent / he Departed this Life on the 7th of Kislev
5553 / which corresponds to the 22^d of Novr 1792 / in the
55 Year of his Age.

Burial Register: 5553 7 Kislev 1792 22 Novr. Emanuel
Baruch Louzada aged 55 years.

　　South of No. 287, two together.

288　　　　ותמת רחל

היא מצבת קברת רחל האשה הצנועה
והנכבדת זוגתו של הנביר הנעלה
עמנואל ברוך לוזאדה נ֗לע יום רביעי
שבעה לחדש ניסן שנת התקע ויהיו ימי
חייה ששים שנה:

תנצבה

SACRED / To the Memory of / MRS RACHEL BARUCH
LOUSADA who departed this Life / on Wednesday the 11th
April 1810 / Aged 60 Years.

*Burial Register: 5570 Nisan 1860 11 April Mrs Rachel
Baruch Louzada aged 60 years.*

289   מצבת

קבורת הגביר הנעלה החסיד וענו
נעים זמירות ישראל ה֗ה דאניאל
ברוך לויזאדא נלע יום ג
לחדש שבט שנת התקלפ בן
ארבעה וארבעים שנה
תנצבה

S A / Do bemaventurado Pio / & Devoto / Daniel Baruch
/ Louzada que servio ou / Cargo de Hazan deste K K / Fo
em 3 de Sebat 5539 q / corresponde a 19 Janeiro / 1779 de
Idade de 44 Anos S B A G D.

*Burial Register: 5539 3 Sebat 1779 19 January Hazan
Daniel Baruch Louzado aged 44 years.*

290 East of above. Stone ornamented with cherubim in
top corners.

Here Rest the Earthly Remains of the Pious & Charitable Mr Matthias Lopez who departed this life on Sunday
the 29th Sivan 5539 Coresponding to the 13th June 1779

Aged 43 years.

יבוא שלום ינוחו על משכבותם הלך נכחו
קבורת הגביר הנעלה איש צדיק תמים
כבוד ה"הר מתתיה לופים אבי יתומים
עוזר דלים מרחם עניים חונן אביונים
חסיד ישר ונאמן ביום א' ערב ראש
חדש תמוז שנת תק"לם ליצירה נ'ל'ע'
וזכרו לברכה תמיד נזכר נשמתו בעדן
ה' כנן רטוב ורוחו ונשמתו תלין בטוב
ויהיו ימי חייו מ"נ שנים

תנ'צ'ב'ה'

S A / Del B:A: Honrado Humilde Caritativo / y virtuozo
el Sor Matitya Lopez / quien passo desta a mejor vida /
para Gozar el fruto de Sus buenas / obras en Domingo Bis-
pera de Rosh / Hodesh Tamuz 5539 de Edad / de 43 Annos /
S.B.A.G.D.G.L.E.G.

Carving: Tree chopped down.

*Burial Register: 5539 29 Sevan 1779 13 June Matthias
Lopez aged 43 years.*

Two ledgers together near wall of warehouse.

291 Hebrew Inscription in border :-

ומשה עלה אל האלקים עלית למרום שבית שבי
ואתה לך לקץ ותנוח
ותעמד לגורלך והיתה נפש אדוני
צרורה בצרור החיים יבא שלום ינוחו על משכבותם
הולך נכחו.

In the centre :-

מצבת
קבורת הגביר הנעלה

122

לשם ולתהלה פרנם
הדור סנהיג הקהילה
הלא הוא האיש משה
לופים נלבע יום ד עשירי
לחדש אייר שנת תקלח
ליצ לפק בן מה שנים
תנצבה

Here Rests the Remains of Mr Moses / Lopez of Speights Town Barbados / whome exchanged this life for a better / in the year of his Wardenship being / one of the Wardens of the Synagogue / on Wednsday the 10th day of the Month / Yar 5538 which Corresponds to the 6th / Day of May 1778 Aged 45 Years.

Carving: Tree Chopped down

Burial Register: 5538 18 Yiar 1778 6 May Parnas - Moses Lopez aged 45 years.

292 Seven lines of Hebrew :-

סצבת

קבורת האשה הכבודה והצנועה
והנכבדת סרת שרה אשת הגביר
הנעלה משה לופים נלע ביום שבת
קדש עשרים ימים לחדש אייר
התקסט לפג בת נו שנים

תנצבה

Here rest the Earthly Remains of / Mrs SARAH LOPEZ widow of / Moses Lopez deceased / who departed this Life on Saturday / the 20th Yar 5549 / Corresponding to the 16th of May 1789 / Aged 56 Years.   S B A G D E G.

Burial Register: 5549 20 Yiar 1789 16 May Sarah widow of Moses Lopez aged 56 years.

Carving at bottom : A hand chopping down a conifer tree.

Near the outside boundary wall of the grave-yard are
three ledgers in a row.   Undoubtedly, the bodies of three
victims of the hurricane of 10 October 1780.

293   מצבת

קבורת הגביר משה די פיזה
נ֗ל֗ע֗ בי֗א לחדש תשרי שנת
התקסא ל֗פ֗ג֗ בן לז שנה
תנצבה

S ᴬ / Do bemaventurado / Mosseh de Piza f.º em / 11 de
Tisry / 5541 que / corresponde a 10 dia / de Outubro 1780
de / Idade de 37 Annos.   S A G D G

*Burial Register: 5541   11 Tisri   1780   10 October   Moses
De Peiza aged 37 years.*

294 In the border :-

Here lies Interr'd Mr Ephraim Baruh Lousada who was
called from this transitory life Octʳ 10 1780 aged 25
years.

מצבת

קבורת הבחור אפרים ברוך
לויזאדה נ֗ל֗ע֗ בי֗א לחדש תשרי
שנת התקסא לפג֗ בן כ֗ה֗ שנה
תנצבה״״״״״

S ᴬ / Do Bemaventurado Mansebo / Efraim Baruh Lousada
Fº em / 11 de Tisry 5541 Corresponde / a 10 de Outubre
1780 de 25 / Anos de Idade / S A G D G.

*Burial Register: 5541   11 Tisri   1780   Oct. 10.
Ephraim Baruch Louzado aged 25 years.*

295 In the border :-

Here lies Interr'd Miss Ester Baruh Lousada who was
called from this Transitory Life the Oct[r] 10 1780 Aged
13 years.

מצבת

קבורת הבתולה הצנועה
אסתר ברוך לויזאדה נל̇ל̇ע̇
ביא לחדש תשרי התקמא לפנ
בת יג̇ שנה
תנצבה ″″″″

S[A] / Da Bemaventurada & honesta / Donzela Ester Baruh
Lousada / F[o] em 11 Tisry 5541 Corresponde / a 10 Outubre
1780 de 13 / Anos de Idade. S A G D G.

*Burial Register: 5541 11 Tisri 10 October 1780 Miss
Ester Baruch Louzado aged 13 years.*

Near to the warehouse on the right are two ledgers.

296 No Inscription visible.

297   מצבת

קבורת הגביר הנעלה דוד
פיניירו נל̇ל̇ע̇ יום ה לחדש
כסליו שנת ה̇ת̇ק̇מ̇ש̇ [!]
תנצבה

S[A] / Do Bemaventurado / David Pinheiro que / faleceu
em 5 de Kislev / 5542 que corresponde / a 23 de Novembro
1781 / de Idade de 47 Annos. / S A G D G

*Burial Register: 5542 5 Kislev 1781 23 Novr. David
Pinheiro aged 47 years.*

125

298 Top broken and missing.

מצבת

קבורת האשה הכבודה יעל

אלמנת של הגביר הנעלה דוד

פינירו נ׳׳לׂעׂ יום י״ח לחדש סיון

שנת החׂקׂמׂב

תנצבה

S^A / Da bemaventurada / Jael Viuva que foy de /
David Pinheiro que / f⁰ em 18 de Sivan 5542 / que corres-
ponde a 2 / de Junho 1782 d' Idade / de 33 Annos. / S A G
D G.

*Burial Register: 5542 18 Sevan 1782 2 June Jail widow
of David Pinheiro aged 33 years.*

299 Discovered when the foundations were being dug for
a new wall in the driveway , near new entrance. White
marble ledger in excellent preservation.

מצבת

קבורת הבחור הנחמד

אברהם די דוד נונס נׂ׳׳לׂעׂ יום

יח לחדש תמוז שנת החׂקׂמׂ

תנצבה

S^A / Do B.A. ABRAHAM de / DAVID NUNES que f⁰ /
em 18 de Tamus 5540 / que corresponde a 21 / de Julho
1780 d' Idade / 56 Annos / S A G D G.

126

BURIAL GROUND ENCLOSURE C

The remaining seventy-four inscriptions are to be found in the enclosure on the left of the pathway leading from the main entrance to the Synagogue.

Commencing at the angle of the wall at the north-eastern corner of the enclosure there are two marble ledgers close together.

300 In the border :-

HERE LYETH INTERR'D THE BODY OF JACOB FROIS LATE MERCH^T OF THIS ISLAND WHO DEPARTED THIS LIFE JAN^Y Y^E 8th 1757 AGED 70 YEARS.

מצבת

קבורת הישיש הנכבד יעקב
פרוייס נ͏ׄלׄעׄ יום י"ו לחדש טבת
שנת ה͏ׄתׄק͏ׄיׄז ליצירה
תנצבה

S^A / Do Bemaventurado y / Temente de D^s o Sr JACOB FROIS que Aos 70 Anos / de Sua Idade Passo para / Milhor vida faleceu em / 16 Tebet de 5517 que Cor- / responde a 8 de Janeiro 1757.   S A G D G

Burial Register: 5517 16 Tebet 1757 8 January Jacob Frois aged 70 years.

301　Seven lines on Hebrew :-

כי שרה שמה

יהודית נסעה סתחחתונים
אשת חיל לבעלה עטרת
וללכת לגור בעליונים
בת ששים ואחת שנה נגזרה
בלב טוב יהודית היא שמרה
ויהודית נחלפה בשרה

SEPULTURA / Dela Bienaventurada y / Charitativa S^{ra}
Jehudith Mul / her que foy ..... Frois / que fue mudado
....mbre / en Sara que ales 61 años / de Su Edad passo
ala mejor / Vida en 11 de Kislev de 5514 / que Corresponde
a 13 de / Deziembro 1753.

One line of Hebrew :-

תנצבה

*Burial Register:　5514　11 Kislev　1753　13 December
Julia wife of Jacob Frois.*

Against the boundary wall there are seven stones.

302　In the border :-

HERE LYETH INTERR'D THE BODY OF REBECCA
MASSIAH WIFE OF ABRAHAM MASSIAH DEPARTED THIS
LIFE MARCH Y 2 D. 1749 AGED 32 YEARS.

והנה רבקה יוצאת

רבקה ששם חנה היתה בוחרת
בקיצור שנותיה קראוה
אשת חיל לבעלה עטרת
לכן קמו בניה ויאשרוה

129

הקריבה נשמתה כטהור שי
ותלך היא לדרוש את ה'

SEPULTURA / De la Bienaventurada y / Charitative
Sʳᵃ Da Ribca / Massiah que fue Mudado Su nombre en Hana
que / a los 32 Anos de su Edad / partio de Esta a mejor /
vida en 5 de Adar Primer Ano de 5510

תׄנׄצׄבׄהׄ

Burial Register: 5510 5 Adar 1749 2 March Rebecca
wife of Abraham Massiah aged 32 years.

303   מצבת

קבורת הבחור הנחמד תם וישר
כהר חזקיהו יונה רודריגים די ליאון
נלעׄ יום ששי עשרה לחדש טבת
שנת התׄקׄי

תנצבה

S ᴬ / Do Bemaventurado Pio / e Recto Mancebo Hisqui /
Yahou Jonah Rodrigues / de Leon Falleceu Sesta / Feye a
10 de Tebet 5510 q' / Corresponde a 8 Decemb: 1749 S V.
S B A G D E G.

Burial Register: 5510 10 Tebet 1749 8 December
Hisquyahu Jonah Rodrigues De Leon.

304   מצבת

קבורת האשה הכבודה והצנועה
[אסתר] אלמנה של הנביר יהודה
סמיאח נלׄעׄ יום כח לחדש [טבת]
שנת התק[מ]ב
תנצרה

S ᴬ / Da B.A. Esther Viuva que / foy de Ieudah

130

Massiah que / fo em 28 de Tebeth 5542 que / corresponde
a 14 de Janeiro / 1782 de Idade de 60 Annos. S A G D G

עון והדר לבושה
ותשחק ל'ום אחרון

*Burial Register: 5542 28 Tebet 1982 14 January Esther
widow of Judah Massiah aged 60 years.*

305 In the border :-

HERE LYETH THE BODY OF MRS RACHEL CARVALHO
WHO DEPARTED THIS LIFE 22 OF MARCH 1791 AGED 80
YEARS.

מצבת

קבורת האשה הנכבדה
והצנועה מרת רחל כרואל'ו
נלע 'ום מו לחדש אדר
שנת התקנא
תנצבה .

S^A / Da bemaventurada / Rachel Carvalho que / F° em
15 de Adar* 5551 / que corresponde a 22* / de Marco 1791
/ de Idade de 80 Annos. S A G D G

*Burial Register: 5551 15 Adar 1791 22 March Mrs Rachel
Carvalho aged 80 years.*

* *The 15 Adar 5551 was 21 March.*

306 In the border :-

HERE LYETH INTERR'D THE BODY OF JACOB HAIM
CARVALLO LATE MERCHANT OF THIS ISLAND WHO DE-
PARTED THIS LIFE Y 30TH DAY OF JUNE 1749 AGED 48 YEARS.

וי'עקב הלך לדרכו'

יעקב וחיים שם זה הגבר

במשה נשתנה כחלותו

גופו ינוח פה בזה הקבר

וברחה למעלה נשמתו

לוקח בעת החן והרחמים

במשפט הצור שפעולו תמים

SEPULTURA / Del bienaventurado / JACOB HAIM CAR-
VALLO / Cuio nombre fue mudado / en Mosseh que falecio /
a los 48 anos de su edad / en 26* de Tamuz Ano de / 5509
que corresponde / a 30 de Junio de 1749.

Carving: Hand from clouds felling tree.

*Burial Register: 5509 26 Tamus 1749 30 June, Jacob
Haim Carvalho aged 48 years.*

* 26 Tamuz 5509 was 12 July 1749.

307 Stone against wall, with no inscription.

In the corner on the right there are four stones :-

308 S^A / Da bemaventurado Moseh / de Morais que f° en 29
de Tebet 5506* que corresponde / A .... de Janro Anno 1746.
S A G D G.

*Burial Register: 5506 29 Tebet 1746 21 January Moses
de Morais.*

309 White marble slab.

In the border :-

HERE LYETH INTERR'D THE BODY OF MR ABRAHAM
ISRAEL NUNES WHO DEPARTED THIS LIFE ON THE 25TH

DAY OF DECEMBER 1745 AGED 46 YEARS.

מצבת

קבורת הגביר הנכבד אברהם
ישראל נונים נ̇ל̇ע̇ יום ה̇ י"ד
לחדש טבת שנת התק̇ו̇
תנצבה

S^A / Do Muy Honrado S^r / ABRAHAM YSRAEL NUNES
Falleceu em 4^d Feira a Noite 14* de Tebett / 5506 q^e
corresponde a / 25 Decembre 1745.   S A G D G.

Burial Register: 5506 14 Tebet 1745 25 December
Abraham Israel Nunes.

* Incorrect.   December 25, 1745, was Tebet 2, 5506.

310 Marble slab broken at the top.

In the border :-

HERE LYETH THE BODY OF MR PHINEAS NUNES LATE
MERCHANT OF THIS ISLAND WHO DEPARTED THIS LIFE
YE 27 AUGUST 1769 AGED 49 YEARS.

מצבת

קבורת הגביר הנעלה פינחם
נונים נפטר לבית עולמו ליל
ב כה לחדש מנחם בשנת
ויעמד פינחם ויתפלל ותעצר
המג̇נ̇פ̇ה !לפק
תנצבה

S^A / Do bemaventurado Y / Honrado Pinhas Nunes /
Faleceu em Domingo a / Noite 27 Agosto de 1769 / que
corresponde a 25 de / Menahem 5529 de Idade / de 49 Annos.
S A G D G

133

Carving: Tree chopped down.

Burial Register: 5529 25 Ab. 1769 27 August Phineas Nunes aged 49 yrs.

311 White marble slab.

In the border :-

HERE LYETH INTERR'D THE BODY OF MR BENJAMIN NUNES WHO DEPARTED THIS LIFE ON THE 22ND DAY OF JUNE 1746 AGED FIFTY YEARS.

מצבת

קבורת הגביר הנכבד בנימין
דניאל נונים נ״לֹעַ יום א" ר״ו
לחדש תמוז שנת ה׳תק׳ו
תֹ׳נֹ׳צֹ׳בֹ׳הֹ

S^A / Do Muy Honrado Sr Benjamin Daniel Nunes / Falecu em Domingo / 15 de Tamuz 5506 q / Corresponde a 22 / Junho 1746 / S A G D G.

Burial Register: 5506 15 Tamuz 1746 22 June Benjamin Daniel Nunes aged 50 years.

Near the eastern bounday wall, three stones.

312 In the border :-

HERE LIES THE BODY OF DAVID BARUH LOUZADA LATE OF THIS ISLAND MERCHANT AND SEVERAL YEARS READER OF THEIR SYNAGOGUE WHO DIED Y^E 5TH KISLEV 5520 W^{CH} ANSWERS Y^E 25TH NOVR 1759 AGED 47^Y 9^M

ויברך דוד את יי לעיני כל הקהל

134

מצבת

קבורת החסיד העניו ר׳ דוד ברוך

לוזאדה נעים זמירות ישראל נלע

באחד בשבת יום ה׳ לחדש כסלו שנת

התקכ שהן ס״ז שנה ותשעה חדשים

יהיה לו שכרו על אשר עבד

את עמו בלא פרם

תנצבה

S^A / Do Bemaventurado DAVID / BARUH LOUZADA que
/ fuy D^s Servido Recolher / para Sy Domingo 5 Kislev 5520
/ que Corresponde a 25 Novem / bro 1759 que Serviu p. Hazan
/ en Esta Sta Kaal diversos años / sin paya de Edade de
A M
47 9 / S B A G D E G

Carving: Tree chopped down.

*Burial Register: 5520 5 Kislev 1759 25 November David
Baruch Louzado aged 47 years & 9 mos.*

313 In the Border :-

HERE LYETH THE BODY OF SARAH LATE WIFE OF
DAVID BARUCH LOUZADA WHO DEPARTED THIS LIFE JULY
Y 17 1755 AGED 35 YEARS

מצבת

קבורת שרה דודתו של הגביר

דוד ברוך לויזאדה נ׳לע׳ ביום

ג׳ לחדש אב שנת ה׳תקי״ט [!]

תנצבה

Da bemaventurada de Sarah / Mulher que foy de David /
Baruh Louzada que f° em / 3 de Ab 5515 que corresponde /
de a 11 de Julho 1755 de / Idade de 35 Annos / S A G D G

Carving: Tree chopped down.

Burial Register: 5515 3 Ab. 1755 11 July Sarah wife of David Baruch Louzado.

314 Touching boundary wall on right.

In the border :-

HERE LYETH THE BODY OF JAEL LEAH BARUH LOUZA-
DA WHO DEPARTED THIS LIFE THE 21 DAY OF NOVEMBER
1751 AGED 12 YEARS AND 6 MONTHS.

ותצא יעל לקראת האלהים

רבות בנות עשו חיל ואת עלית על כלנה
מיעל שהיתה שמה בלאה שמה נשתנה
הבתולה הצנועה והיקרה מכל בנות דריה
קרבה בשנים ושלמה בסידותיה ובדבריה
סבת שתים עשרה שנה וששה חדשים נטרפה
לקבל שכר מעשיה סיוצרה

תנצבה

S^A / Da B.A. Donzela Jael Lea / Filha de David Y
Sarah Baruh Louzada qual f° / em 15 Kislev 5512 que cor /
responde a 21 Novembro: 1751   S A G D G.

*Burial Register: 5512 15 Kislev 1751 21 November Jail
Leah child of David & Sarah Baruch Louzado aged 12 yrs &
6 mos.*

*Note: Error in Hebrew date in inscription. 15 Kislev
5512 was 2nd December 1751.*

South of last stone, two together against wall.

315 In the Border :-
HERE LYETH THE BODY OF MR DAVID NUNES MERCHANT

WHO DEPARTED THIS LIFE ON THE 15 DAY OF JUNE 1764
IN THE 67TH YEAR OF HIS AGE.

מצבת

קבורת הישיש הנכבד הגבור
הנעלה דוד נונים נלע עשק מו(?)
לחדש סיון שנת התקכד

תנצבה

Do bemaventurado Pio / Y devoto David Nunes / que f°
en 15 de Sivan / 5524 que corresponde a 15 de Junio 1764
sendo / de Idade de 67 Annos. / S A G D G

*Burial Register: 5524 15 Sevan 1764 15 June David
Nunes aged 67 years.*

316 S^{A} / De la Bienaventurada y / mui anciana Ss^{ra} /
DEBORAH NUNES falecio / em mercoles 12 de Sebat / 5513
y 17 de Enero de / 1753 de Edad de 86 Annos / S B A G D
L G.

*Burial Register: 5513 12 Sebat 1753 17 January
Deborah Nunes aged 86 years.*

Returning to the western wall, in a line with Nos:
301 and 302.

317 In the border :-

HERE LIES INTERR'D THE BODY OF THE ANCIENT
JACOB HEZEKAL GARCIA DEPAZ WHO DEPARTED THIS LIFE
MARCH THE 17TH 1752*.

מצבת

קבורת הישיש הנכבד יעקב

137

חזקיהו גרסיא די פאז נ֖ל֞ע י֞א
לחדש אדר שני שנת התק֞י֞ג
תנצבה

S^A / Del Bienaventurado JACOB HISQUIAHU GARCIA DE
PAZ / que fue D^s Servido Recojer / para su Santa Gloria en
/ dia de Sabath de Veadar / 5513 que Corresponde a / 7 de
Marco 1752.* / S A G D G A .

Carving: Hand from clouds felling tree.

*Burial Register: 5513   11 Veadar   Jacob Hezekiah Garcia
De Pas.*

*If the Hebrew date 11 Veadar 5513 is correct, the civil
date should be 1753, and not 1752, as it appears on the
stone.*

318 In the border:-

HERE LYETH INTERR'D THE BODY OF ESTHER DACOSTA
SPINSTER WHO DEPARTED THIS LIFE THE 29TH of OCTOBER
1755 AGED 43 YEARS.

מצבת
קבורת הבתולה הצנועה
והנכבדה מרת אסתר שרה דא
קושטא נ֖ל֞ע ביום ד" כ֞ד לחדש
חשון שנת התק֞י֞ו
תנצבה

S^A / Da Bemaventurada / Pia Y honesta Donzela /ESTHER
SARAH DACOSTA que faleceu em 4^a fiera / 24 de Hesvan a
5516 / de Edade de 43 Annos / S A G D E G

Carving: Tree chopped down.

*Burial Register: 5516   24 Hesvan   1755   29 Octr.   Miss
Ester Sarah DaCosta aged 43 years.*

319 Almost indecipherable.

לספד לשרה ולבכתה

שרה ... בצדק וביושר
נפטרה מעולם ...
עשתה צדקה שהיא לבושה
... לרוכב בערבות
שם נפשה פרחה למנוחתה
לפיכך ... מקום קבורתה

SEPULTURA / De La Bien aventurada / y Charitativa
S^{ra} SARAH / DA COSTA de Andrade / que ales 56 Anos de
Su / Edad fallecio y fue Sepul- / tada en Viernes 17 de /
Kisleu de 5513 que Corres / ponde de 23 de Novembro /
de 17[-]2.

תנצבה

Burial Register: 5513 17 Kislev 1752 23 November
Mrs. Sarah Da Costa de Andrade, aged 56 years.

320 In the border :-

HERE LIES INTERRED Y^e BODY OF ABRAHAM LINDO
SEN^R LATE MERCHANT OF THIS ISLAND WHO DEPARTED
THIS LIFE FEB^{RY} 11TH 1763 AGED 42 Y^{RS} & 2 MONTHS

ויצא יעקב מבאר שבע וילך חרנה
אברהם איש תמים שנשתנה יעקב
שמו כחלותו טוב שם משמן טוב
הנה קנה במעשיו הטובים וצדקתו רך
בשנים זקן הוא בבינה והגיעה עת
דודים לנשמתו ויהי בימי ארבעים
שנים של שנותיו נתבקש למעלה
במקום שומרי עידותיו

SEPULTURA /Del Bienaventurado Prudente / Honrado
Honeste Virtuoso y / Charitative ABRAHAM de DAVID LINDO
que en su En / -fermedad fue Mudado su / Nombre en Jahacob
que en los / 42 Anos y 2 Mezes de su Edad / passo de Esta
Vida ala de la Bienaventurama 28 de Se / -bath Anno de
5523 q corres / ponde a 11 de Febrero 1763 / S A G D E G.

Burial Register: 5523   28 Sebat   1763   11 February
Abraham Lindo Snr., aged 42 yrs & 2 mos.

321   In the border :-

HERE LYETH THE BODY OF SARAH WIDOW OF REV
MEHIR A COHEN BELINFANTE WHO DEPARTED THIS LIFE
31 OCTOBER 1785 AGED 63 YEARS.

מצבת

קבורת האשה הצנועה והנכבדה
מרת שרה אלמנת של הה̄ הדיין
המצויין הישיש הנכבד מהיר
הכהן בלינפנטי ז̄ל̄ נ̄ל̄ע̄ יום כ"ז
לחדש חשון שנת ה̄ת̄ק̄מ̄ו̄ פק
תנצבה

De la bienaventurada S^{ra}. / Sarah Vuida que fue del /
B.A.Y Reverendo Sabio / Mehir Acohen Belinfante / que f^o
en 27 de Hesvan / 5546 que corresponde a / 31 de Outubro
1785 de la / Edad de 63 Anos. / S A G L G.

Burial Register: 5546   27 Hesvan   1785   31 October
Sarah widow of Haham Myer à Cohen Belinfante aged 63 yrs.

322   In the border :-

HERE LIES INTERR'D Y^e BODY OF Y^e MOST PIOUS
& CHARITABLE Y^e REV^D MEHIR ACOHEN BELINFANTE WHO
WAS READER TO Y SINAGOGUE TEN YEARS & WAS BELOVED

BY ALL WHO KNEW HIM HE DEPARTED THIS LIFE THE
25TH of SEP 1752 AGED 48 YEARS.

Sunk oval with crown and hands of the Cohen raised
in the act of blessing, in relief.

מצבת

קבורת החכם הנעלה נעים זמירות ישראל מוהל
זריז סופר
מהיר ותוקע ותיק אשר הרביץ תורה בק"ק נדחי
ישראל כה"רך
מאיר הכהן בילאינפאנטי נת[ב]קש בישיבה של
מעלה ביום שלא
נאסר בו כי טוב לחדש תשרי וכמו השחר עלה לפק
ליצירה
והוא גם בן חיל שנה במותו
תנצבה

Do Bemaventurado Haham Anehela Nehim Zemirot Israel
Kebod Riby / Mehir Acohen Belinfante com sua meliflua e
suave voz como Hazan / admirava como deligente Mohel davao
S^{to} Firmamento como experto / Sopher escrevia a Divina Ley
Como atente Mestre a ensinava e Como / excellente Tokeah
Amoestava as Pecador Passou de ester e / trabalhosa Vida
a Eterna e Gloriosa que lhe adquiriram sua Devo - / caõ
Piedade e Caridade em Segunda feyra 17 de Tisry 5513 que /
Corresponde a 25 Septembro 1752 havendo administrado o
Posto / de Hazan neste K K de Nidhe Israel Des Annos com
todo Zelo e devoçaõ Soffreu as affrontes com paciencia
offences com / Tolerancia Sacrificou a Propria Convenencia
do Publico Beneficio / despediu - se do Posto por ver se
com isso socegava a Paixão e / odio e cessavão as contendas
e discordancias mas oh Desgraça / humana Faleceo quando
Ellas quedao vivas Passageiro / Lhe contempla e admira se
queres como Elle Gozar da Gloria Vive Como Elle nem Sempre
o melhor vive mais nem se vive para / outros não puderão
em outros tantos. / S B A G D E G.

141

האיש רוכב על כנפי שם   סוף סוף שכב ארצה ולן

סופר מהיר ונעים זמר   תקע שופר הוא סוהלן

גם ליסד דעת את העם   סבו סכלות הוא הצילן

שמו גנפו במסרה   לירות חצים הוא סבלן

Three carved panels :-

1. Man's figure, in knee-length skirted coat, blowing a shofar.

2. Hand holding a quill pen, symbolic of his being scribe.

3. Bottle, spatula, scissors, forceps, needle and other marks of the Mohel's art.

Burial Register: 5513 17 Tisri 1752 25 Sep. Haham Meher A-Cohen Belinfante, aged 48 years.

323 Broken across the middle. In the border :-

HERE LYETH THE BODY OF JAELL LATE WIFE OF MR DAVID NUNES CASTELLO WHO DEPARTED THIS LIFE THE 2^D OF SEPTEMBER 1760 AGED 31 YEARS & 7 MO^S .

מצבת

קבורת האשה הכבודה והצנועה

סרת יעל אשת הגביר דוד נונס

קאשטילו נלע ביום ד' כ"ב לחדש

אלול שנת התקכ

תנצבה

S^A / Da B A Virtuoza Honesta / & Caritativa Yael mulher que foy de David Nunes Castello f.º em 22 Elull 5520 / que corresponde a Settem. / 1760 de Idade de 31 Anno. / S A G D G.

Carving: Tree chopped down.

Burial Register: 5520 22 Elul 1760 2 Septr. Jail
Nunes widow of Castello aged 31 yrs & 7 mos.

324 IMMERSED / Beneath this Tomb / Rest the Body of /
MOSES BURGESS / Whose Life was Mark'd / with Charitable
Customs / he died on the sixteenth day of / September /
One thousand seven hundred / And Ninety four / Aged /
Forty Years ten Months and fourteen days / Lamented by his
Friends / And all who knew him / And his widow. /   In
Memory to his Remains / hath placed this Stone / The Last
Gift / of her / AFFECTIONS.

Burial Register: 5555 Elul 1795 [sic] *16 September.*
Moses Burgos aged 40 years & 10 days [sic].

325 Broken across the middle.   In the border :-

HERE LYETH THE BODY OF ...ANNAH NUNES CASTELLO
WHO DEPARTED THIS LIFE THE 17 OF SEPTEMBER 1752
AGED 28 YEARS & 4 M^S.

ואת!חנה יתן סנה אחת אפים
חיל וטוב עשו בנות רבות
ואת שרה על כלנה עלית
ולחזות בנועם אהובות
בערב יום כפור לרום עלית
אוחך בחן וחסד אל קנה
ושרה נחלפה בחנה

S^A / De la· bienaventurada Y / Encortada Doncella
Sarah / Nunes Castello que f^o. de / Edad de 28 Anos Y 4
Me^s / Y fue sepultada vispera de / Kipur Ano 5513 que
cores / ponde a 17 Setiem^e 1752 / S A G D G.

Carving: Tree chopped down.

Burial Register: 5513   9 Tisri   1752 17 September.
Mrs Hannah Nunes Castello aged 28 yrs. & 4 mos.

מצבת

קבורת הזקנה הצנועה והנכבדה סרת
לאה למוב נׄלׄעׄ יום כׄב לחדש ניסן
שנת הׄתׄקׄכׄג בת שלשה ושבעים שנה

תׄנׄצׄבׄה

S^A / De la bienaventurada / LEAH LETOB que fue / Dios
Servido Recojer para / fu Santa Gloria en 22 del / mez Nisan
Año 5523 que / Corresponde a 5 de Abril 1763 de la Edad de
73 Anos. S B A G D L E G^a.

*Burial Register: 5523 22 Nisan 1763 5 April Leah
Letob aged 73 years.*

327 Oval Ornamentation, with one line of Hebrew :-

~ וישב העפר אל הארץ כשהיה ~

Then shall the dust return to ye Earth as it was.

תחת זאת המצבה נטמן גוף איש חסיד ישׁר
ונאמן נטע נעמן ואב רחמן אהוב לשמים
ולבריות זקן ונשוא פנים הׄה ירמיהו ברוך
לוזאדה נפטר בשם טוב לבית עולמו כׄב
לחדש טבת שנת התקנג ויהיו ימי חייו
שמנה ושמנים שנה

תנצבה

Underneath this Tomb rests Secure / the last Remains
of / Mr JEREMIAH BARUH LOUZADA / who was Universally
known / to be Religious & Honest / a loving Husband & a
tender Parent / he Departed this Life the 22^d of Tibeth
5533 / which corresponds to the 6th of Jan^{ry} 1793 / in the
88 Year of his Age.

Burial Register: 5553 22 Tebet 1793 6 January
Jeremiah Baruch Louzado aged 88 years.

328 Broken across the centre.   In the border :-

HERE LYETH ... THE BODY OF SARAH LATE WIFE
OF JEREMIAH BARUH LOUZADA WHO DEPARTED THIS LIFE
NOV.R Yᵉ 22 1754 Aged 42 Years

מצבת

קבורת שרה זוגתו של הגביר
ירמיהו ברוך לויזאדה נ̇ל̇ע̇ יום ח'
לחדש כסליו שנת התקטו

תנצבה

S A / Da bemaventurada Sarah / Mulher que foy de
Yimiahu / Baruh Lousada qual fọ . . . . cor /
responde .. 22 November 1745 / da Idade de 42 Annos. /
S A G D G .

Carving: Tree Chopped down.

Burial Register: 5515 8 Kislev 1754 22 November
Sarah widow of Jeremiah Baruch Louzado aged 42 years.

Returning to western wall.   Space, and then three
together.

329   בני אברהם ספדו למרה
                  ביום מותה נפלה עטרה
                  עטרת משפחתה ויודעיה
                  תפארת מכיריה וריעותיה
                  בחייה היתה בסר ואנחה
                  ובמותה הלכה לגן מנוחה
                  נשמתה גנוזה לחולקא טבה

145

לרשת שכרה לחיי עולם הבא

מצבת

קבורת הכבודה והצנועה הבתולה שרה בת אהרן

פירירה הינריקים נ͏ִ͏ל͏ִ͏ב͏ִ͏ע͏ יום ב יא לחדש אדר

שנת ת͏ִ͏ק͏ִ͏ל͏ִ͏ד͏ִ͏ בת ל͏ִ͏ו͏ִ שנה

ת͏ִ͏נ͏ִ͏צ͏ִ͏ב͏ִ͏ה͏ִ

Here lies till happy Resurrection / A maid Possessed
of every perfection / cutt off in the prime of youth &
life / Er'e her Virtues could Shine as wife / Her loss
much regreted by all / Her Friends afflicted at her fall /
This Consolation thear thought Imploy / Her Soul perfect
fele̲city doth Injoy / Sarah Pereira Henriques departed
this / Life on Monday being the 11th of Month Adar / in
the Year 5534 which Corresponds to / the 22nd Feby 1774
Aged 36 Years & 4 months.

Carving: Tree chopped down.

Burial Register: 5534 11 Adar 1774 22 February
Miss Sarah Pereira Henriques aged 36 yrs & 4 mos.

330 S^A/ Da bemaventurada Y devota / Abigail Henriquez
que fo em / Sabat R.H. Tamus 5520 que / Corresponde a 14
de Junio 1760. S A G D G .

Burial Register: 5520 1 Tamus 1760 14 June
Abigail Henriques.

331 In the border :-

HERE LYES THE BODY OF ESTER FRANCO NUNES
WIDOW WHO DEPARTED THIS LIFE THE 19TH OF FEBRU-
ARY 1759 AGED 75 YEARS.

SEPULTURA / Da muy Honrado e / Virtuoza S^{ra}. ESTER
FRANCO NUNES faleceo / em 22 de Sebat 5519 que /

146

Corresponde a 19 de Feb? / 1795 da Idade de 75 Años. /
S B A G E G .

Three ledgers in a row.

332   In the border :-

HERE REST THE EARTHLY REMAINS OF MRS JAEL
WIDOW OF MR ABRAHAM GOMES WHO DEPARTED THIS LIFE
ON THE 9TH DAY OF FEBRUARY 1769 AGED 54 YEARS.

מצבת

קבורת הכבודה והצנועה
אשת חיל רבת פעלים יעל
סנשים באהל תבורך כפה
פרשה לעני וידיה שלחה לאביון
מים שאל חלב נתנה ותורת חסד
על לשונה הה אלמנתו של
הנביר הנעלה אברהם גומיס
אינריקים בע נלע יום ה' שני
ימים לחדש אדר ראשון שנת
ובהעלותי אתכם מקברותיכם
ימי לפ"ק בת נ"ד שנים

תנצבה

Da B.A. Pia humilde & Virtuo^sa S^ra Yahel Viuva do
R A S. Abraham Gomes Henriques / a qual faleceu em 5^a f^a
de / Adar p.° do Anno 5529 que / Corresponde a 9 Febre.^ro
1769 / de Idade de 54 Annos / S B A G D E G .

HERE LYETH INTERR'D THE BODY OF MR ABRAHAM
GOMES HENRIQUES WHO DEPARTED THIS LIFE THE 30TH
OF JULY 1762 AGED 54 YEARS.

ה̃יה̃

אברהם סבקש ממך מחילה
חטאתי עויתי פשעתי
וסלחת לעוני כי רב הוא
ידעתי ה' כי צדק משפטיו ואמונה עניתני
ה' ה' אל רחום וחנון ארך אפים ורב חסד ואמת
יבאוני רחמיך ואחיה כי תורתך שעשעי
לולי תורתך שעשעי אז אבדתי בעניי
ה' אמת משה עבדו אמת ותורתו אמת

מ̃צ̃ב̃ת̃

קבורת החסיד העניו ובעל תמובה כה"ר
גומיש איניריקים שנפטר סן העה̃ לבית עולמו
לחיי העה̃ב בליל שמי עשרה לחדש מנחם
שנת התקכב לפק̃ : ויהי במנת חמישים וארבעה
של אברהם נתבקש בישיבה של מעלה

תנצבה

S^A / Do B.A. & Devoto Sr. ABRAHAM / GOMES HENRI-
QUES que/ Faleceo em noite de 6.ª f^{o.} / 10 do Mez menahem
Año / 5522 de Idade Annos [54].

Carving: Tree Chopped Down.

Burial Register: 5522   10 Ab.   1762   20[!] July
Abraham Gomes Henriques.

HERE LYETH INTERR'D THE BODY OF MR JACOB
GOMEZ HENRIQUES WHO DEPARTED THIS LIFE THE 2^d OF
FEBRUARY 1757 AGED 43 YEARS & 8 MONTHS.

מצבת

קבורת הנביר הנעלה יעקב
חזקיהו נוסים אינריקוס נ״לע ביום
ד שנים עשר להדש שבט שנת
התק״יז ליצירה

תנצבה

S^A / Do Bemaventurado Y / Honrado Sr JACOB HIZ
QUIAU / GOMES HENRIQUES fal^e. / ceu em 4.^{a} feira 12 de
Sebat / 5517 Y 2 de Feb^o. 1757 de / Idade de 43 Anos Y 8
Mezes. / S A G B E G .

Carved panel in relief :- Ladder with Angels des-
cending from the clouds, figure at foot (Jacob) with
head lying on a stone.

Burial Register: 5517 12 Sebat 1759 2 February
Jacob Gomes Henriques aged 43 yrs & 8 mos.

335 Broken across the top.   In the border :-

HERE LYETH INTERR'D THE BODY OF MR AB^M.
BRANDON LATE MERCH^T OF THIS ISLAND WHO DEPARTED
THIS LIFE ON THE 10TH OF AUGUST 1756 AGED 54
YEARS.

מצבת

קבורת הנביר הנכבד והנעלה כהר
אברהם בראנדון נ״לע ביום ג׳ יד׳ לחדש
מנחם שנת התקיו ליצירה
תנצבה

149

Do Bemaventurado Pio Y / Devoto Sr ABRAHAM BRANDON / Que faleceu em 3.ª feyra 14 / do Mez de Menahem a / 5516 de Idade de 54 Annos / S B A G D E G

Carving: Tree chopped down.

Burial Register: 5516   14 Ab.   1756   10 August   Abraham Brandon.

Two stones together.

336   Broken at the right bottom corner.   In the border :-

HERE LYETH THE BODY OF MRS REBECCAH NUNES
WIDOW OF MR PHINEAS NUNES LATE MERCHANT OF THIS
ISLAND WHO DEPARTED THIS LIFE APRIL Y^e 4 1774
AGED 59 YEARS.

מצבת

קבורת האשה הכבודה והצנועה
סרת רבקה נונים נלע' יום ג' ד'
לחדש ניסן שנת התקלה,

תנצבה

S^A / Da bemaventurada / Ribcah Viuva que foy / de Pinhas Nunes que / faleceu em 4 de Nisan 5535 que Corresponde a / 4 de Abril 1775 de Idade / de 59 Annos. / S A G D G .

Burial Register: 5535   4 Nisan   1775   4 April   Rebecca widow of Phineas Nunes aged 59 yrs.

337   In the border :-

HERE LYETH INTERR'D THE BODY OF MRS LUNAH
VALVERDE WHO DEPARTED THIS LIFE MONDAY (!)

7TH DAY OF AUGUST 1756 AGED 66 YEARS.

מצבת

קבורת האשה הכבודה הזקנה
מרת לונה ואלוירדי נל״ע ביום שבת
קודש יא׳ לחדש מנחם שנת התק״ יו
ליצירה

תנצבה

S^A / Da Mui Honrada S^{ra} / LUNAH VALVERDE feleceu /
em Sebat 11 do mez de / Menahem 5516 Y 7 de Agos- / -to
1756 de Idade de 66 Annos / S A G D E G .

Carving: Tree chopped down.

Burial Register: 5516 11 Ab. 1756 7 August Mrs. Luna
Valverde aged 66 yrs.

338 In the border :-

HERE LYES INTERRED THE BODY OF MOSES PINHEIRO
LATE MERCHANT OF THIS ISLAND WHO DEPARTED THIS
LIFE JULY THE 14TH 1755 AGED 60 YEARS.

מצבת

קבורת הישיש הנכבד הנביר הנעלה
משה פנירו נל״ע ביום ב׳ ששה ימים
לחדש מנחם שנת התק״ט ו

תנצבה

Del Bienaventurado y / Caritativo Sr MOSEH /
PINHEIRO falecio en dia / de Lunes 6 del mez de /
Menahem del a 5515 que / Corresponde a 14 de Julio / 1755-
S A G D L G .

Carving: Tree chopped down.

Burial Register: 5515 6 Tamus [sic] 1755 14 June[sic]
Moses Pinheiro aged 60 yrs. [*The date given in the inscription is correct.*]

Adjoining the eastern boundary wall, two together.

339 In the border :-

HERE REST THE EARTHLY REMAINS OF MRS REBECCA
WIDOW OF MR ABR.^M PINHEIRO WHO DEPARTED THIS LIFE
ON THE 31st OF DECEMBER 1768 AGED 56 YEARS.

מצבת

קבורת הכבודה והצנועה מרת
רבקה אלמנתו של הנביר הנעלה
אברהם פיניירו נלע יום שני כ
לחדש חשון שנת התקכט בת
נו שנים

תנצבה

S^A / Da B.A. e virtuosa S.^ra Ribca / viuva de B.A. S^r
Abraham / Pinheiro a qual faleceu / em 2^a. f^a 20 de
Hesvan do / Anno 5529 que corresponde / a 31 Outubro [sic]
1768 de / Idade de 56 Annos / S B A G D E G

Burial Register: 5529   20 Hesvan .... *Rebecca widow
of Abraham Pinheiro aged 56 yrs.*

340 In the border :-

HERE LYETH INTERR'D THE BODY OF AB.^M PINHEIRO
LATE MERCHANT OF THIS ISLAND WHO DEPARTED THIS
LIFE THE 5TH OF MARCH 1755 AGED 29 YEARS.

ואברהם כבד מאד

אברהם איש תמים שנשתנה
ביהושע שמו כחלותו
טוב שם מסמן טוב הנה קנה
במעשיו טובים וצדקתו
רך בשנים זקן הוא בבינה
והגיעה עת דודים לנשמתו
בשנים שהיה עשרים ותשע
וילך יחושע אל גן ישע

Del Bien - aventurado Prudente / Honesto honrado
virtuoso y / Chari^{vo}. ABRAHAM PINHEIRO / que en Su
enfermedad fue / mudado sunombre en Jehosu.^a / que en los
29 Anos de Sua / edad paso de esta vida a la / dela bien-
aventuranza en 22 / de Adar Ano de 5515 que / Corresponde
a 5 de Marzo / de 1755.

תִּנְצְבָה

Carving: Tree chopped down.

Burial Register: 5515 22 Adar 1755 5 March Abraham
Pinheiro aged 29 years.

Returning to the western wall, near a tree-stump,
three together.

341   מצבת

קבורת הגביר הנעלה החסיד העניו
איש תם וישר בעל צדקות יצחק גארסיאה
נע נלע בארבעה ימים לחדש אדר שני
שנת התקכא לפ׳ג בן נ׳ה שנים
תִּנְצְבָה

S^A / Del B.A. Humilde Caritativo / y virtuozo el S.^R

153

ISHAC GARSIA quien passo / desta a mejor vida en 4 / de
Veadar 5521 que Cor- / responde a 10 de Marco / 1761 de
Edad de 56 Años / S B A G E .

*Burial Register: 5521 4 Veadar 1761 10 March Isaac
Garcia aged 56 years.*

Note: Difference in age in Hebrew (55) & Port. (56).

342   *Very faint lettering:*

S^A / Do B.A. Rachel Mulher / que foy de Ishac Garsia
/ qual f.º em 3 de Elul 5519 / que corresponde a 28 / Agosto
1759 de Idade / 60 Annos. / S A G D G.

*Burial Register: 5519 Elul 1759 28 August Rachel wife
of Isaac Garcia aged 60 years.*

343   Broken in three places and very indistinct.

S^A / Da bem aventurada Sarah / ... Porto que f .....
/ Adar 5522 que correspond / a 27 Fevreiro Anno 1762. /
S A G D G .

מצבת

קבורת שרה די פורטו נלע יום ד
לחדש אדר שנת התקכב

תנצבה

*Burial Register: 5522 Adar [Hebrew epitaph gives 4th
Adar] 1762 27 February Sarah de Porto.*

About the centre of the enclosure near the base of a
tamarind tree is a stone without any inscription.   Adjoining is No. 344.

344   In the border :-

HERE LIES INTERR'D Y^e BODY OF Y^e MOST CHARI-
TABLE PIOUS & WELL BELOVED MOSES DE PAZ WHO DE-
PARTED THIS LIFE Y^e 11 of FEBY 1764 AGED ABOUT 48
YEARS & WAS LAMENTED AND WELL RESPECTED BY ALL
THAT KNEW HIM.

ויקרא אל משה ביום השביעי ומשה
עלה אל האלהים ויקרא אליו אלהים

מצבת

קבורת הנביר החסיד ועניו רודף צדקה וחסד משה
די פאם זכר צדיק לברכה אשר נתבקש בישיבה של
מעלה ויקרא אל משה ביום השביעי והאיש משה
עניו מאוד ומשה עלה אל האלהים לחזות בנועם
ה' ולבקר בהכלו בן מאב שנים נפמר לבית עולמו ח'
לאדר ראשון שנתאך מוב וחסד ירדפוני כל ימי חיי
ושבתי בבית ה' לאורך ימים ליצירה

תנצבה

S^A / Del Bienaventurado Humilde / Caritativo y
virtuoso / MOSEH de PAZ quien passo / desta a mejor vida
para gozar / el Fruto de sus buenas obras / en 8 de Adar
Rison 5524 / que corresponde a 11 de / Febrero 1764 de
Edad de 42 / para 47 Años / S B A G D E G .

*Burial Register: 5524, - Adar 1764, 11 February
Moses De Pas aged 42 years.*

East of tree, five stones.

345 Broken across the centre.

SA / Da bemaventurada Sarah / de Morais que f^o em
28 de / Adar seny 5518 que corres- / -ponde a 6 de Abril
1758.

Burial Register: 5518 28 Adar 1758 6 April Sarah de Morais.

346   Broken in three pieces.   In the border :-

HERE LYETH YE BODY OF SARAH WIDOW OF MR JOSEPH ABARBANEL WHO DEPARTED THIS LIFE THE 9 OF NOVEMBER 1764 AGED 57 YEARS.

S^A / Da bemaventurada Sarah / Viuva que foy de Joseph Abarbanel que f.º em 14 de / Hesvan 5525 que corresponde / a 9 de Novembro 1764 de Idade de 57 Annos   S A G D G .

Burial Register: 5525 14 Hesvan 1764 9 November Sarah widow of Joseph Abarbanel aged 57 years.

347   מצבת

קבורת הגביר הנעלה יוסף אברבנאיל
נ״ע ביום כ״א לחדש ניסן שנת התקכא
בן נ״ו שנה

תנצבה

Do bemaventurado Ioseph / Abarbanel que f.º em 21 de / Nisan 5521 que corresponde / a 25 de Abril 1761 de Idade / de 56 Annos.   S A G D G .

Burial Register: 5521 21 Nisan 1761 25 April Joseph Abarbanel aged 56 years.

348   Broken in three places.   In the border :-

HERE LYETH THE EARTHLY REMAINS OF MRS LUNAH WIDOW OF THE LATE MR MOSES PINHEIRO WHO DEPARTED THIS LIFE THE 17 OF MARCH 1770 AG^D 68 YE^S.

מצבת

קבורת הזקנה הכבודה
והצנועה סרת לונה אלמנתו
של הגביר הנעלה משה
פיניירו נ̇ל̇ע̇ ביום ש̇ק̇ כ לחדש
אדר שנת הת̇ק̇ל̇

תנצבה

Da bemaventurada y / Honrada Sra Lunah / Viuva que
foy de B.A. S.ʳ Mosseh Pinheiro que / faleceu em Sabath 20
/ de Adar 5530 que corresponde a 17 de Mar.ᶜᵒ / 1770 de
Idade de 68 Ann.ᵒˢ / S A G D G .

*Burial Register: 5530 20 Adar 1770 17 March Luna
widow of Moses Pinheiro aged 68 years.*

South of Tamarind tree, three slabs in a row.

349 A very fine stone.

מצבת

קבורת הבחור הנחמד יעקב
מונטיפיורי סוחר סעיר לונדון
אשר נ̇ל̇ב̇ע̇ באחד בשבת כ̇ט̇
לחדש האביב

בשנת

ה̇לא צבא̇ לא̇נש ע̇לי אר̇ץ
ויהיו ימי שני חייו עשרים ושמונה שנה

תנצבה

SACRED to the memory of / Mr JACOB MONTEFIORE /
of London Merchant, / who departed this Life for /

everlasting Glory / on Sunday the 12 of April 1801, / Aged
28 Years and 2 Months / and whose earthly Remains are deposited / beneath this Tomb: / His loss is sincerely lamented by his / numerous Relations, Friends and / Acquaintance, for his filial Duty, Affections, / friendship,
Integrity and / Philanthropy.

    Carving (since cut out and taken away): Sunk panel
    with partly-clad figure lying on couch, with angel
    ministering to him.

               Moses Ancona   Sculp.
                   London.

*Burial Register: 5561 Nisan 1801 12 April Jacob
Montefiore aged 28 years and 2 months.*

350 Broken across the middle and both lower corners, and
one piece (lower left corner) missing.   In the border :-
(on 4 sides)

    ...eth Interred the Body of Abr.^m Lindo Junr Esqr
formerly of LONDON & lately of this Island Merchant Whose
Probity & Charitable Deeds are much better Monument to his
Virtues then any that could be Erected here who Departed
this life 30 March 1784 Aged 60 Years.

מצבת

הישיש הנכבד הגביר הנעלה
בעל צדקה עוזר דלים ונומל
חסדים אברהם די יעקב לנדו נ״לע״
יום ג״ ח׳ לחדש ניסן שנת ה[תק]מ̇ד̇ לפ̇ק̇
בן ס״ שנים

תנצבה

S^A / De el Bienaventurado Caritativo y / Honesto
Varon Abraham de / Jachacob Lindo que fue Dios / Servido

Recoger a sua Santa / Gloria en 8 de Nisan Año 5544 / que
Corresponde a 30 de Marco / 1784 de Eddad de 60 Años y 3 /
Mezez / S A G D L E G .

*Burial Register: 5544 8 Nisan 1784 30 March (Tuesday)
Abraham Lindo aged 60 years & 3 mos.*

351 In the border : -

HERE LYETH INTERR'D Y BODY OF MRS BRANCA LINDO
WIFE OF Yᵉ LATE MR JACOB LINDO WHO DEPARTED THIS
LIFE THE FIRST DAY OF AUGUST 1765 AGED 77 YEARS.

מצבת

קבורת הצדקת הצנו[ע]ה והנכבדה סרת
בראנקה אשת זוגתו של הנביר הנעלה
יעקב לינדו נ̇לע ב̇לע ביום חמישי י̇ד לחדש
מנחם שנת התקכה ויהי ימי בראנקה[ן
שבעים ושבעה שנים

הנצבה

Da Bemaventurada Caritativa / Y Honesta Sᵗᵃ Branca
Mulher / q̃ foy Do Bemaventurado Sᵗ / Jahacob Lindo de
Haedo que / Passo desta a Melhor Vida em / 5 fᵗᵃ 14 de Mez
Menahem 5525 / que Corresponde a 1º Agosto / de Idade de
77 Annos. / S B A G D E G .

*Burial Register: 5525 14 Ab. 1765 1 August Branca
widow of Jacob Lindo - aged 77 years.*

Two together beside the east wall.

352 In the border : -

HERE LYETH INTERR'D THE BODY OF MRS RACHEL
LINDO WIFE OF THE LATE MR DAVID LINDO WHO

159

DEPARTED THIS LIFE THE 31 OF JULY 1766 AGED 73
YEARS.

מצבת

קבורת הצדקת הצנועה והנכבדה
מרת רחל זונתו של הישיש הנכבד
הנביר הנעלה דוד לינדו נלע ביום
ה כה לחדש מנחם שנת היא מצבת
קבורת רחל לפק ויהיו ימי רחל שלוש
ושבעים שנה

תנצבה

Da Bemaventurada Caritativa / & Honesta S.^{ra} Rachel
Viuva / que foy .. bemaventurado S^r / David Lindo
...assou desta a / Milhor Vida em 5.^{a} f.^{ra} 25 de / Menahem
A^{o}5526 que Corres / ponde a 31 de Julho 1766 / da Idade
de 73 Annos. / S B A G D E G .

*Burial Register: 5526 25 Ab. 1766 13[!] July Rachel
wife of David Lindo aged 73 years.*

353   In the border : -

HERE LYETH THE BODY OF MR DAVID LINDO MERCHANT
WHO DEPARTED THIS LIFE SUNDAY THE 20 DAY OF MAY
1759 IN THE 65 YEAR OF HIS AGE.

מצבת

קבורת הישיש הנכבד ונשוא
פנים הנביר הנעלה דוד לינדו
אשר נפטר בשם טוב מעולמו ביום
א כב לחדש אייר שנת התקיט
בן סה שוה

תנצבה

160

S.^A / Do Bemaventurado Pio e / Temerozo de D.ª o
Venerado / velho David Lindo o recoleo / D.ª para sua
Eterna Gloria / em Domingo a noite as 12 / horas sendo 22
de Yiar 5519 / que corresponde a 20 de / Mayo 1759 de
Idade de 65 A.ᵒˢ   S B A G D G .

Burial Register: 5519   22 Yiar   1759   20 May   David Lindo
Note: 5519, Yiar 22 = May 19, 1759.

South of No. 353 are two slabs with indistinct inscriptions, 354 and 355.

Returning to west wall and working in easterly
direction.

356   Broken in two pieces.

Mr DAVID ABOAB / Merchant / departed this Life the
5.th Sep.^r / 1800 / Aged 58 Years.

Burial Register: 5560   Tisri   1800 5 Sep.   David Aboab
aged 58 years.

Two Slabs together - 357 and 358.

357   מצבת

קבורת הגביר יצחק לופים נלעׄ
ביום כ לחדש שבת(1) שנת התׄקׄסׄדׄ
בן נׄבׄ שנים

תנצבה

In Memory of / ISAAC LOPEZ / died 20.th Sebat 5564
/ Corresponding to the / 2.nd February 1804 / Aged 52 Years/

Burial Register: 5564   20 Shebat   1804   2 February
Isaac Lopez aged 52 years.

161

358 Around the sides and top :-

HERE RESTS THE REMAINS OF DABORAH LATE WIFE
OF M.ᴿ ISAAC LOPEZ JUNᴿ WHO DEPARTED THIS LIFE ON
SUNDAY THE 20 OF JULY 1783 IN THE 34 YEAR OF HER
AGE.

Carving: Sunk panel with hand from the clouds pick-
ing a flower.

מצבת

קבורת הצנועה הנכבדה והצדקת
דבורה אשת הנביר יצחק לופּיס
נלֹעֹ יום ראשון כ תמוז תקֹסֹגֹ
בת לד שנה

תנצבה

Sᴬ / Da benaventurada Cari- / tativa y temente de
D.ˢ / Dna Deborah mulher de / Isaac Lopez f.º em Domin.ᵍº /
20 de Tamuz 5543 que cor- / responde a 20 d' Julho de /
1783 de Idada de 34 Annos.   S B A G D G .

Carving: Sunk panel with hand from the clouds felling
tree.

*Burial Register: 5543 20 Tamus 1783 20 July Deborah
wife of Isaac Lopez Jnr. aged 34 years.*

Three slabs together :-

359   מצבת

קבורת הצנועה והנכבדה סרת
הבתולה אסתר בת יעקב פּינײרו
נלֹעֹ יום יג לחדש תמוז שנת
התקסג בן [!]כֹ שנים

Here Rests the Remains of / Mis [sic] ESTHER PIN-
HEIRO / Resigned in Death cut off in the / Flower of her
Age regretted by / all her Friends on the 3.^{d} July / 1803
in the 20th Year of her Age.

Burial Register: 5563   26 Tamus 1802 3 July Esther
daughter of Jacob Pinheiro aged 20 years.

360 Broken across the centre and right corner of base.

מצבת

קבורת האשה הכבודה והצנועה

הנכבדה מרת אסתר אשת הנביר

הנעלה אברהם דא קושטא די

אנדראדא נלﬞﬞﬞ ביום ראש חדש

ניסן התקנﬞﬞﬞא לפﬞﬞﬞג בת ששה

וששים שנה וששה חדשים

תנצבה

Here rests the Earthly remins / of [repaired with
cement] worthy / ESTHER widow of ABRAHAM / DA COSTA
[de Andrade]who departed this / transitory Life for those
Blessed / Regions where departed Souls / enjoy in lasting
felicity the Just / Reward of Virtuous Deeds and / Good
actions on Tuesday 1st of / Nisan 5551 corresponding to /
the 5th April 1791 Aged 66 / Years and 6 Months.   S B A G
E G .

Carving: Tree chopped down.

Burial Register: 5551 1 Nisan 1791 5 April Esther
widow of Abraham Da Costa de Andrade 66 yrs and 6 mos.

361 In the border :-

HERE LIETH THE BODY OF ABRAHAM DA COSTA DE
ANDRADA WHO DEPARTED THIS LIFE ON THE 2^{d} OF

JANUARY 1783 IN THE 66th YEAR OF HIS AGE.

מצבת

קבורת הישיש הנכבד
אברהם דא קוסטא די
אנדראדא נ׳ל׳ע׳ יום כח
לחדש טבת שנת התקמג

תנצבה

S^A. / Do bemaventurado / Abr.^m da Costa d'Andrada /
que Faleceu em 28 de / Tebeth 5543 que cor / responde a
2 de Jane.^{ro} / 1783 de Idade de 66 / Annos.   S A G D G .

Burial Register: 5543   28 Tebet   1783   2 January
Abraham Da Costa De Andrada aged 66 yrs.

362   The lower half is broken in six pieces.

מצבת קבורת הבתולה שרה נוניס קאסטילו

Beneath this Stone / lies interred / All that was
mortal of / Miss SARAH NUNES CASTELLO / Daughter of /
DAVID AND RACHEL NUNES CASTELLO / Whose fortitude
in her last illness / Could only be equalled / by her /
unspotted carrear thro her small portian / of Sublunary
existance / Adorned with every charm of person and mind /
her life was truly valuable / to her Parents / And Friends
/ who by her death were rendered inconsolable / but for
the hope / inspired by her / unaffected Piety & unexampled
resignation dur^g / ... a most painful illness / in full
confidence / that as her infant child soared to heaven /
& looked up for bliss eternall / so it there enjoys sera-
phic joys and with Angels now join the heavenly choir /
in praises / of that omnipotent being with whom she now
rests / She departed this life the 3rd day of Elull /
5542 which corresponds to the 13th day / of August 1782
Aged 12 Years.

עוז והדר לבושה ותשחק ליום אחרון

363 Broken in many pieces, and parts missing.

ומשה עלה אל האלהים

מצבת

קבורת הנביר הנעלה משה
אבוהב נ׳ל׳ע׳ יום י׳ם׳ לחדש
מנחם שנת התקמב ליצירא(!)

תנצבה

..urado
.....faleceo
... m de...
... ade a ..
... nos ..

364 Under a genip tree. Broken in many pieces. In the border :-

SACRED TO THE MEMORY OF THE LATE MR DAVID
VALVERDE WHO WAS SUMMONED TO APPEAR BEFORE ....
OF THE ALMIGHTY ON MONDAY THE 8 OF JULY 1782 AGED
30 YEARS & 7 . .

מצבת

קבורת הנביר הנעלה דוד ואלוירדי
נ׳ל׳ע׳ ביום שני׳ כו יום לחדש תמוז
שנת התקמב ויהיו ימי הייו שלשים
שנה ושבעה חדשים

תנצבה

165

S^A / Del bienaventurado David / Valverde de que fue
D^s Servido / tamar a su S^a Gloria en Lunes / 26 de Tamuz
5542 que corres / ponde a 8 Julio 1782 tiendo de / Edad
de 30 Años Y 7 Meses / S B A G D L E G .

Carving: Tree chopped down.

*Burial Register: 5542 26 Tamus 1782 8 July David
Valverde aged 30 yrs. & 7 mos.*

365 Broken across middle.

מצבת /

קבורת הגביר הנעלה בנ̇יאמין
אברבניל נלע̇ יום ש̇ק̇ ה' לחדש
סיון שנת התקמב ליצירה

תנצבה

S^A / Del bienaventurado Binjamin / Abarbanel que
falecio en 5 de / Sivan 5542 que corresponde / a 18 de
Mayo 1782 de Edad / de 40 Annos / S A G L G .

Oh Binjamin / de Dios querido y Estimado Paes a su
Santa Ley / Fuites siempre afficionado / Desta trabjosa
vida / Fuistes por Dios llamado / Para en el Mansion
Celeste / Ser con Gloria Beatificado.

*Burial Register: 5542 5 Sevan 1782 18 May
Benjamin Abarbanel aged 40 years.*

Two together near east wall.

366 ותהי אסתר נושאת חן בעיני כל רואיה

And Esther obtained grace / in the sight of all that
beheld her. / Here lieth the body of Mrs / Esther Widow
of Mr Benjamin / Massiah who departed this / Life the 13
of Elul 5555 / which answers to the 27 of August 1795
aged 73 years.

166

367

תחת המצבה הזאת נקבר שארית חומר
הגביר הנעלה היׁשיׁש הנכבד בנימין מׁשיח
אׁשר היה סוחר טוב באי הזאת אהוב ונׁשוא
פנים מכל יודעיו ובמותו היה כל העם הולך
ובכה ויׁשא קינה ונהי ׁשנים רבות התפלל
בפני קהל ועדה ויעל לדוכן לזמר כחזן
חנם אין כסף וימל את הילדים ומהולל
מאוד על זה כי ׁשכל את ידיו וינוע וימת
ויאסף אל עמיו בעׁשׁק כׁמ לחדׁש אדר
בׁשנת לׁבׁנׁיׁׁסׁיׁן אמר ידיד יׁי יׁשכון
לבטח עליו ויהיו ימי חייו תׁשע וׁשׁשים
ׁשנה וׁשמנה חדׁשים

Underneath this Tomb lies interred / the Earthly
Remains of Benj[n]. Massiah / late Merchant of this Island
who was / universally beloved and respected / by all that
knew him whose death / was much lamented He had been /
Reader of the Jews Synagogue for / many Years without Fee
or Reward / and performed the Office of a / Circumciser
with great Applause / and Dexterity He departed this /
Life on the 29 Adar 5542 Corres / ponding to the 15th of
March 1782 Aged 69 Years and Eight months.

Back to western boundary and near to the pathway.

368 Broken across the middle.

לבנימין אמר ידיד ... יׁשכן לבטח...

מצבת

קבורת הבכור בנימין די יצחק
ישראל נוניס נ׳׳ל׳׳ע ביום יד׳ לחדש
תמוז שנת התקנ׳׳ו בן ל״ב שנ[ה]

תנצבה

Here rests the Remains of / Mr BENJAMIN NUNES /
Merchant, born in London / 3 d of September 1764 died /
in this Island of Barbados / the 19th of July 1796 / in
the 32^d year of his Age.

Script letters :-
[Indistinct].....   can declare
   ... rests the relics of a man sincere
   By virtue led, resigned to fortunes fate
               ... great
One God..   breath
    .... at the hour of death.

Burial Register: 5556 Tamus 1796 19 July Benjamin
[son of Isaac] Israel Nunes aged 32 years.

369   Broken in three pieces.

מצבת

Here Rests the Earthly / Remains of Matthias son of /
Mr Isaac Lopez who departe^d / this transitory Life for
the / Enjoyment of a better on / Thursday 14 Elul 5553
corres / ponding to 22 August 1793 / Aged 10 Years 2 Months
& 25 days.

Burial Register: 5553 14 Elul 1793 22 August
Mathias child of Isaac Lopez aged 10 yrs 2 mos and 25 days.

370   Carving: Hand from clouds chopping down tree.

Lamentation and Bitter weeping Rachel weeping for
her children and refused to be comforted for her children

because they were not - Refrain thy voice from weeping and thine Eyes from tears for thy work shall be rewarded.

In one single arched line :-

ויהי בהקשתה בלדתה היא קבורת רחל עד היום
הזה היא בית לחם

Then :-

סצבת

האשה הכבודה והצנועה הנכבדה סרת אשת
חיל סבורכת צדקה וחסד ורב פעלים ותורת
חסד על לשונה רחל אשת הנגיר המרומם
והנעלה משה לופים יצו אמן נפטרה לבית
עולמה ביום שבת קדש ארבעה ימים
לחדש אלול שנת התקמז לבריאת
עולם: בת שלושים שנים וארבעה חדשים

תנצבה

Here rest the Earthly remains of the most charitable / virtuous and worthy Rachel late wife of Moses / Lopez who departed this transitory world in child / birth for her immortal soul to enjoy the reward / of her good deeds in future Felicity on Saturday / the 4th Elul 5547 Corresponding to the 18 August 1787 / Aged 30 Years and 4 Months / S B A G D E G .

Burial Register: 5547 14 Elul 1787 18 August Rachel wife of Moses Lopez aged 30 years and 4 mos.

Four stones together.

371 Broken across the top. In the border :-

BENEATH THIS .... THERE RESTS INTERR'D THE .....AND PIOUS REMAINS OF MR MORDECAY MASSIAH WHO DEPARTED THIS LIFE IN HOPES OF ENJOYING A

BETTER ON THE ... TAMUZ 5552 WHICH CORRESPONDS
TO THE 23 OF JUNE 1792.

ד׳ נתן וד׳ לקח יהי שם ד׳ סברך

*Burial Register: 5552 3 Tamus 1792 23 June Mordecai
son of Benjamin Massiah aged 35 years.*

372 Broken across the middle.

מצבת

קבורת הגביר הנעלה מיאר(!)
הכהן נ׳ל׳ע׳ יום א׳ לחדש
אלול שנת התקנ׳א׳ בן נ׳ו׳
שנים

תנצבה

Here lieth the Body / of Mr Myer Cohen / who departed
this / life the 30 of August / 1791 which Answers / to the
1st of Elul 5551 Aged 56 Years.

Burial Register: 5551 1 Elul 1791 30 August Myer Cohen

373 One line of Hebrew : -

מצבת קבורת הישיש הנכבד
דוד בורגום נ׳ל׳ע׳ ביום ז׳ שבט שנת
התקנ׳ח׳ בן נב שנים   תנצבה

S^A / Do bien aventurado / DAVID BURGOS /que f°
em 7 de Sebat 5558 / que corresponde a 24 de / Janeiro
1798 de Idade / 52 Annos. / S A G D G.

Here lieth Interr'd / the remains of Mr DAVID
BURGOSS / Merchant of this Island / A Man / whose words
spoke the sentiments / of his Heart Just were the actions
/ and upright his ways / Heaven call'd him from this

170

world / to a better / 24 January 1798 / Aged 52 Years.

374 In the border :-

UNDERNEATH THIS TOMBSTONE LIETH THE BODY OF
MRS RACHEL WIDOW OF MOSES BURGOSS SHE WAS A
LOVING MOTHER TO HER CHILDREN MAIN^{ED}. THEM WITH
HER DAILY LABOUR WAS ESTEEMED OF ALL HER FRIENDS
& ALWAYS READY TO SERVE THEM DEPARTED THIS LIFE
THE 12 OF MAY 1791 AGED 63 YEARS.

היא מצבת קבורת רחל עד היום

מצבת

קבורת מרת הזקנה רחל בורגוס נפטר ביום ח'
לחדש אייר התקנ"א שלוש ושמים שנה
מפרנים את בניהם כל ימיה בכבוד וענוה
וריחמה עניים

תנצבה

S^A / Da bemaventurada Rachel Burgoss / mulher que
foy Do B A Moseh Burgoss / fo. em 8 Iyar 5551 Corresponde
con 12 / de Mayo 1791 de Idade de 63 years / amroza mae
para seus Filhos toda sua / Vida os manteve con toda
Honra / Pia doza Sobreos Povres y temeroza de / Deos /
S A G D G .

171

APPENDIX I

Entries in the Burial Register relating to the Jews which was deposited in the Central Registry at Bridgetown, Barbados, and which have no corresponding memorial in the graveyard.

Page 968

5435	26 Adar			Moses Cohen De Leon
5453	17 Nisan			Emanuel Carco
5454	13 Tebet			Davis child of Isaac and Sarah Suares aged 12 months
5454	13 Nisan			Hannah, wife of Samuel Aboab Cordoza
5454	24 Sevan			Sarah Suares
5459	12 Tamus			Aaron Simeon
5463	27 Sebat	1702	3 February	Sarah Nunes
5465	16 Elul			Mrs. Rachel Fonsequa
5466	23 Kislev			Sarah of Jacob and Esther Suares
5467	28 Adar			Abraham Válverde
5470	Tisri	1709		Manuel Sebo* Eliau son of David Villoa
5470	11 Tisri			Isaac De Piza
5470	11 Tisri			Elias son of Daniel Villao
5472	11 Tisri			Abraham Pacheco
5474	22 Hesvan			Isaac Haim Millado
5478	26 Nisan	1718	15 April	Moses Pereyra Brandon
5481	6 Yiar	1721	22 April	Isaac child of Matatya de Leao aged 2 years and six months.
5493	13 Ab	1733	14 July	Hanah Ester Lopez
5495	23 Nisan	1735	4 April	Sarah Baruch Henriques aged 76 years
5496	10 Nisan	1736	9 March	Abraham Haim Israel De Penna
5501	22 Sebat	1741	29 January	Elias Raphael son of Abraham and Ester Valverde
5504	16 Adar	1744	18 March	Isaac De Morais

---

* *Very probably a corruption of* mancebo *"youth"!*

5506	10 Tamus			Solomon Baruch Louzado
5512	21 Ab	1752	21 July	Judio Raphael Baruch Louzado aged 12 years and 6 months
5532	5 Elul	1772	3 September	Joseph child of Benjamin and Judith Abarbanel aged 3 years and 1 month
5534	29 Kislev	1773	14 December	Joshua Frois
5536	1 Yiar	1776	20 April	Ester child of Jacob and Lunah Valverde aged 6 years 6 months and 27 days.
5546	27 Ab	1786	21 August	Judith wife of Phineas Nunes aged 34 years
5553	1 Sebat	1793	25 January	Abraham Mendes Da Costa
5555	20 Adar	1795	12 March	Angel wife of Emanuel De Peiza aged 38 years
5555	10 Sebat	1795	30 January	Parnas Aaron Pinheiro aged 56 years
5556	8 Hesvan	1795	9 November	Isaac Pinheiro aged 74 years
5557	4 Tisri	1796	6 October	David Brandon aged 62 years
5557	Sebat	1797	10 January	Jacob Israel Nunes aged 66 years
5557	18 Nisan	1797	14 April	Hazan David Sarfatty De Pina
5560	5 Nisan	1800		Abraham Buzaglo aged 67 years
5561	19 Sevan	1801	31 May	Mordecai Burgos Massiah aged 34 years
5562	21 Yiar	1802	23 May	Isaac Israel Nunes aged 75 years
5562	1 Sevan	1802	1 June	Hazan Daniel Da Costa de Andrada aged 45 years
5563	21 Adar	1803	16 March	Mrs. Hannah Lealtad aged 75 years
5563	7 Nisan	1803	31 March	Jacob Pinheiro aged 74 years
5564	Tisri	1803	3 October	Beatrice child of Abraham and Sarah Nunes aged 19 months
5564	17 Tamus	1804	26 July	Isaac son of Jacob Pinheiro aged 39 years
5564	7 Elul	1804	14 September	Leah wife of Isaac Lealtad aged 35 years
5564	24 Elul	1804	31 August	Isaac son of Moses Levy aged 14 years
5566	Adar	1806	4 March	Isaac Lindo jnr aged 21 years and 7 months

5567	5 Tisri			Mrs. Rebecca of Jacob Massiah
5567	12 Tisri	1807	19 May	Isaac Lindo aged 49 years
5567	16 Nisan	1807	23 April	David son of David Israel and Leah Brandon aged 18 years and 10 months
5567	18 Ab	1807	17 August	Mrs. Lebanah Lopez
5567	6 Elul	1807	September	Simcha child of Eleazar and Judith Montefiore aged 9 months
5568	7 Tisri	1807	9 October	Rachel de Haim Abinun Lima
5568	14 Tisri	1807	16 October	Miss Rebecca Baruch Louzado aged 61 years
5568	1 Elul			Leah of Isaac Israel Nunes
5569	13 Tisri			Esther Baruch Louzado
5570	21 Tebet			Esther Ullao
5571	9 Sevan	1811	1 June	Raphael Gomez
5571	14 Ab			Lebana De Crasto
5572	21 Adar			Abigail Ullao
5573	5 Tisri	1812	11 September	Hazan Abraham de David Brandon
5573	19 Tisri	1812	25 September	Eve child of Benjamin Elkin aged 17 days
5573	20 Nisan	1813	20 April	Rebecca Carvarlho
5574	27 Adar	1814	19 March	Sarah widow of Joseph Barrow aged 72 years
5574	23 Nisan	1814	13 April	Haim Abraham Lurio aged 34 years
5574	27 Nisan			Rebecca Ullao
5574	10 Tisri	1814	24 September	Joseph son of Jacob Pinheiro aged 39 years.
5575	30 Tisri	1814	14 October	Joseph Haim a Cohen Belenfante aged 66 years
5575	3 Yiar			Lebanah Ullao
5576	18 Nisan			Miriam Ullao
5576	13 Tamus	1816	9 July	Mary Miriam wife of Mozley Elkin aged 26 years[+]
5576	3 Elul			Judah Massiah
5576	8 Elul			Daniel Cohen son of Benjamin Cohen D'Azevedo
5577	4 Hesvan	1816	26 October	Judith wife of Moses Burgos aged 65 years
5577	26 Tebet	1816		Hanah wife of Judah Aarons

[+]*Mozley of Isaac Elkin married 29.4.1816 Miriam of Jacob Simmonds.*

174

5578	29 Veadar	1818	16 April	Sarah wife of Benjamin Hisquiau (B.R:Henriques) Da Costa aged 61 years 9 months and 20 days.
5578	2 Sevan	1818	6 June	Hanah widow of Jacob Pinheiro aged 91 years
5579	26 Tisri			Abraham Valverde
5579	28 Hesvan			Rachel Massiah
5579	4 Tebet	1819	19 March	Jacob De Peiza
5579	1 Elel	1819	21 August	Jacob child of Benjamin Elkin aged 1 year 1 month 19 days
5580	2 Yiar	1820	14 March	Mrs. Bathsheba de David Brandon
5580	24 Elul	1820	3 September	Sarah wife of Daniel Pass*
5581	22 Tebet	1821	27 December	Hazan Moses Henriques Julian
5581	19 Tamus	1821	19 July	Benjamin child of Joshua Levi
5582	9 Kislev	1821	3 December	(Mary Ann) Miriam Hanah child of Daniel Pass aged 3 monts and 8 days
5582	10 (Kislev) (B.R.11)	1821	5 December	Jacob Joseph Levi aged 51 years
5582	4 Tebet	1821	28 December	Parnas Abraham son of David Lindo aged 35 years
5581	1 Yiar	1822	22 April	Miss Simcha of David Valverde
5582	15 Sevan	1822	4 June	Miss Rachel Pinheiro aged 85 years
5583	5 Sebat	1823	18 January	Isaac Massiah
5584	7 (Tisri) (B.R.11)	1823	12 September	Sarah wife of Haim Barrow (B.R:Baruch) aged 82 years
5584	10 Hesvan	1823	15 October	Nathaniel son of Abraham Israel Keys
5584	27 Adar	1824	26 Bebruary	Aaron Baruch Louzado
5584	24 Yiar	1824	22 May	Miss Lunah of Jacob Pinheiro aged 73 years.
5584	21 Tamus	1824	17 July	Jacob son of David Lindo aged 27 years
5584	Elul	1824	9 September	Sarah of Abraham Massiah
5585	10 Kislev	1824	1 December	Hazan and Parnas Israel De Peiza Massiah aged 61 years.
5585	16 Tebet	1825	20 January	Moses son of Abraham Israel Keys
5585	13 Sebat	1825	1 February	Luna wife of Phineas Nunes aged 54 years

*Daniel of Naphtali Pass married 20.101819 Sarah of Moses de Castro

5585	21 Sevan	1825	8 December	Abigail of Mordecai Massiah
5585	27 Sevan	1825	13 December	Sarah of David Massiah
5586	27 Sebat	1826	14 February	Hisquiau Isaac Rodrigues Miranda
5586	15 Adar	1826	22 February	Parnas Phineas Nunes aged 71 years
5586	3 Sevan			Zachariah Bar Menahem
5586	17 Elel	1826	19 September	Benjamin of Jacob Israel Nunes
5587	23 Nisan	1827	19 April	Sarah wife of Isaac Lealtad aged 52 years.
5587	21 Yiar	1827	18 May	David of Isaac Lindo aged 64 years
5587	5 Elel	1827	21 August	Jacob of Benjamin Israel Nunes
5588	1 Hesvan	1827	22 October	Jacob Simmons
5588	3 Adar	1828	17 February	Miss Luna of Benjamin Israel Nunes aged 81 years
5588	5 Adar	1828	19 February	Sarah of Joshua Massiah
5588	26 Nisan	1828	10 April	Levinia Haya de Isaac Lopez Brandon
5588	24 Tamus	1828	6 July	Judith wife of Joshua Levi
5588	23 Ab	1828	3 August	Miss Deborah of Benjamin Israel Nunes aged 70 years
5589	10 Tisri	1828	18 September	Mrs. Esther Gar(c)ia
5589	29 Tisri	1828	8 October	Leah wife of Daniel Moses Lobo aged 24 years 2 months and 15 days
5589	7 Hesvan	1828	15 October	Isaac child of Mordecai Lealtad
5589	21 Yiar	1829	24 May	Rebecca of Simon Barrow (B.R: Baruch)
5590	8 Tisri	1829	5 October	Napthteli child of Daniel Pass
5590	24 Tamus	1830	15 July	Isaac Hisquiau Da Costa aged 51 years
5590	10 Ab	1830	30 July	Henry son of Judah Aarons
5591	29 Yiar	1831	12 May	Jacob of David Valverde
5591	21 Sevan	1831	1 June	Alfred son of Abraham Rodrigues Brandon
5591	23 Sevan	1831	4 June	Miss Hannah Ullao
5591	25 Sevan	1831	6 June	Parnas Abraham Rodrigues Brandon aged 65 years
5591	2 Elul	1831	11 August	Miss Jail of Jacob Pinheiro aged 71 years

5591	2 Elul	1831	11 August	Sarah of Isaac and Leah Lealtad aged 27 years
5592	10 Adar	1832	1 February	Moses son of Daniel Pass
5592	10 Sevan	1832	8 June	Mordechay of Isaac and Leah Lealted
5593	20 Tamus	1833	7 July	Daniel son of Naphteli Pass De Leon
5594	Kislev	1833	December	Daniel Pass
5594	11 Kislev	1833	November	Haim of Isaac & Leah Lealtad
5594	23 Sevan	1834	30 June	Isaac de Abraham Lealtad
5594	14 Ab	1833	19 August	David son of Raphael and Judy Lindo
5595	17 Hesvan	1834	19 Nove	Judith of Isaac and Sarah Lealtad.
5596	27 Adar	1836	16 March	Hirschell Elkin child of Joseph Hart aged 6 months and 13 days
5596	10 Yiar			Miriam of Judah Eleazar Levi
5596	28 Sevan	1836	13 June	Rachel De Paiza aged 103 years (B.R: 102)
5596	17 Ab	1836	1 August	Miss Elizabeth Hart aged 51 years
5597	5 Tisri	1836	16 September	Michael son of Joshua and Judith Levi aged 12 years 8 months and 18 days.
5597	15 Nisan	1837	19 April	Edward child of Joshua and Hannah Hart aged 3 years 1 month and 27 days.
5597	26 Nisan	1837	1 May	Jacob Da Costa child of Hart and Sarah Miriam Lyon aged 4 years 6 months and 15 days. *
5598	16 Hesvan			Isaac of Isaac Lindo
5598	18 Sebat	1838	13 February	Rachel daughter of Isaac and Leah Lealtad
5598	19 Yiar	1838	14 May	Parnas Meyer son of Benjamin Abraham(s) aged 56 years
5598	7 Tamus (B.R. 18)	1838	1 July	Elias Rodrigues Miranda aged 39 years. (Elias of Hisquiau Isaac Rodrigues Miranda married 3rd March 1833 Rachel of Jacob Frois de Meza)

* *Hart Lyon married 8.4.1829 Miriam Sarah Da Costa.*

5598	4 Ab	1838	25 July	Miss Leah Da Costa de Andrada
5599	5 Iyar	1839	19 April	Miss Jail of Isaac Israel Nunes
5599	5 Sevan	1839	18 May	Raphael of Moses and Sarah Lindo aged 46 years and 6 months
5601	18 Tisri	1840	14 (B.R:15) October	Leah of Isaac and Sarah Lealtad
5601	24 Adar	1841	17 March	Julia child of Jacob and Esther Abarbanel Lindo
5601	29 Tamus	1841	18 July	Isaac Cardoso Baeza
5602	21 Tisri	1841	6 October	Jacob Peynado Alvares Correa
5604	28 Hesvan	1843	22 November	Jacob of Isaac and Sarah Lealtad
5604	30 Elul	1844	13 September	Isaac Aarons child of Jacob and Clara Lewis aged 2½ months
5606	17 Nisan	1846	14 April	Gabriel name changed to Michael child of Jacob and Clara Lewis
5606	27 Nisan	1846	24 April	Judith widow of Raphael Lindo
5605	8 Ab	1846	31 July	Isaac of Moses Lopez
5607	14 Adar	1847	1 March	Esther widow of Myer Abrahams
5607	25 Tamus	1847	9 July	Rachel widow of David Lindo
5609	23 Hesvan	1848	19 November	Jael widow of Daniel Pass (daughter of Moses Pinheiro)
5610	11 Kisliv	1849	26 November	Abigail of Isaac and Sarah Lealtad
5610	12 Sevan	1852	30 May	Moses of Joseph Tolano aged 38½ years
5612	19 Tamus	1852	6 July	Leah widow of Moses Pinheiro aged 96 years
5612	9 Ab	1852	25 July	Rahel widow of Elias Rodrigues Miranda aged 35 years and 8 months
5613	1 Yiar	1853	9 May	Hazah Samuel Elias son of Elias and Hannah Daniels aged 48 years
5613	6 Elul	1853	9 September	Isaac Valverde aged 77 years
5614	24 Tisri	1853	26 October	Esther of Isaac and Leah Lealtad aged 53 years
5614	11 Sevan	1054	7 June	Lewis Samuel (died of cholera)

5614	28 Sevan	1854	24 June	Moses child of Lewis and Leah Catharine Samuel
5615	25 Tebet	1855	16 January	Esther Nunes aged 86 years
5618	15 Elul	1856	7 September	Rachel child of Ephraim Joseph Polack aged 6 months
5621	10 Tisri	1860	26 September	Parnas Sampson de Abraham Shannon aged 60 years
5623	3 Elul	1853	18 August	Sarah widow of Moses Lobo aged 92 years
5629	18 Adar	1869	1 March	Abigail widow of Isaac Lobo
5630	25 Ab	1870	22 August	Reyna of Isaac and Leah Lealtad
5631	1 Tisri	1870	25 September	Moses D'Azevedo son Isaac and Abigail Lobo aged 35 (Isaac Lobo, son of Moses Lobo married 26 March 1834 Abigail, daughter of Benjamin Cohen d'Azevedo)
5635	19 Ab	1875	19 August	Samuel son of Moses Myers aged 45 years 1 month and 19 days
5637	17 Tebet	1877	2 January	Moses son of Marks Schloss (of Surinam) aged 34 years 2 months and 2 days died at 5 after 5 a.m.
5638	23 Yiar	1878	26 May*	Benjamin son Moses and Hannah Cohen D'Azevedo died at St. Pierre Martinique at 2 of a.m. aged 62 years 6 months and ?
5641	13 Tamus	1881	10 July	5 p.m. Reyna widow of Benja. C. D'Azevedo died at St. Pierre Martinique aged
5642	14 Tisri	1881	7 October	1 a.m. Philip son of Moses and Leah Rubins aged 75 years
5640	12 Hesvan	1879	29 October	Sophia widow of Samuel Elias Daniels died at Philadelphia U.S.A. aged 65 years 1 month and 28 days
5646	8 Sebat	1886	14 January	Solomon Baber Isaacs (B.R: died in London).

*Interred at Barbadoes on the 14th February 1883 corresponding
with the Eve of the 18th Sebat 5644.

APPENDIX II

Another record of burials commences at page 978 of the bound volume, from which the following additional names and information have been extracted.

Page 978

5581	3 Sevan	1821	13 June	Hannah wife of David Aboab Furtado
5582	4 Tebet	1821	28 December	Abraham Lindo (Parnas Presidente)
5585	11 Kislev	1824	1 December	Isaac Depiza Massiah (Parnas Presidente)
5586	1 Sebat	1826	9 January	Judah Serug a Cohen
5589	13 Tisri	1828	21 September	Miher (Mehir) of Joseph A Cohen Belinfante
5588	21 Ab	1828	2 August	Joshuah de Jacob a Levi
5588	11 Hesvan	1828	20 October	Hazan Abraham Israel Keys *
5589	22 Sebat	1829	26 January	Isaac Haim a Levi
5591	12 Sevan	1831	24 May	Hannah D. Haim Isaac a Levi
				Isaac Baruch Lousada
				Abraham De Naphtali Pass De Leon
5592	18 Tamus	1832	16 July	Judah Eleazar a Levi
5594	24 Sevan	1834	1 July	Isaac Lealtad aged 76 years and 6 months
5598	7 Tamus	1838	30 June	Leah of Abraham De Leon aged 75 years
5601	27 Iyar	1841	18 May	Abraham of Solomon De Leon (home St. Croix)
5603	9 Hesvan	1842	31 October	E. H. Hacham Ashalem Revd. Solomon Hershell (in London)
5608	27 Tebet	1848	2 January	Benjamin Elkin aged 65 years (died in London)
5600	26 Sebat	1840	31 January	Sarah wife of Benjamin Elkin 46 years §

---

* *Abraham Israel Keys married 30.1.1811 Jael de Moses Rodrigues Brandon.*

§ *Sarah de Jacob Levi married Benjamin Elkin 30 January 1811.*

5609	29 Adar	1849	23 March	Hananel de Castro (BR: P.B.) aged 54 years, in London
5610	6 Elul		23 August	L.M. Lobo in Philadel- phia aged 44 years
5610	18 Elul	1850	26 August	Isaac of Moses Lobo aged 43 years and 2½ months
5614	3 Ab	1854	28 July	Jacob Jessurun D'Olivayra aged (in Soufrière, St. Lucia)
5615	16 Tamus	1855	12 December	Isaac Lopez Brandon (New York)
5618	15 Elul	1856	7 September	Rachel Polack aged 8 months
5621	10 Tisri	1860	26 September	Sampson Shannon aged 62 years
5622	8 Kislev	1861	11 November	Moses de Benjamin Cohen D'Azevedo p.p. K.K.N.I. Philadelphia
5625	19 Sebat	1865	15 February	Isaac de Benjamin Cohen D'Azevedo, St. K.(itts?) (B.R.: S. Thomas)
5628	28 Iyar	1868	19 May	Julia wife of David Baeza Junr., Surinam
5627	17 Sebat	1867	23 January	Sarah wife of Daniel Moses Lobo, Philadel- phia*
5620	30 Tebet	1859	26 December	Hazan Ephraim Joseph Polack - Surinam
5576	8 Elul			Daniel de Benjamin Cohen D'Azevedo aged 17 years
5630	2 Tamus	1870	1 July	David Moses Cordoza Baeza died in Surinam, July 1st 1870 69 years and 10 months
5630	6 Sebat	1870	8 January	Abraham son of Samuel Isaac and Rachel Finzi died at Philadelphia U.S.A. aged 69 years and 9 months
5645	4th day of Passover		Friday morning, ½ past 4,	Judith daughter of Moses Cohen D'Azevedo, widow of Abraham Finzi died at Philadelphia U.S.A. aged 68 years and 28 days §

---

* *David Moses Lobo married Jan. 15 1834 Sarah de Samuel I. Finzi.*

§ *Abraham son of Samuel Finzi married March 26 1834 Judith daughter of Moses Cohen d'Azevedo.*

APPENDIX III

Additional names from the original Burial Register kept
by the Congregation, now Bevis Marks MS 325

5452	19 Yiar			Abigail de Fonseca
5461	28 Adar			David son of Pinhas Abarbanel
5462	15 Sebat	1701-2		Leah wife of Jacob Baruch Louzado
5464	14 Adar			Sarah daughter of Emanuel Israel
5465	3 Sevan			Mrs. Rebecca Valverde
5483	6 Nisan			Moses son of Jacob Frois
5496	10 Nisan	1736	9 March	Abraham Haim Israel de Peiza
5513	10 Tisri	1752	17 September	Mrs. Hanah Nunes Castello aged 28 years and 4 months
5516	14 Tamus	1756	12 July	Jacob Valverde aged 43 years
5522	15 Ab	1762	3 August	Lunah Arrabas
5525	26 Tisri	1764	23 October	Deborah wife of Jacob de Fonseca aged 55 years
5540	13 Ab			Leah Aboah Furtado, aged 64 years
5557	17 Elul	1797	8 September	Hazan Israel Abaddy
5572	16 Kislev			Simha Abarbanel
5572	13 Nisan			Daniel Ullao
5649	8 Nisan	1889	9 April	Anna Baeza (born Levi) widow of D.M.C. Baeza, daughter of Joshua and Judith Levi aged 72 years 3 months and 18 days – buried at Westbury cemetery
5662	13 Kislev	1901	24 November	Miriam (born Lobo) widow of Jacob Abarbanel Lindo aged 62 years, 1 month and 2 days
5666	12 Elul	1906	7.45 p.m. 1 September	Eleanor Jane daughter of David Moses and Anna Baeza, née Levi aged 59 years 6 months and 20 days, buried at Westbury cemetery by C.D. Davies
5685	Tamus	1925	9 July	Joshua Baeza son of David Moses Cordoza and Anna Baeza née Levi aged 82 years six months and twentyfive days.

INDEX

OF

PERSONAL NAMES

NOTES

The tombstones have been numbered consecutively. Numbers having three digits or less denote a reference to the individual tombstones.

The Roman figures I, II & III denote a reference to entries in Appendices I, II & III respectively; numbers having four digits denote a reference to the (Jewish) year of burial. References to Introd., refer to the Introduction & Preface.

References to persons mentioned on tombstones other than their own, and to persons mentioned in the Burial Register otherwise than in respect of their own burial, appear in parentheses.

The following abbreviations have been used: for father (f), wife (w), son (s), daughter (d), husband (h), mother (m), child (c), B.R. = Burial Register, als. = alias, p.p. = Parnas President, K.K.N.I. = Kahal Kados Nidhe Israel, i.e. Barbados Congregation.

*   *   *

A

Aarons: *see also* Lewis
  Hanah (w of Judah), I, 5577
  Henry (s of Judah), I, 5590
  Isaac (c of Jacob & Clara
    Lewes), I, 5604
  Judah (h of Hanah, I, 5577);
    (f of Henry, I, 5590)

Abaddy:
  Abigail (w of Israel, *Hazan*),
    268
  Israel, *Hazan* (h of Abigail,
    268), III, 5557

Abarbanel:
  Benjamin, 365; (f of Joseph,
    I, 5532)

Abarbanel: *(continued)*
  David (s of Pinhas), III, 5467
  Joseph (c of Benjamin & Judith),
    I, 5532
  Joseph (f of Pinhas Hisquiau,
    144); 347; (h of Sarah,
    346)
  Judith (m of Joseph, I, 5532)
  Leah (w of Pinhas), 37
  Pinhas (h of last), 37: (f of
    David, III, 5461)
  Pinhas Hisquiau (s of Joseph
    & Sarah, B.R.: of
    Joseph & Sarah Abraham)
    144

Abarbanel: *(continued)*
Sarah (m of Pinhas Hisquiau), 144
Simha, III, 5572

Abarbanel Lindo:
Esther (m of Julia), I, 5601
Jacob (f of Julia), I, 5601
(s of David & Sarah of London), 115
Julia (c of Jacob & Esther), I, 5601
Perla (d of Jacob & Esther), 112
Miriam (w of Jacob), III, 5662

Abinun Lima:
Haim (f or h of Rachel), I, 5568
Rachel (de Haim), I, 5568

Aboab:
David, *Merchant*, 356
Moses, 363

Aboab Cordoza:
Hannah (w of Samuel), I, 5454
Samuel (h of Hannah), I, 5454

Aboab Furtado:
David (h of Hannah), II, 5581
David, *Merchant*, (h of Esther, 74), 75
Emanuel, 8 a.
Esther (w of David), 74
Esther (w of Isaac), 49
Hannah (w of David), II, 5581
Isaac (h of Esther), 49
Leah, III, 5540

Abraham(s):
Benjamin (f of Meyer), I, 5598
Esther (w of Meyer), I, 5607
Meyer, *Parnas* (s of Benjamin) I, 5598; (h of Esther), I, 5607

Abudiente (or Gideon):
Abraham (s of Gideon), 189: (h of Rachel, 190)
Gideon (f of Abraham, 189)
Pagdiel, *B.R.:* Rachel, 187
Rachel (w of Abraham), 190
Rowland, Introd. p. x
Sampson, Introd. p. x.

Acosta, David de, Introd. p. 5

Aguila:
Dr. Daniel Haim de, 60

Alvares:
Hanah, 212

Alvares Correa:
Jacob Peynado, I 5602

Andrade: *see also* Costa de Andrade
Rebecca de, 148

Antunes:
Esther, 164

Arrobas:
Lunah, III, 5522. Introd. p viii

Azevedo: *see also* Finzi, Lobo
Abigail Cohen d', (d of Benjamin, m of Isaac Lobo, I, 5631)
Benjamin Cohen (f of Menasseh Cohen d', 128); (f of Daniel Cohen d', I, 5576)
Benjamin Cohen d', (f of Moses Cohen d', II, 5622); (f of Isaac Cohen d', II, 5625)
Benjamin Cohen d', *died at St. Pierre Martinique** (s of Moses & Hanah Cohen d'), 121°, 121a; I, 5638, (h of Reyna d', I, 5641)
Daniel Cohen d' (s of Benjamin Cohen d'), II, 5576

Interred at Barbados

Azevedo: *(continued)*
Hannah [*died ?*] *in Phila-*
delphia (w of M[oses]
d'), II, 5609
Hannah Cohen d', (m of
Benjamin Cohen d',
121, 121a)
Isaac Cohen d', *St. K.* [sic]
(de Benjamin Cohen d'),
II, 5625
Judith Cohen d' (m of
Menasseh Cohen d', 128)
Judith Cohen d' *died at*
Philadelphia (d of
Moses Cohen d', w of
Abraham Finzi d'),II,
5645
Menasseh Cohen d' (son of
Benjamin & Judith
Cohen d'), 128
M[oses] d' (h of Hannah d',
II, 5609)
Moses d' (s of Isaac and
Abigail Lobo), I,
5631
Moses Cohen d' (f of
Benjamin Cohen d',
121, 121a)
Moses Cohen d', *p.p. K.K.*
N.I.; in Philadelphia
(de Benjamin Cohen d'),
II, 5622; (f of Judith
Cohen d' - w of
Abraham Finzi, II,
5645)
Reyna d', *died at St. Pierre,*
Martinique (w of Ben-
jamin Cohen d'), I,
5641

B

Baber Isaacs:
Isaac, *died in Tobago**
(s of Judah), 110
Judah (f of Isaac, 110)
Solomon, I, 5646

Baeza: *see also* Cordoza Baeza
David *Junr.* (h of Julia, II,
5628)
Julia, *of Surinam* (w of
David *Junr.*), II,
5628

Baeza *see* Cordoza Baeza

* *Interred in Barbados*

Bar Menahem:
Zachariah, I 5586

Barrasse, Abraham, Introd.
p.x.

Barrow: *(Baruch)*
Bella (w of Simon), 281
Haim, *Merchant*, 265, (h of
Sarah, I, 5584)
Joseph (h of Sarah, I, 5574)
Rebecca (w or d of Simon), I,
5589
Sarah (w of Joseph), I, 5574
Sarah (w or d of Haim), I,
5584
Simon, 280; (h of Bella, 281)
Simon (f or h of Rebecca, I,
5589)

Barscoe (= *Belasco ?*), Introd.
p.x

Baruch Henriques:
Abraham, 5; (f of Isaac, 211)
Isaac (s of Abraham), 211
Rachel, 131
Sarah, I, 5495

Baruch Louzada:
Aaron, 17; (h of Rachel, 18)
Aaron, I, 5584
Aaron (h of Esther Sarah, 11)
Daniel, *Hazan*, 289
David, *Hazan, Merchant*, 312;
(h of Sarah, 313); (f of
Jael Leah, 314)
Eliau (s of Jacob & Rebecca),
208
Emanuel (h of Esther, 286),
287
Emanuel (h of Rachel, 288)
Ephraim, 294
Esther, 295
Esther, I, 5569
Esther (w of Emanuel), 286
Esther Sarah (w of Aaron) 11
Isaac [no date], II
Isaac (s of Jacob & Rebecca),
209
Jacob (h of Rachel, 146)

186

Baruch Louzada *(continued)*
   Jacob (h of Rebecca, 163);
      (f of Eliau, 208);
      (f of Isaac, 209)
   Jael (w of Solomon), 69
   Jael Leah (d of David and
      Sarah), 314
   Jeremiah, 327; (h of Sarah,
      328)
   Jeremiah (h of Rachel Hanah,
      143)
   Julio Raphael, I, 5512
   Leah (w of Jacob, III, 5462)
   Moses, 217
   Rachel (w of Aaron), 18
   Rachel (w of Emanuel), 288
   Rachel (w of Jacob), 146
   Rachel Hanah (w of Jeremiah),
      143
   Rebecca, I, 5568
   Rebecca (w of Jacob), 163;
      (m of Isaac, 209)
   Sarah (w of David), 313;
      (m of Jael Leah, 314)
   Sarah (w of Jeremiah), 328
   Solomon, I, 5506
   Solomon Raphael, 68; (h of
      Jael, 69)

Belasco: *see also* Barscoe
   Abraham (f of Moses, 126)
   Moses, *Hazan*, (son of
      Abraham), 126

Belinfante:
   Deborah (widow [w ?] of
      Mehir a Cohen), 1
   Joseph a Cohen (f of Mehir,
      II, 5589)
   Joseph Haim a Cohen, I,
      5575
   Mehir a Cohen, *Mohel and
      Hazan* (h of Deborah ;
      1); (f of Rebecca,
      270); (h of Sarah,
      321); 322
   Mehir (s of Joseph a Cohen),
      II, 5589
   Rebecca (d of Mehir a
      Cohen), 270
   Sarah (widow [second w] of
      Mehir a Cohen), 321

Belisario: *see* Mendes Belisario

Brandao *see* Brandon

Brandon: *see also* Lopez Brandon;
      Rodrigues Brandon
   Abraham, *Hazan* (de David),
      I, 5573
   Abraham, *Merchant*, (h of
      Esther Abigail, 2);
      (h of Sarah, 92); 335
   Bathsheba (de David), I,
      5580
   David, I, 5557; (f of Abraham,
      I, 5573); (f or h of
      Bathsheba, I, 5580)
   David (s of David Israel &
      Leah), I, 5567
   David Israel (f of David,
      I, 5567)
   Esther Abigail (widow [w ?]
      of Abraham), 2
   Leah (m of David, I, 5567)
   Moses (h of Rachel, 70)
   Moses Pereira, I, 5478
   Rachel (w of Moses), 70
   Sarah (w [widow ?, second w ?]
      of Abraham), 92

Bueno Henriques:
   Abraham (h of Rachel, 147)
   Daniel, 161
   Rachel (w of Abraham), 147

Bueno Frances:
   Jacob (h of Rebecca, 58);
      145
   Rebecca (w [widow ?] of Jacob),
      58

Burgos: *see also* Burgos Mas-
      siah, Burgos de Piza
   Aaron Haim, 30
   David, *Merchant*, 373; 245
   Deborah, 245; *B.R. possibly:*
      David, I, 5448
   Esther (w of Jeremiah), 52
   Jeremiah (h of Esther, 52);
      (f of Samuel, 198)
   Jeremiah Emanuel, 54
   Judith (w [widow ?] of Moses),
      I, 5577
   Luna (widow of Mordecay), 99

Burgos *(continued)*
Mordecay (h of Luna, 99)
Moses, 324; (h of Judith, I, 5577)
Moses (h of Rachel, 374)
Rachel (widow of Moses), 374
Samuel (s of Jeremiah),198
Illegible, 168

Burgos Massiah:
Mordecai, I, 5561

Burgos de Piza:
Mordecai, 98

Burnett: *see also* Lobo
Edward (s of Isaac and Abigail Lobo), I, 5610

Buzaglo:
Abraham (h of Simha, 284); I, 5560
Simha (w of Abraham), 284

C

Caceres
Esther de, 184
Brothers, Introd. p. vii

Cahanet: *see also* Peyxoto
Deborah Sarah (w of Moses Cohen Peyxoto), 150

Campos:
Abraham Hisquiau de, 95
Isaac de (h of Rachel Hana de, 93)
Rachel Hanah de (w of Isaac de), 93
Rebecca de (widow of Samuel Raphael de), 140
Samuel Raphael de (h of Rebecca de, 140); 141

Campos Pereira:
Isaac de (h of Sarah Leah de, 94)
Sarah Leah de (w of Isaac de), 94

Capes: *(? Campos)*
See Abraham Hisquiau de, 95

Carco:
Emanuel, I, 5453

Cardoso:
Haim, 200

Cardoza Baeza, *see* Cordoza Baeza

Carigal:
Raphael Haim Isaac, *Rabbi*, 256; Introd., p. x

Carvalho: *see also* Nunes Carvalho
Jacob Haim, *Merchant*, 306
Rachel, 305
Rachel Sarah, 139
Rebecca, I 5573

Caseres *see* Caceres

Castello: *see also* Nunes Castello
David (f of Raphael, 323)
Hannah (or Sarah), 325
Yosiyahu Raphael (c of David), 232

Castro: *see* Crasto
Moses de (f of Sarah m Daniel Pass) I, 5580

Chillão, Chillon
Abraham, Introd., p.vi
David, 170

Ciudad Real: *see* Rodrigues Ciudad Real

Clarke: .
Mary Elizabeth, III, 5667

Cohen: *see also* Azevedo, Belinfante, Peyxoto, Sarug
Myor, 372

Cordoza: *see* Aboab Cordoza, Cardoso

Cordoza Baeza: *see* Daniels

Anna (widow of David Moses), III, 5649, *nee* Levi

David Moses, *died in Surinam* (h of Rachel, 125); (f of Eleanor Jane, III, 5666), II, 5630

Eleanor Jane (d of David Moses & Anna), III, 5666

Isaac, I, 5601

Joshua, (s of David Moses & Anna), III, 5685

Rachel (w of David Moses), 125

Correia : *see* Alvares Correa

Costa: *see also* Lyon; Mendes da Costa

Benjamin Hisquiau (Henriques) da (h of Sarah da, I, 5578)

Esther Sarah da, 318

Isaac Hisquiau da, I, 5590

Jacob da (c of Hart & Sarah Miriam Lyon), I, 5597

Sarah da (w of Benjamin Hisquiau Henriques da), I, 5578

Costa de Andrade:

Abraham da (h of Esther da, 360); 361

Anjelah da (w [widow ?] of David Hisquiau da), 9

Daniel da, *Hazan*, I, 5562

David Hisquiau da, *Hazan*, (h of Anjelah da, 9); 63

Esther da (widow of Abraham da), 360

Leah, I, 5598

Sarah da, 319

Costa Gomes:

Ester (de Jacob) da, 124

Jacob da (f or h of Esther da, 124)

Coutinho:

Moses Haim, 33

Crasto:

Benjamin de (husband of Esther-de, 275)

Esther de (w of Benjamin de), 275

Gabriel de *Junr.*, 276

Hananel de, [*died ?*] *in London*, II, 5609

Lebana de, I, 5571

D

Daniels:

Annie Marie (c of Edward Samuel & (Sophia) Mary), 109

Edward Samuel, (s of Samuel & Sophia), 108; Introd. p.

Elias (f of Samuel Elias, I, 5613)

Hannah (m of Samuel Elias, I, 5613); (widow of Elias, w of Moses Cohen d'Azevedo)

Mary Elizabeth, (als. Sophia or Sophia Mary), 108; m of Annie Marie, 109)

Samuel Edward (h of Sophia Mary, 108)

Samuel Elias, *Hazan*, 122; (s of Elias & Hannah), I, 5613; (h of Sophia, I, 5640); (f of Edward Samuel, 108)

Sophia (d of Joshua & Jane Levi, widow of Samuel Elias) *died at Philadelphia*, I, 5640; (m of Edgar Samuel, 108)

Sophia Mary (m of Annie Marie) alias Mary Elizabeth Clarke, (widow of Samuel Edward), 108

De Meza: *see* Frores de Meza

Dias:

David Ys[hac], 219

Emanuel Israel (f of Sarah, 169)

Judica Israel, 185

190

Frances: *see also* Bueno
    Frances
  Rebeccah, 86

Franco Nunes:
  Esther, 331
  Esther (w of Moses), 79
  Jacob, *Merchant*, 25, (h of
    Lunah, 26)
  Lunah (w of Jacob), 26
  Moses (h of Rachel, 46)
  Moses, *Merchant*, (h of
    Esther, 79); 80
  Rachel (w of Moses), 46

Franks, Benjamin, Introd.
    pp.

Frois:
  Jacob, *Merchant*, 300; (h
    of Jehudith, 301);
    (f of Moses, III,
    5483)
  Jehudith, *B.R.:* Julia (w
    of Jacob), 301
  Joshua, I, 5534
  Moses (s of Jacob, III,
    5483)

Frois (or Frores) de Meza:
  Jacob (h of Rachel, 127)
  Jacob (f of Rachel
    Elias Rodrigues Miran-
    da, I, 5598)
  Rachel (w of Jacob), 127

Frores de Meza: *see* Frois de
    Meza

Furtado: *see* Aboab Furtado

G

Gabay Letob:
  David (h of Rebecca, 165)
  Rebecca (w of David), 165

Gabay Risson:
  Aaron, 248
  Isaac (h of Judith, 158);
    230
  Judith (de Isaac), 158
  Sarah, 233

Gaon:
  Esther, 243

Garcia:
  Esther, I, 5589
  Isaac, 341; (h of Rachel,
    342)
  Rachel (w of Isaac), 342

Garcia de Paz;
  Jacob Hisquiau, 317

Gideon, *see* Abudiente

Gomes: *see also* Costa Gomes
  Benjamin (h of Esther
    Rachel, 71)
  Benjamin (h of Hester
    Abigail, 3)
  Deborah (m of Moses, 88)
  Esther Rachel (w of Ben-
    jamin), 71
  Hester Abigail (w of
    Benjamin), 3
  Isaac (f of Moses, 88)
  Moses (s of Isaac and
    Deborah), 88
  Raphael, I, 5571

Gomez: *see* Gomes

Gomes Henriques:
  Abraham (h of Jael, 332);
    333
  Isaac (h of Venida, 29)
  Jael (widow of Abraham),
    332
  Jacob Hisquiau, 334
  Venida (w of Isaac); 29

H

Haedo: *see* Lindo de Haedo

Halevy: *see* Levy

Hamis:
  Moses, 240

Hart: *see also* Elkin
  Edward (c of Joshua and
    Hannah), I, 5597

Hart: *(continued)*
  Elizabeth, I, 5596
  Hannah (m of Edward, I, 5597)
  Joseph (f of Hirshell Elkin,
    I, 5596)
  Joshua (f of Edward, I, 5597)
  Moses (f of Samuel, 282)
  Samuel, *Merchant,* (s of
    Moses), 282

Hayaya:
  Joshua (h of Sarah, 215);
    216
  Sarah (widow of Joshua),
    215

Hayne, Samuel, Introd. pp ix - xiii

Henriques: *see also* Baruch
         Henriques; Flores;
         Gomes Henriques;
         Jessurun Henriques;
         Julian; Pereira
         Henriques; da Costa
  Abigail, 330
  Rachel Esther, 247

Hershell:
  Solomon *E.H.* [sic=He-?]
    Hacham Ashalem Revd.,
    II, 5603

I

Idanha: *see also* Ydana
  Rachel, 196

Isaacs: *see* Baber Isaacs

Israel: *see also* Piza
  David, 250
  Sarah (d of Emmanuel), II,
    5464

J

Jacob, Abraham, Introd. p

Jessurun Henriques:
  Ephraim, 251

Jessurun de Leon:
  Daniel (husband of Sarah,
    35)
  Sarah (w of Daniel), 35

Jessurun Mendes:
  Abraham (s of Joseph and
    Jael), 207
  David, 221
  David (son of Joseph and
    Jael), 205
  Jacob (s of Joseph and
    Jael), 231
  Jael (m of David, 205);
    (m of Abraham, 207);
    (m of Rachel, 210);
    (m of Jacob, 231)
  Joseph, (alias Lewis Dias)
    Introd.,
    (f of David, 205);
    (f of Moses, 206);
    (f of Abraham, 207);
    (f of Rachel, 210);
    (f of Jacob, 231)
  Moses (s of Joseph & Jael),
    206
  Rachel (d of Joseph & Jael),
    210

Jessurun D'Olivayra:
  Jacob [died ?] in *Soufrière,*
    St. Lucia, II, 5614

Joseph:
  Eve (widow of Jacob), 283
  Jacob, 277; (h of Eve, 283)

Julian:
  Moses Henriques, *Hazan,* I,
    5581

K

Keys:
  Abraham Israel, *Hazan,* (f
    of Nathaniel, I, 5584);
    (f of Moses, I, 5585);
    II, 5588
  Moses (s of Abraham Israel),
    I, 5585
  Nathaniel (s of Abraham
    Israel), I, 5584

Kidd, Captain, Introd., p. xi

L

Lealtad:
  Abigail (d of Isaac & Sarah),
    I, 5610

Lealtad: *(continued)*

Abraham (f of Isaac, I, 5594); II, 5594

Esther (d of Isaac & Leah), I, 5614

Haim (s of Isaac & Leah), I, 5594

Hannah, I, 5563

Isaac (de Abraham), I, 5594; II, 5594

Isaac (c of Mordecai), I, 5589

Isaac (h of Leah, I, 5564);
(f of Sarah, I, 5591);
(f of Mordecai, I, 5592);
(f of Haim, I, 5594);
(f of Rachel, I, 5598);
(f of Esther, I, 5614);
(f of Reyna, I, 5630)

Isaac (h of Sarah, I, 5587);
(f of Judith [?], I, 5595);
(f of Leah), I, 5601);
(f of Jacob, I, 5604);
(f of Abigail, I, 5610)

Jacob (s of Isaac & Sarah), I, 5604

Judith (d of Isaac and Sarah), I, 5595

Leah (d of Isaac & Sarah), I, 5601

Leah (w of Isaac), I, 5564;
(m of Sarah, I, 5591);
(m of Mordecai, I, 5592); (m of Haim, I, 5594); (m of Rachel, I, 5598); (m of Esther, I, 5614); (m of Reyna, I, 5630)

Mordecai (f of Isaac, I, 5589)

Mordecai (s of Isaac & Leah), I, 5592

Rachel (d of Isaac & Leah), I, 5598

Reyna (s of Isaac & Leah), I, 5630

Samuel (f[?] of Isaac), I, 5595

Sarah (d of Isaac & Leah), I, 5591

Sarah (w of Isaac), I, 5587;
(m of Judith [?], I, 5595); (m of Leah, I, 5601); (m of Jacob, I, 5604); (m of Abigail, I, 5610)

Leao: *see* Leon

Leo: *see* Leon

Leon: *see also* Jessurun de Leon; Pass de Leon; Pereira de Leon; Rodrigues de Leon

Abraham de (f of Leah de, II, 5598)

Abraham de, *home St. Croix* (s of Solomon de), II, 5601

Daniel Joshua de (h of Sarah de, 35)

Isaac de (c of Matatia de), I, 5481

Leah de (w or d of Abraham de), II, 5598

Matatia de (f of Isaac de, I, 5481)

Moses Cohen de, I, 5435

Moses Hisquiau de, *Hazan*, 269

Sarah de (w of Daniel Joshua de), 35

Solomon de (f of Abraham de I, 5601; II, 5601)

Letob: *see also* Gabay Letob
Leah, 326

Levi:

Benjamin (c of Joshua), I, 5581

Hannah a (de Haim Isaac a), II, 5591

Haim Isaac a (f or h of Hannah a, II, 5591)

Isaac Haim a, II, 5589

Jacob a (f of Joshuah a, II, 5588)

Jacob Joseph, I, 5582

Joshuah a (s of Jacob a), II, 5588

Joshua (f of Rebecca, 113); (f of Sarah, 114); 116; (f of Benjamin, I, 5581); (h of Judith, I, 5588 and f of Anna Baeza, III, 5649); (f of Michael, I, 5597)

Judah Eleazar a, II, 5592; (f or h of Miriam a, I, 5596)

Levi: *(continued)*

Judith (m of Rebecca, 113);
(m of Sarah, 114); (w
of Joshua), I, 5588;
(m of Anna Baeza, III,
5649); (m of Michael,
I, 5597)

Michael (s .f Joshua and
Judith), I, 5597

Miriam (w or d of Judah
Eleazar), I, 5596

Rebecca (d of Joshua and
Judith), 113

Sarah (d of Joshua and
Judith), 114

Sophia (d of Joshua and
Jane) *see under*
Daniels

Levi Rezio: *see* Rezio

Levi Ximenes, *see* Ximenes

Levy:

Isaac (s of Moses), I,
5644

Isaac Hisquiau, *of London*,
(s of Pinhas), 137

Moses (f of Isaac, I, 5564)

Pinhas (f of Isaac Hisquiau,
137)

Lewis: *see also* Aarons

Clara (m of Isaac Aarons, I,
5604); (m of Gabriel,
I, 5606)

Gabriel, name changed to
Michael (c of Jacob &
Clara), I, 5606

Jacob (f of Isaac Aaron, I,
5604); (f of Gabriel,
I, 5606,)

Lima: *see* Abinun Lima

Lindo: *see also* Abarbanel
Lindo; Elkin; Lindo
de Haedo

Abraham *Junr.*, *Merchant of
London*, (de Jacob),
350

Abraham, *Parnas Presidente*
(s of David), I, 5582;
II, 5582

Abraham *Senr.*, *Merchant*
(de David), 320

Lindo: *(continued)*

Branca (w of Jacob), 351

David (f of Abraham, I,
5582; II, 5582); (f
of Jacob, I, 5584)

David (h of Rachel, I,
5607)

David (s of Isaac), I, 5587

David (son of Raphael and
Judy), I, 5594

David, *Merchant*, (f of
Isaac, 271); (f of
Abraham, *Senr.*, 320);
(h of Rachel, 352);
353

Elias (f of Isaac, I, 5598)

Isaac, I, 5567

Isaac (f of David, I, 5587)

Isaac (s of Elias), I, 5598

Isaac (s of David), 271

Isaac *Junr.*, I, 5566

Jacob (f of Abraham *Junr.*,
350); (h of Branca,
351)

Jacob (s of David), I, 5584

Jacob, *of London*, 115

Joseph Jacob, 259

(probably) Judith (widow
of Isaac), 273

Judith (widow of Raphael),
I, 5606; (m of David,
I, 5594)

Moses (f of Raphael, I,
5599)

Perla, (d of Jacob and
Esther Abarbanel), 112

Rachel (widow of David),
352

Rachel (widow of David), I,
5607

Raphael (f of David, I,
5594); (s of Moses and
Sarah), I, 5599; (h
of Judith, I, 5606)

Sarah (m of Raphael, I,
5599)

Lindo de Haedo, Jacob, 351

Lindon: *see* Lindo

Lion: *see* Leon

Lobo:
  Abigail (m of Edward Burnett,
    I, 5610); (widow of
    Isaac), I, 5629; (m of
    Moses D'Azevedo, I,5631)
  Daniel Moses (h of Leah,
    I, 5589)
  Daniel Moses (h of Sarah,
    II, 5627)
  David (f of Rachel m David
    M C Baeza), 125
  Isaac (f of Edward Burnett,
    I, 5610); II, 5610; (h
    of Abigail, I, 5629);
    (f of Moses D'Azevedo,
    I, 5631); (s of Moses
    Lobo, h of Abigail
    Cohen D'Azevedo), I,
    5631
  Leah (w of Daniel Moses),
    I, 5589
  L.M. (P.P.) [died] in
    Philadelphia, II,
    5610
  Miriam, widow of Jacob
    Abarbanel Lindo
  Sarah (widow of Moses), I,
    5623; (d of Samuel I.
    Finzi, II, 5627)
  Sarah, Philadelphia (w of
    Daniel Moses), II,
    5627

Lopez:
  David (h of Sarah Leah, 134)
  Deborah (w of Isaac Junr.),
    358
  Esther Hanah (w of Moses),
    96
  Hanah Esther, I, 5493
  Isaac, 357; (h of Deborah,
    358); (f of Mathias,
    369)
  Isaac (s of Moses), I, 5606
  Lebanah, I, 5567
  Mathias, 290
  Mathias (s of Isaac), 369
  Moses (f of Isaac, I, 5606)
  Moses (h of Esther Hanah,
    96)
  Moses (h of Rachel, 50)
  Moses (h of Rachel, 370)

Lopez: (continued)
  Moses of Speightstown,
    Parnas, 291; (h of
    Sarah, 293)
  Moses Senr., 151
  Rachel (w of Moses), 50
  Rachel (w of Moses), 370
  Sarah (widow of Moses),
    292
  Sarah Leah (w of David),
    134

Lopez Brandon:
  Isaac, New York (f or h
    of Levinia Haya, I,
    5588); II, 5615
  Lavinia Haya (de Isaac),
    I, 5588

Lopez Pereira:
  Abraham, 224

Louzada: see also Baruch
    Louzada
  Jacob (h of Leah, 153)
  Leah (wife of Jacob), 153

Luiz:
  Jacob, 159

Lurio:
  Haim Abraham, I, 5574

Lyon: see also Costa
  Hart (f of Jacob da Costa,
    I, 5597)
  Sarah Miriam (m of Jacob
    da Costa, I, 5597)

M

Marques: see Rodrigues Mar-
    ques

Massiah: see also Burgos
    Massiah; Piza Mas-
    siah; Messias
  Abigail (w or d of
    Mordecai), I, 5585
  Abraham (h of Rebecca, 302)
  Abraham, Merchant, 266;
    (f or h of Sarah, I,
    5584)

Massiah: *(continued)*
Abraham *Senr.*, (h of Rachel, 14)
Angel (w [widow ?] of Jacob) 73
Benjamin, *Hazan, Merchant, Mohel*, (h of Esther, 366); 367; (f of Mordecai, 371)
Daniel, 10; (h of Sarah, 61)
Daniel (s of Simeon & Sarah), 171
David (f or h of Sarah, I, 5585)
Deborah, 195
Esther, 267
Esther (widow of Benjamin), 366
Esther (widow of Judah), 304
Isaac, 15
Isaac, I, 5583
Jacob (h of Angel, 73); 194
Jacob (h of Rebecca, I, 5567)
Joshua (f or h of Sarah, I, 5588)
Judah, I, 5576
Judah (h of Esther, 304)
Mordecai (f or h of Abigail, I, 5585)
Mordecai (h or Sarah, 13); (f of Sarah, 160)
Mordecai (s of Benjamin), 371
Rachel, I, 5579
Rachel (w of Abraham *Senr.*), 14
Rebecca (w of Jacob), I, 5567
Rebecca (w of Abraham), 302
Samuel Moses, 8b.
Sarah, 101; (m of Daniel, 171)
Sarah (d of Mordecai and Sarah), 160
Sarah (w or d Abraham), I, 5584
Sarah (w or d David), I, 5585
Sarah (w or d Joshua), I, 5588
Sarah (w of Daniel), 61
Sarah (w of Mordecai), 13; (m of Sarah, 160)

Massiah: *(continued)*
Simeon, *Mohel,* 64; (f of Daniel, 171)

Medina:
Abraham de, 252
Solomon de, 188

Medina, *see* Robles de ---, --

Mendes: *see also* Jessurun Mendes
Abraham Aaron (s of Joseph), 186
Esther (d of Joseph), 237
Isaac (s of Joseph), 173
Joseph, 41; (f of Isaac, 173); (f of Abraham Aaron, 186); (f of Moses, 241); (f of Esther, 237)
Moses (de Solomon, h of Sarah Abigail, 32)
Moses (s of Joseph), 241
Sarah Abigail (w of Moses de Solomon), 32
Solomon (f of Moses, 32)

Mendes Belisario:
Abraham Hisquiau, 136

Mendes da Costa;
Abraham, I, 5553

Mercado:
Aaron de, 227
Abraham de, Introd., p. vi
David Raphael de, *Merchant,* 178

Messias, Abraham, Introd., p. vi

Meza: *see also* Fonseca Meza; Frois de Meza
Isaac de (h of Rachel de, 166); 172
Rachel de (widow of Isaac de), 166

Millado:
Isaac Haim, I, 5474

Miranda: *see* Rodrigues Miranda

Nunes: *(continued)*
Luna (m of Isaac Haim, 87)
Luna (d of Benjamin Israel),
I, 5588
Luna (w of Phineas), I,
5585
Moses (f of Isaac Haim, 87)
Moses (h of Abigail, 4)
Moses (h of Leah, 84)
Moses Haim (s of Abraham),
142
Phineas (h of Judith, I,
5546)
Phineas, *Merchant*, 310; (h
of Rebecca, 336)
Phineas, *Parnas* (h of Lunah,
I, 5585); I, 5586
Rebecca (widow of Phineas),
336
Sarah, I, 5463
Sarah (m of Beatrice, I,
5564)

Nunes Carvalho:
(probably) Benjamin, 138
Benjamin (c of David & Sarah),
130
David (f of Sarah, 130)
Sarah (c of David & Sarah),
130
Sarah (m of Sarah, 130)

Nunes Castello:
Angel (widow of Ephraim),
274
David, 272; (f of Sarah,
362)
David (h of Jael, 323)
David, *Merchant*, 149
Ephraim (h of Angel, 274)
Hanah, III, 5513
Jael (w of David), 323
Judith (widow of Moses Haim)
77
Moses Haim, 76; (h of
Judith, 77)
Rachel (m of Sarah, 362)
Sarah (d of David & Rachel),
362

O

Olivayra D': *see* Jessurun
D'Olivayra

P

Pacheco:
Abraham, I, 5472
Dynah, 203
Hisquiau, (h of Sarah, 62)
Jacob, 213
Rebecca, 214
Sarah (w of Hisquiau), 62

Pass:
Daniel (h of Sarah, I,
5580); (f of Miriam
Hanah, I, 5582); (f
of Naphtali, I, 5590);
(f of Moses, I, 5592);
I, 5594; (h of Jael,
I, 5609); (s of Naph-
tali and w of Sarah,
I, 5580)
Jael (widow [2nd w ?] of
Daniel), I, 5609
(Mary Ann) Miriam Hanah
(c of Daniel), I,
5582
Moses (s of Daniel), I,
5592
Naphtali (c of Daniel),
I, 5590; (f of Daniel,
I, 5580)
Sarah (w of Daniel), I,
5580; (d of Moses de
Castro)

Pass do Leon:
Abraham (de Naphtali), II
[no date]
Daniel (s of Naphtali), I,
5593
Naphtali (f of Abraham,
II [no date]); (f of
Daniel, I, 5593)

Paz: *see also* Garcia de Paz
Moses de, 344

Pazer: *see* Piza

Peiza: *see* Piza

Penha: *see also* Sarfatty de
  Penha
  Abraham Haim Israel de, I,
    5496
  Isaac de la (h of Luna de
    la, 55)
  Luna de la (w of Isaac de
    la), 55

Penna: *see* Penha

Pereira: *see also* Brandon;
    Campos Pereira; Lopez
    Pereira; Rodrigues
    Pereira
  Aaron Hisquiau, 135

Pereira Henriques:
  Aaron (f of Sarah, 329)
  Sarah (d of Aaron), 329

Pereira de Leon:
  Abraham (s of Moses, 174
  Benjamin (h of Sarah, 39);
    40
  Lebanah(wife [widow ?] of
    Matatia), 97
  Matatia Raphael, 91; (h of
    Lebanah, 97)
  Moses (f of Abraham, 174)
  Moses (f or h of Sarah Esther,
    236)
  Sarah (w of Benjamin), 39
  Sarah Esther (de Moses, 236

Pereyra: *see* Pereira

Peyxoto: *see also* Cahanet
  Moses Cohen (h of Deborah
    Sarah Cahanet, 150)

Pina: *see* Penha

Pinha: *see* Penha

Pinheiro:
  Aaron, *Parnas*, I, 5555
  Abraham Joshua, *Merchant*
    (h of Rebecca, 339);
    340
  David (f of Moses, 123);
    297; (h of Jael, 298)
  Esther (d of Jacob), 359

Pinheiro: *(continued)*
  Hanah (widow of Jacob),
    I, 5578
  Isaac, I, 5556
  Isaac (s of Jacob), I,
    5564
  Jacob (f of Esther, 359),
    I, 5563; (f of Isaac,
    I, 5564); (f of
    Joseph, I, 5575); (h
    of Hanah, I, 5578);
    (f of Lunah, I, 5585);
    (f of Jael, I, 5591)
  Jael (d of Jacob), I, 5591
  Jael (widow of David), 298
  Joseph (s of Jacob), I,
    5575
  Leah (widow of Moses), I,
    5612
  Lunah (d of Jacob), I, 5584
  Lunah (widow of Moses),
    348
  Moses (husband of Leah, I,
    5612)
  Moses (f of Jael m Daniel
    Pass, I, 5609)
  Moses (s of David) 123
  Moses, *Merchant*, 338; (h
    of Lunah, 348)
  Rachel, I, 5582
  Rebecca (widow of Abraham),
    339

Piza: *see also* Burgos de Piza
  Abraham de (s of Isaac
    Israel de), 199
  Abraham Haim Israel de, III,
    5496
  Abraham Israel de, 100
  Angel de (w of Emanuel de),
    I, 5555
  David de (s of Isaac Israel
    de), 83
  Emanuel de (h of Angel de,
    I, 5555)
  Isaac de, I, 5470
  Isaac Israel de (f of
    Abraham de, 199)
  Isaac Israel de (f of David
    de, 83); 275; (h of
    Rachel de, 258); (f
    of Moses de, 261)

199

Piza: *(continued)*
Jacob de, I, 5579
Moses de, 293
Moses de (h of Sarah de,
260); (de Isaac Israel
de), 261
Rachel de, I, 5596
Rachel de (w of Isaac
Israel de), 258
Sarah de (w of Moses de),
260
Sarah Simha Israel de, 235

Piza Massiah:
Israel de, *Hazan and Parnas
Presidente*, I, 5585,
II, 5585

Polack:
Ephraim Joseph, *Hazan,
Surinam*, (f of Rachel,
I, 5618); II, 5620
Rachel (c of Ephraim Joseph)
I, 5618 aged 6 years
[but in II, 5618 given
as 8 months]

Porto:
Sarah de, 343

R

Real: *see* Ciudad Real

Rezio:
Isaac Levi, 225
Jacob Abraham Levi, 226

Risson: *see* Gabay Risson

Rizio: *see* Rezio

Robles de Medina:
David (h of Hanah, 264)
Hanah (de David), 264

Rodrigues:
Esther, 181

Rodrigues Brandon:
Abraham, *Parnas*, I, 5591;
(f of Alfred, I,
5591)
Jael (d of Moses), II,
5588

Rodrigues Brandon: *(continued)*
Alfred (s of Abraham), I,
4491

Rodrigues Ciudad Real:
Sarah, 197

Rodrigues de Leon:
Hisquiau Jonah, 303
Moses Hisquiau, *Hazan*,
III, 5530

Rodrigues Marques:
Jacob, 57

Rodrigues Miranda:
Elias, I, 5598; (h of
Rachel, I, 5612)
Hisquiau Isaac, I, 5586:
(f of Elias, I, 5598)
Rachel (widow of Elias,
d of Jacob Frois de
Meza, I, 5598), I,
5612

Rodrigues Pereira:
Sarah, 44

Rodrigues Suares:
Solomon, 204

Rubins:
Leah (m of Philip, I,
5642)
Moses (f of Philip, I,
5642)
Philip (h of Sarah, 117);
(s of Moses & Leah),
I, 5642
Sarah (w of Philip), 117

S
Samuel:
Alexander, Hebr: Pinhas,
of London (s of James
Hebr: Simon), 120
James Simon (f of Alexander
Pinhas, 120)
Leah Catharine (m of Moses,
I, 5614)
Lewis, I, 5614; (f of Moses,
I, 5614)
Moses (c of Lewis and Leah
Catharine), I, 5614

[*masons,*] *Sidney St.,
Mile End, London*

Valverde: *(continued)*
Abraham Jedidyah *Junr.,
Merchant,* 43
David, 364; (f of Simha, I,
5581); (f of Jacob, I,
5591)
David, [*B.R.:* Daniel] (f of
Elias, 42); (f of Jael
Hanah, 48); (h of Simha
Abigail, 48a)
David Israel (h of Rachel,
19); 66
Elias (s of David, *B.R.:*
Daniel & Simha Abigail)
42
Elias Raphael (s of Abraham
& Esther), I, 5501
Esther (c of Jacob and
Lunah), I, 5536
Esther (m of Elias Raphael,
I, 5501)
Esther (widow of Abraham
Hisquiau), 21
Isaac, I, 5613
Isaac Haim, *Merchant,* 24
Jacob, 78
Jacob (h of Rachel, 47)
Jacob (s of David), I, 5591
Jacob Hisquiau, *Merchant*
(h of Lunah, 263); (f
of Esther, I, 5536)
Jacob Joshua, *Merchant,* 22,
(h of Simha Sarah, 23)
Jael (w of Abraham), 45;
(m of Moses, 228); (m
of Rebecca, 242)
Jael Hanah (d of David &
Simha), 48
Lunah, 337
Lunah (w of Jacob Hisquiau)
263; (m of Esther, I,
5536)
Moses, 132
Moses (s of Ab[raham] and
Jael), 228
Rachel (w of David Israel
Junr.), 19
Rachel (w of Jacob), 47
Rebecca, 90
Rebecca, Mrs.,III, 5465

Valverde: *(continued)*
Rebecca (d of Ab[raham]
and Jael), 242
Simha (w or d of David), I, 5581
Simha Abigail (m of Elias,
42); (m of Jael Hanah,
48); (w of David), 48a
Simha Sarah (w of Jacob *Junr.)*
23

Villao: *see* Villoa

Villoa:
Daniel (f of Elias, I, 5470)
Daniel Haim (h of Esther,
156); 157
David (h of Rebecca, 34);
(f of "Manuel Sebo"
Eliau [on whom see
below], I, 5470)
Elias (s of Daniel), I,
5470
Esther (w [widow ?] of
Daniel Haim), 156
Manuel Sebo [?] Eliau
[corruption for
Mancebo Eliau] (s of
David), I, 5470
Rebecca (w of David), 34

W

Walduck,T., Introd. p. vii

X

Ximenes, Abraham Levy,
Introd.. p.x

Y

Ydana: *see also* Idanha
Abraham (s of Jacob), 239
Jacob (f of Abraham, 239)

Surname illegible

Abraham (f of Esther, 253)
Esther (d of Abraham and
Rebecca), 253
Jacob, 54b
Rebecca (m of Esther, 253)

202

INDEX

OF PLACES

Place names other than Bridgetown, Barbados, referred to on the tombstones or in the Burial Register.

*　　*　　*

A

Amsterdam, Introd., p. vi

B

Bevis Marks, Introd.　p. vii, x.
Boston
  Carry, A, [stonemason], Boston. (130)

C

Curacao, Introd.,　p. vi, xii, xxix.

F

Falmouth, Introd.,　p. ix

L

London:
  Ancona, Moses, *Sculptor,* London (349)
  Castro, Hananel de, in London (II, 5609)
  Elkin, Benjamin, in London (II, 5608)
  Isaac, Solomon Baber, in London (II, 5696)
  Levy, Isaac Hisquiau, son of Pinhas, of London (137)
  Lindo, Abraham *Junr.*, de Jacob, *Merchant,* formerly of
    London, and lately of Barbados (350)
  Lindo, Jacob, born in London, died in Barbados (115)
  Montefiore, Jacob, *Merchant,* of London (349)
  Nunes, Benjamin, *Merchant,* son of Isaac Israel, born
    in London, died in Barbados (368)
  Samuel, Alexander, Hebr.: Pinhas, son of James, Hebr.:
    Simon, of London (120)
  Samuel, [monumental mason], Sidney St. Mile End,
    London (110)

N

New York:
  Lopez Brandon, Isaac, New York (II, 5615)
  Hart, Samuel, 282

Newport, Rhode Island:
  Hart, Samuel, 282

P

Philadelphia:
  Azevedo, D', Hannah, wife of M[oses], in Philadelphia
    (II, 5609)
  Azevedo, D', Judith, daughter of Moses Cohen, widow of
    Abraham Finzo, died at Philadelphia (II, 5645)
  Azevedo, D', Moses de Benjamin Cohen, p.p., K.K.N.I.
    Philadelphia (II, 5622)
  Daniels, Sophia, widow of Samuel Elias, died at Phila-
    delphia, U.S.A. (I, 5640)
  Finzi, Abraham, son of Samuel Isaac and Rachel, died
    at Philadelphia (II, 5630)
  Lobo, L.M., in Philadelphia (II, 5627)

S

Soufrière (St. Lucia):
  Olivayra, Jacob Jessurun D', in Soufrière, St. Lucia
    (II, 5614)
Speightstown (Barbados):
  Introd.   p. vii.
  Lopez, Moses, *Parnas*, of Speightstown, Barbados (291)
Surinam:
  Baeza, Julia, wife of David *Junr.*, Surinam (II, 5628)
  Cordoza Baeza, David Moses, died in Surinam (II, 5630)
  Polack, *Hazan* Ephraim, Surinam (II, 5620)
  Schloss, Moses, son of Marks, of Surinam (I, 5637)
  Soesman, Isaac Eleazar, born in Surinam, died in
    Barbados (118)
St. Croix:
  Leon, Abraham of Solomon de, home St. Croix (II, 5601)
St. K[itts ?]
  Azevedo, Isaac de Benjamin Cohen, D', St. K[itts ?]
    (II, 5625)
    [Alternatively St. Thomas]

St. Pierre (Martinique):
  Azevedo, Benjamin, D', son of Moses and Hanah Cohen,
    died at St. Pierre, Martinique, interred at Bar-
    bados (121, I, 5638)
  Azevedo, D', Reyna, widow of Benjamin Cohen, died at
    St. Pierre, Martinique (I, 5641)

St. Thomas;
  Azevedo, Isaac D', son of Benjamin Cohen, died at St.
    Thomas, alternatively St. K[itts] (II, 5625

T

Tobago:
> Baber Isaacs, Isaac, died in Tobago, interred in Barbados, (110)

W

Westbury:
> Anna Baeza, buried at, III, 5649